Common
Florida Mushrooms

Common
Florida Mushrooms

James W. Kimbrough
Mycologist, Plant Pathology Department

UNIVERSITY OF
FLORIDA

EXTENSION
Institute of Food and Agricultural Sciences

ISBN 0-916287-30-0

Kimbrough, James W.
    Common Florida mushrooms / James W. Kimbrough.
        p. cm.
    Includes bibliographical references (p.).
    1. Mushrooms--Florida--Identification. 2. Mushrooms--Florida--
    Pictorial works. 1. Title.
QK605.5F6 K56 2000
579.6'09759--dc21   00-032116

Editor: Ray Ford
Designer/illustrator: Katrina Vitkus

The Florida Cooperative Extension Service at the University of Florida's Institute of Food and Agricultural Sciences is a partnership of county, state and federal government which serves the citizens of Florida by providing information and training on a wide variety of topics. In Florida, the Extension Service is a part of the University of Florida's Institute of Food and Agricultural Sciences with selected programs at Florida Agricultural and Mechanical University (FAMU). Extension touches almost everyone in the state from the homeowner to huge agribusiness operations in such areas as food safety, gardening, child and family development, consumer credit counseling, youth development, energy conservation, sustainable agriculture, competitiveness in world markets, and natural-resource conservation.

IFAS/Extension Bookstore
Building 440, Mowry Road
PO Box 110011
Gainesville, FL 32611
352-392-1764 • 352-392-2628 fax
{800-226-1764 VISA/MasterCard orders only}
Shop our on-line catalog of educational resources at
http://ics.ifas.ufl.edu/ForSaleResources

NOTE: The University of Florida is not liable in any way for the consumption or resulting complications of eating mushrooms by any persons referring to this identification text or photographs.

Preface

The inland regions of the southeastern U.S. were settled by a mixture of Scotch-Irish, Highland Scots, and a few Anglos and Germans. In general, these settlers and their descendants had a great aversion to mushrooms. The mycophobia of the Anglo-Saxons is widely known and dates back a few centuries (Baker, 1990). Florida differs from other areas of the Southeast, however, in that it has had a highly varied population of ethnic groups all along, due to the rapid influx of people along the coastal areas. This trend continues as more and more people migrate to the sunbelt. Today, Floridians have a keen interest in mushrooms and other fleshy fungi for food and for recreational use.

While serving as extension mycologist at the University of Florida for almost 36 years, more than 75% of my requests have been for the identification of poisonous and edible mushrooms, or the instructions for cultivating them. Learning to identify Florida mushrooms has not been an easy task since it is believed that more kinds of mushrooms occur in the southeastern U.S. than in other areas of comparable size. The plant flora of Florida is a rich mixture of temperate and tropical species which support a great variety of both saprobic and ectomycorrhizal mushrooms. There are estimates that between 3,000 to 5,000 species of mushrooms occur in the South. Nearly 1,000 species have been described as new species from Florida, almost exclusively through the efforts of Dr. W. A. Murrill.

Murrill, as he was fondly called around Gainesville, developed a keen interest in mushrooms from Dr. George F. Atkinson at Cornell University, where he received his Ph.D. in 1900. Four years later Murrill became Assistant Curator of the New York Botanical Garden, where he was in charge of the cryptogamic collections. During his 20-year tenure at the Garden, he traveled extensively throughout the U.S., including Florida, and in various European and South American countries. He collected extensively in these countries, identifying nearly 75,000 fungi, 1,700 of which he considered new species. Battling physical exhaustion, medical and financial problems, and depression, Murrill resigned from the Garden in 1924. Before leaving the Garden, Murrill visited Florida in 1923, collecting mushrooms and plants in various coastal and inland cities. During these excursions, he was accompanied by D. Fairchild, C. Deering, and H. C. Beardslee. After leaving the Garden, he went into semi-seclusion at a homeplace near Staunton, VA.

In subsequent years, he made a number of visits to Florida, which became more frequent and of longer duration. By 1930 he had decided to make Gainesville his home, and spent almost 28 years around the University of Florida, actively collecting mushrooms throughout north central Florida and occasionally in south Florida, as his many friends were happy to take him to favorite collecting areas (see Weber, 1961).

Within a few years, publications on Florida mushrooms began to appear, and between 1938 and 1955 Murrill published almost 75 papers dealing largely with gilled mushrooms. More than 8,000 of his collections were accessioned in the University of Florida Mycological Herbarium before his death in 1957. Prominent mycologists such as R. Singer, L. R. Hesler, G. Burlingham, H. C. Beardslee, J. L. Lowe, and others visited the University of Florida to consult with Murrill. Subsequent to his death, dozens of agaricologists have continued to visit the Mycological Herbarium to study his collections, and we still receive from 10-25 requests annually for the loan of Murrill's type specimens.

Mushroom hunting in Florida can be done year-round in many areas of the state. Because of the mild, subtropical climate, saprobic species will emerge after adequate rainfall during any season of the year. Ectomycorrhizal species, however, are very seasonal; the greatest populations occurring during very rainy summer months, but reappearing in late fall and during winter months as the winter weather fronts provide rain. While the same genera can be found during summer and winter rainy seasons, the composition of species changes greatly. For example, an abundance of *Agaricus* species occurs during summer months but very rarely in the winter. Species of *Cortinarius* are rare in summer months, but abundant during the winter. There are two extremely dry seasons along most of the Florida peninsula, March to June and late September to early November. Even though hurricanes and other weather phenomena may bring unusual rainfall during these months, few ectomycorrhizal species will be found.

While assembling information and photographs to incorporate in a field guide to Florida mushrooms, I soon realized that a majority of the species described by Murrill had no illustrations at all. Most of his descriptions stressed field characters, lacking many of the microscopic and microchemical properties used in modern taxonomy. During his latter years in Gainesville, he was unable to travel to other herbaria and museums, the university library dropped many of the journals during the years of WW2, and Murrill's memory was not as keen as in previous years. As a result of these and other problems, Murrill made a number of mistakes in identification and was unsettled in his classification. However, as many of the major mushroom genera were subsequently monographed by modern agaricologists, most of Murrill species have stood the test of time.

Acknowledgments

I would like to thank the Plant Pathology Department of the University of Florida for creating a mycology position in 1964 and allowing me to be the first to assume that role. For the past 36 years, my teaching, research, and extension activities have been limited to the study of fungi. Much of the extension work has involved the identification of mushrooms and other fleshy fungi. Through the encouragement of the Cooperative Extension Service of the Institute of Food and Agricultural Sciences (IFAS), I initiated work on a book of Common Mushrooms of Florida. I appreciate the financial support they provided for me to work on the project and fund the printing of the book.

A special thanks goes to my wife, **Jane**, who not only gave me great encouragement over the years, but who also trudged with me through the hills, hollows, and trails around the state, keeping records of the various species we photographed and collected. I thank **Dr. Gerald L. Benny**, and **Loren Kimbrough** for assisting with preserving, packeting, and accessioning material in the Mycological Herbarium.

Several individuals have been kind enough to loan me slides of several mushrooms that were not in my collection. These include **Dr. Brian Akers**, **Dr. Henry Aldrich**, **Sherri Angels**, **Dr. Tim Baroni**, **Dr.** and **Mrs. Gerald Benny**, **Terry Henkle**, **Dr. Greg Mueller**, **Dr. Walter Sundberg**, and **Robert** and **Rosemary Williams**. I would also like to thank the following staff of the IFAS Communications Services Department for the editing, graphic design, scanning, and other activities involved in getting this publication in print, **Mr. Mike Allen**, **Mr. Ray Ford, Jr.**, **Ms. Katrina Vitkus** (design and illustration), and **Mr. James Petterson** (photo-manipulation).

Lastly, I would be remiss if I did not acknowledge the late **Dr. W. A. Murrill** who described more than 700 new species of mushrooms here in northern Florida. Having these type specimens here in my building has made what could have been a hard task of species confirmation a relatively easy one.

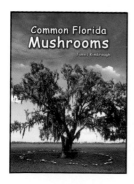

On the Cover:

Thanks to **Dr. Henry Aldrich** for the striking photograph of *Chlorophyllum Molybdites* as the foreground photo and **Milt Putnam** for the live oak photo. The clouds are a stock photo. The original *Chlorophyllum Molybdites* had a shrub type tree surrounded by the fairy ring with a house in the background (right). Photos merged by **Katrina Vitkus**.

Contents

Introduction

With their large, conspicuous sporulating structures, yet ephemeral in their appearance, mushrooms have long been a fascination and mystery to mankind. There is evidence that man has used mushrooms for food, medicine, and in religious practices for more than 4,000 years. The recent discovery that the "ice man" in the Austrian/Italian Alps had in his pouch, among other things, mushrooms, dates their use for more than 6,000 years. We still are fascinated and mystified by mushrooms, as evidenced by the increasing number of individuals who seek to find them, study them, and to use them for food, medicine, and pleasure.

What are mushrooms?

First of all, mushrooms are fungi, and as such, their vegetative phase is composed of microscopic threads called **mycelium**, common to the layman as **spawn** or **mold**. Mycelial cells of mushrooms are walled, contain nuclei and other membrane-bound organelles, but do not contain chlorophyll. Thus, they cannot manufacture their own food and must get nutrition from another source. They must also absorb their food because with walled cells they can not engulf food as we do. Many may live as **saprophytes**, utilizing decaying plant material; a few as **parasites** which can invade living plants, and lastly, others are **symbiotic**, i.e. they have established a beneficial type of parasitism in which both the parasite (the mushroom) and the host (the higher plant) receive benefit from this companionship. A majority of mushrooms are symbionts and have an intimate mycelial/root association referred to as **mycorrhizae**. Such mushrooms are either **ectomycorrhizal** or **ectendomycorrhizal,** and are associated with members of most families of tree species. Thus, the "body" of a mushroom is buried in the soil, around roots, or in decaying plant debris. It is the sporulating phase that "sticks its head out" only on special occasions, and it is this phase that distinguishes mushrooms from other fungi. Sporulating structures of mushrooms are called **basidomata**, so named because their spores are borne on microscopic club-shaped structures called **basidia** within the **lamellae** (gills) or pores of mushrooms. This feature links together a Phylum of Fungi we called Basidiomycota in which mushrooms and some of the other fleshy fungi make up a sizable component.

Mushroom basidiomata are usually fleshy, parasol-like, with a conspicuous **pileus** (cap) and **stipe** (stalk). In most species the stipe is central (fig. 1a), but in others it may be eccentric (off center) (fig. 1b), laterally attached (fig. 1c), or missing, in which case the pileus is attached directly to the substrate on which it is growing. The spore-bearing tissue is a **hymenium** (layer of basidia) lining the surface of **lamellae, pores,** or **folds** beneath the pileus. Groups of fungi with these features were traditionally placed in the order Agaricales, but with more research, we find mushroom-like fungi now placed in the Agaricales, Russulales, Boletales, Cantharellales, and some Aphylloporales (Pegler, 1983). Because of the variation in configuration of the hymenium on which basidia and spores are formed, mushrooms are often confused with wood-rotting bracket fungi belonging to the Aphyllophorales (commonly called polypores), a group that also has pores, lamellae, and folds. How then are mushrooms and polypores distinguished? It is generally accepted that mushrooms have a **monomitic** tissue structure composed of vegetative, generative hyphae, whereas most polypores have a more complex tissue structure, rarely monomitic but commonly **dimitic,** with generative and binding hyphae, or **trimitic**, with generative, binding, and skeletal hyphae. Thus, mushrooms are more succulent and decompose quickly, while polypores are tougher, leathery and persist longer. Mushrooms also have determinant growth and synchronous spore production, while the polypores have indeterminant growth and asynchronous spore production. Simply, mushrooms develop, expand to a certain diameter, drop their spores within a short period of time, and then putrify. Polypores continue to grow, sometimes for several years, adding new hymenia, producing spores periodically, and liberating spores on a daily basis if environmental conditions are proper.

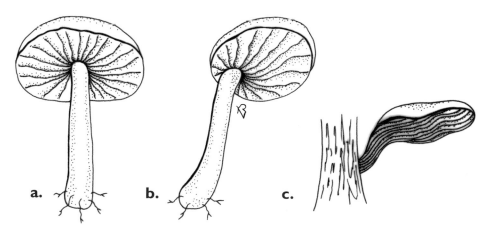

Fig. 1. Attachment of pileus to the stipe: (a) central, (b) eccentric, and (c) lateral.

Morphology and Development of Mushrooms

Formation of the mushroom from vegetative mycelium or spawn is controlled by the interaction of a large number of factors, especially water, temperature, and available nutrients. Results from extensive studies on the commercial production of a variety of mushrooms have shown that a critical volume of mycelium must be produced before **primordia** (pins or buttons) will form. Primordia are composed of an aggregate of highly branched mycelium that become tightly interwoven into globose structures. Primordia of most mushrooms may look similar in their early stages (fig. 2a-d), but they soon enlarge, elongate and take on the configuration of a mushroom. There is limited cell division in developing primordia; most of the expansion is due to cell differentiation and elongation. The mycelium of mushrooms is dikaryotic, i.e., two nuclei with different mating types, and many have **clamp connections**. These are recurving of cells which at cell division act as bridges to allow passage of nuclei form the terminal to subterminal cell and thereby maintaining the dikaryon.

The size and shape of mushrooms are highly variable, and the structures present on the pileus and stipe may be strikingly different. Much of this is due to the fact that there are four distinct types of basidiomatial development. Traditional agaric literature has used plant terms, such as gymnocarpic, angiocarpic, etc. to refer to developmental patterns. I would prefer to use the term hymenial, since fungi do not have carpels but do have layers (hymenia) of basidia. The four types of development are gymnohymenial (fig. 2a), pseudoangiohymenial (fig. 2b), hemiangiohymenial (fig. 2c), and angiohymenial (fig. 2d). **Gymnohymenial** is the simplest type in which the hymenium (lamellae or pores) is exposed throughout development. Mushrooms with this type of development would not have an **annulus** or a **volva**, and the lamellae would often be decurrent. **Angiohymenial** is the most complex type in which the embryonic mushroom develops inside a **universal veil** (fig.2d, uv). After the primordium ruptures through the universal veil, portions of the veil usually remain behind as a **volva** (2d, v), or appear as **volval patches** (fig. 2d, vp) covering the pileus. In the genus *Amanita*, an **inner veil** (fig. 2d, iv) develops between the lamellae and stipe. As the cap expands, the inner veil usually breaks around the margin and forms an apron type annulus around the stipe. Such an annulus is referred to as a **superior annulus** (fig. 2d, sa), since it differs from an annulus formed in other mushrooms. **Pseudoangiohymenial**, as the name implies, appears to be angiohymenial but in actuality is gymnohymenial. In this type of development, the hymenium is initially exposed but the pileus ex-

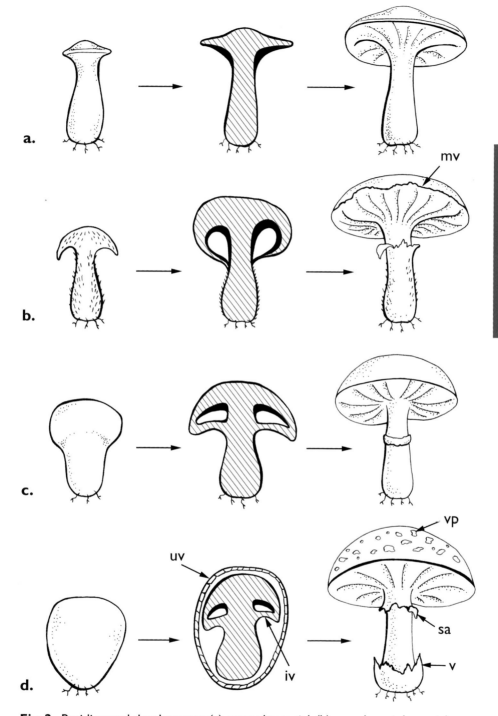

Fig. 2. Basidiomatal development: (a) gymnohymenial, (b) pseudoangiohymenial, (c) hemiangiohymenial, and (d) angiohymenial. (mv=marginal veil, uv=universal veil, iv=inner veil, vp=volval patches, v=volva, sa=superior annulus). *(Adapted from Alexopoulos et. al., 1996. Introductory Mycology. John Wiley & Sons., NY)*

pands early, turns downward (fig. 2b), and the edge adheres to the stipe. As the pileus expands, this adhesion is broken, often leaving behind a fragile annulus which is often movable, or a **marginal veil** (fig. 2b, mv) on the edge of the pileus. The annulus from such development may be membraneous, slimy (= **pellicular veil**) (fig. 9c), or a cobwebby veil (= **cortina**) (fig. 9b). **Hemiangiohymenial** is somewhat like angiohymenial in that hymenial development takes place within the enclosed, expanding pileus. There is no universal veil, and differentiation takes place as the stipe elongates. In hemiangiohymenial development there is a very firm attachment of the edge of the pileus to the stipe, and whenever the pileus expands a well developed, immovable annulus is commonly left on the stipe.

Characteristics of the Pileus

Size: Size of the pileus is often used to separate species in different genera, but cap size alone is rarely used to accurately identify a mushroom.

Shape: Shape of the pileus is mostly characteristic for a given species and can be somewhat variable depending on growth condi-

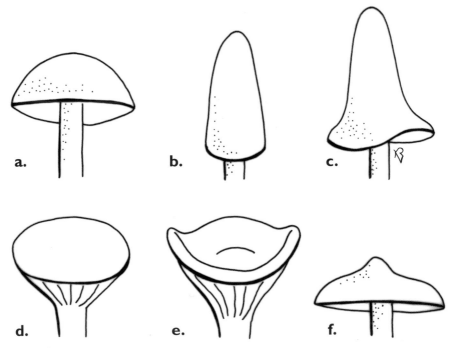

Fig. 3. Pileus shapes: (a) convex, (b) conic, (c) campanulate, (d) plane, (e) depressed, and (f) umbonate.

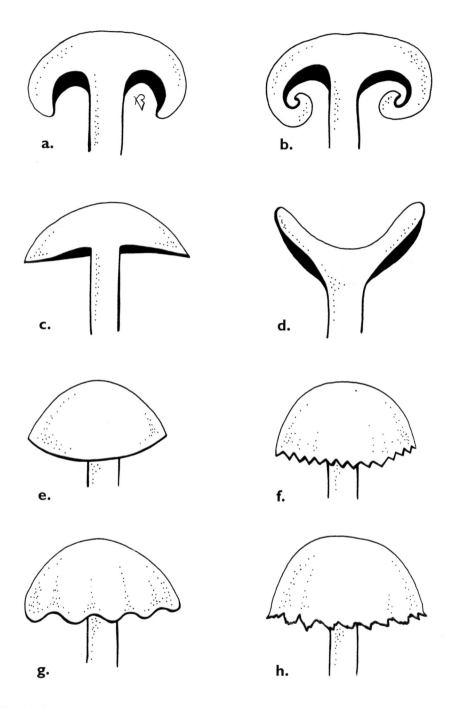

Fig. 4. Margin of the pileus: (a) incurved, (b) inrolled, (c) straight, (d) upturned, (e) even, (f) crenate, (g) undulate, (h) appendiculate.

tions. Across the spectrum of mushrooms, pileus shape is extremely variable. One of the most common shapes is **convex** (fig. 3a) in which the width is usually greater than its height. If the height is greater than the width, it is termed **parabolic**. The pileus in many mushrooms may be **conic** (fig. 3b) at first, but later the margins may flare and become bell-shaped or **campanulate** (fig. 3c). Margins of the pileus may become raised and referred to as flat or **plane** (fig. 3d), or extend further upward to be **uplifted** (fig. 3e). When viewed from the top, those with uplifted margins will usually appear **deeply depressed** (fig. 3e). Several mushroom groups may have **slightly depressed** caps; yet others will have a raised center termed **umbonate** (fig. 3f).

Margin of Pileus: Margins of the pileus are variable. Sometimes the margin is useful in distinguishing certain genera, but more often in characterizing species. It may be **incurved** (fig. 4a), **inrolled** (fig. 4b), **straight** (fig. 4c), or **upturned** (fig. 4d). The edge of the pileus may be **smooth** (fig. 4e), **crenate** (fig. 4f), **undulate** (fig. 4g), or **append-iculate** (fig. 4h) as a result of a **marginal veil**.

Surface of the Pileus: The surface of the pileus is often characteristic of a species or a group of species within a genus. The pileus may be dry, moist, or viscid, and it may be smooth (**glabrose**), hairy (**hirsute, villose**), or scaly (**squamulose**).

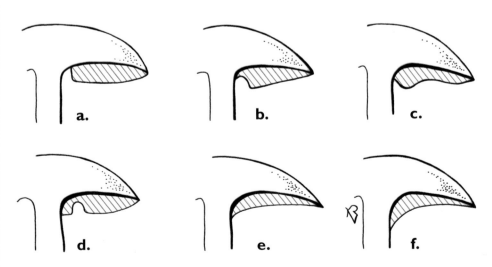

Fig. 5. Lamellae attachment: (a) free, (b) adnexed, (c) emarginate, (d) sinuate, (e) adnate, (f) decurrent.

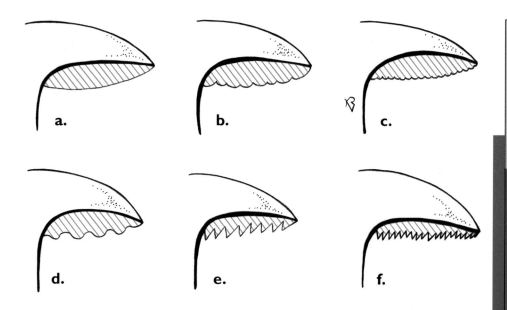

Fig. 6. Margin of lamellae: (a) smooth, (b) crenate, (c) crenulate, (d) wavy, (e) serrate, and (f) serrulate.

Characteristics of Lamellae

Attachment: Lamellar attachment is very important in helping to characterize many genera. They may be **free** (fig. 5a) when they are unattached to the stipe, **adnexed** (fig. 5b) when they appear as if they are attached at only a portion of their width, **emarginate** (fig. 5c) when they are sharply adnexed, **sinuate** (fig. 5d) when they appear to have a notch removed at the point where they meet the stipe, **adnate** (fig. 5e) when they are squarely attached to the stipe over the width of the lamellae, and **decurrent** (fig. 5f) when the lamellae run down the stipe.

Margin of Lamellae: Lamellae margins are often used in separating genera. The margins are said to be **marginate** if the edge of the lamella is of a different color from the lamella itself. The edge may be **smooth** (fig. 6a), **crenate** (fig. 6b), **crenulate** (fig. 6c), **wavy** (fig. 6d) or undulate, **serrate** (fig. 6e), or **serrulate** (fig. 6f).

Characteristics of the Stipe

Shape: Shape of the stipe may vary according to the species. If it is of equal diameter from the apex to the base, it is called **equal**

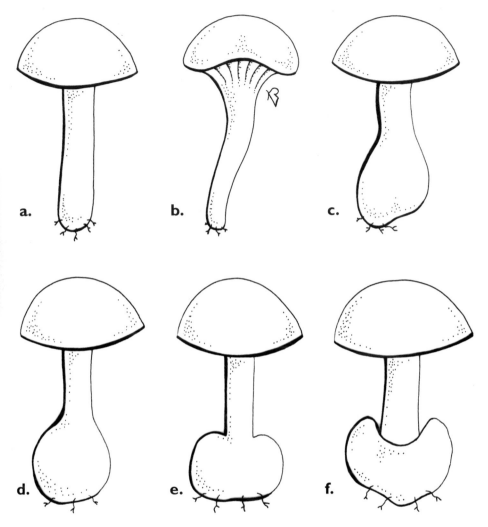

Fig. 7. Shape of the stipe: (a) equal, (b) tapered, (c) clavate, (d) bulbous, (e) abruptly bulbous, (f) emarginate bulb.

(fig. 7a). Many, however, are **tapered** (fig. 7b) in one direction or the other. If tapered to the point of being club-shaped, they are said to be **clavate** (fig. 7c). In many cases, stipes will become extremely swollen at the base and are said to be **bulbous** (fig. 7d). The bulb may become **abruptly bulbous** (fig. 7e) when the bulb is sharply defined, or **emarginate** (fig. 7f) if there is a distinct margin around the edge of the bulb.

     Surface of the Stipe: There are many features of the stipe surface that help to distinguish genera and species. In some of the Boletales, the stipe becomes **glandular dotted** (fig. 8a) with tufts of matted

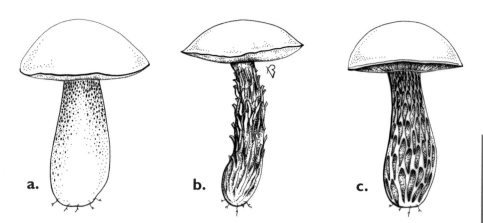

Fig. 8. Surface of the stipe: (a) glandular dotted, (b) scabrous, and (c) reticulate.

hairs. Those that bear scales are called **scabrous** (fig. 8b), while others that form distinct raised net-like ridges are said to be **reticulate** (fig. 8c). Others have raised lines or deep lacerations which, along with different coloration, often help to distinguish genera and species.

Consistency of the Stipe: Stipe consistency is often used in distinguishing certain groups of mushrooms. The stipe of most mushrooms is **fibrous** or **fleshy**, while others are **cartilaginous** and will snap when broken. In a few groups the stipe becomes **woody, corky,** or **leathery**.

Presence or Absence of Veils on the Stipe: The **partial veil** is a membrane that covers the lamellae from the stipe to the pileus margin. In many species, it breaks away from the pileus margin when it expands and remains as a ring or membraneous **annulus** (fig. 9a) on the stipe. In some, the partial veil is cobwebby, resulting in a **cortina** (fig. 9b), and in others very slimy, forming a **pellicular veil** (fig. 9c). In other mushrooms the partial veil breaks away from the stipe and remains as a **marginal veil** (fig. 9d). In most mushrooms the annulus is **central** (fig. 9a), but in others the annulus is attached at the top of the stipe and is said to be **superior** (fig. 9e), or at the bottom where it is said to be **inferior** (fig. 9f).

Types of Volvas: When the universal veil leaves a loose membraneous, cupulate volva around the base of the stipe it is termed **saccate** (fig. 10a). In many instances the volva will become **fragile** (fig. 10b), or completely **mealy**. In some, the volva **adheres** (fig. 10c) completely to the base of the stipe, sometimes flares at the border, or forms a **circumsessile ring** (fig. 10d).

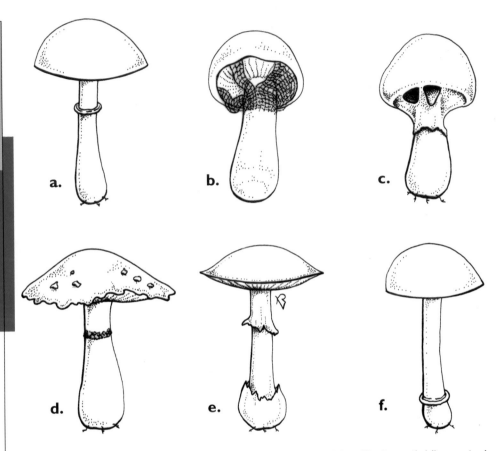

Fig. 9. Veils of the stipe: (a) central annulus, (b) cortina, (c) pellicular veil, (d) marginal veil, (e) superior annulus, and (f) inferior annulus.

Types of Basidiospores

Spore color: One of the most important features of mushrooms needed for accurate identification of families and genera is that of spore color *en masse*. This cannot accurately be judged from gill color, but must be determined by making a **spore print,** unless you are lucky enough to find a fresh spore deposit beneath the specimen you have collected in the field. Spore prints are best made by cutting off the stipe at the apex and placing a mature pileus, gill or pore surface downward, onto a piece of white paper or cardboard. White paper is best because off shades of white may appear white on a dark background. Cover the pileus with a small bowl, dish, or wax paper to prevent wind currents that will disperse the spores. Spore prints may also be made in the field by putting a hole in a sheet of white paper, running the stipe through the hole, raising the paper to beneath the

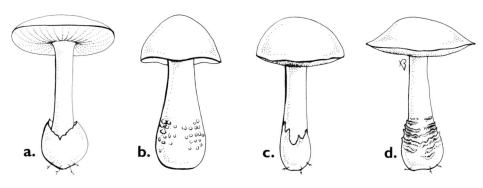

Fig. 10. Types of volva: (a) saccate, (b) fragile, (c) adhering, and (d) circumsessile rings.

pileus, folding the excessive paper over the top of the pileus, and placing the specimen carefully in your collecting container. There is usually a spore print by the time you reach home. Spore prints should be made before the mushroom is refrigerated.

There are five basic patterns of spore coloration: (1) White to cream (sometimes faintly lilac, yellow, or green); (2) salmon to pink or flesh colored; (3) yellow-brown, clay-brown, cinnamon-brown, burnt orange, or rusty-brown; (4) purple-brown to chocolate-brown; and (5) smoke to dark grayish-brown or black.

Spore Shape, Wall thickness, and Surface: The shape and surface of spores, combined with color, can be some of the most important features used to distinguish a number of genera of mushrooms. It is necessary to have a microscope in order to determine these features. One is sometimes able to determine spore color under the microscope, but often the color does not compare to that of the spore print. White to slightly pigmented spores will appear colorless (**hyaline**) under the microscope.

The following different wall characters occur among various genera of agarics and boletes: (1) thin-walled, smooth, and hyaline; (2) thin-walled, roughened, and hyaline; (3) thin-walled, nodulose, and hyaline; (4) thick-walled, hyaline, without a germ pore; (5) thin-walled, slightly roughened, and faintly pigmented; (6) thin-walled, tuberculate to reticulate, hyaline to yellowish, amyloid (turns blue in iodine); (7) thick-walled, distinctly pigmented, smooth; (8) thick-walled, tuberculate or wrinkled, truncate (blunt at one end); (9) thick-walled, angular, nodulose to spiny, pigmented; (10) thick-walled, smooth, hyaline, with a distinct germ pore (a thin area in one end of the spore); (11) thick-walled, smooth, pigmented, truncate; (12) thick-walled, rough, pigmented, truncate; (13) smooth, compressed pigmented, truncate; (14) angular, compressed, pigmented, truncate.

Collecting Mushrooms in Florida

Because of its hot, humid climate, collecting mushrooms during summer months in Florida can be extremely uncomfortable. It is good to plan collecting trips in the early morning and return by noon since the heat and humidity increase by midday, and daily thunderstorms push inland from the coasts by early afternoon. Become familiar with collecting sites and gain permission to collect on public and private land. Keep a compass and map of the area handy in case you loose your orientation. Beware of dangers in the fields and woods such as poisonous plants, snakes, and spiders, as well as mosquitoes, chiggers, and ticks. Certain species of mosqitoes carry the encephalitis virus and other human diseases, seed ticks may carry Lyme diseases or ehrlichiosis, and chiggers are a constant irritation. The bottom line is to keep a supply of insect repellent and dress properly. Ticks seem more difficult to avoid, so I recommend wearing long pants and shirts, tucking pants inside your socks, and applying both spray repellent and powdered sulfur around shoes, socks, waistline and sleeve cuffs.

Some basic equipment needed to collect mushrooms include an open collecting basket or similar container with a durable handle and flat bottom, a knife or small trowel for removing mushrooms from their substrate, waxed sandwich bags or wax paper in which to keep specimens, and a pencil or pen with notebook or cards to keep notes. Avoid using baggies or plastic containers, since they will retain moisture and cause early spoilage of specimens. Do not place mushrooms loosely in a basket, otherwise they will easily become fragmented and mixed with other species; packet them separately.

If possible, collect both young and mature specimens so that the full complement of features will be present. Be careful removing specimens from the substrate, as not to disturb or destroy a volva or a deeply rooting structure. Do not mix collections, keeping careful notes on each group of specimens. Note the habitat, whether it is saprophytic or on the soil and likely mycorrhizal. If saprophytic, with what type of wood or plant debris is it associated? If mycorrhizal, what is the likely host species? Note the size, shape, and color of the pileus, stipe, and structures thereon. Does the specimen change colors when bruised? Does it emit an odor or exude milk when bruised? If present, what color is the milk? Does the color change with time? Chew a small piece of the mushroom to determine if the taste is mild, bitter, peppery, or another distinct taste. Good field notes are vital for accurate identification of most mushrooms. Many characteristics of fresh mushrooms may change with refrigeration or drying. However, during summer months, specimens should be kept in a cooler if you are going to be in the field for several hours.

Recognizing Edible and Poisonous Mushrooms

The layman often refers to edible specimens as "mushrooms" and poisonous ones as "toadstools", but these terms are meaningless scientifically. Essentially every family of Agaricales, Russulales, and Boletales contain both edible and toxic species. The only sure way to determine if a specimen is safe to eat is to identify it correctly, examine the history of the species, and note if it has been determined safe. Amateurs should definitely have identifications confirmed by an authority before they attempt to eat species they have collected. The types of toxins found in mushrooms and the common species in which each type is found will be discussed in a later section (p. 320).

Identifying Mushrooms

In order to accurately identify a particular mushroom, it is essential that a person can use and accurately interpret the keys to families, genera, and species. To do so, one must be familiar with the various characteristics used to diagnose a particular group. First, one must determine whether the fleshy fungus is a mushroom or a mushroom "look alike." To assist in this determination, I have provided an illustration to the common groups of fleshy fungi that could be confused with mushrooms (fig. 11). One of the more common groups of fleshy Basidiomycota is the Polyporaceae, a group of wood-rotting bracket fungi, depicted here by the genus *Inonotus* (fig. 11a). Several members of the Polyporaceae are tender, succulent species and have proven to be desirable for food. One of the groups of mushroom look-alikes is the Hydnaceae, or toothed fungi. Many of them grow from the soil, are stiped and superficially resemble mushrooms. Beneath the pileus, however, the hymenium is covered with downwardly projected teeth as depicted in *Hydnellum* (fig. 11b). Most species of the Hydnaceae are distasteful or too tough for consumption. The Clavariaceae or "coral fungi" have upright basidiomata, many of them fleshy and brightly colored, but are mostly highly branched as depicted in *Ramaria* (fig. 11c). The Clavariaceae have both toxic and edible species. Members of the Phallales are remarkable because of their bright color and offensive odor, much like decaying flesh; thus, the common name of "stink horns." Many of them such as *Clathrus* (fig. 11d) develop angio-hymynially, and the fertile receptacle that pushes out somewhat resembles mushrooms. Despite the repulsive odor, the button stages of several species of Phallales are choice edibles in Asia. Closely related to the Phallales are a number of puffballs belonging to the Lycoperdales. Those such as species of *Calvatia* (fig. 11e) are highly prized as food. In collecting puffballs for food, however, one must be sure they are not dealing with an embryonic stage of an *Amanita,* or a hard-skinned puffball, *Scleroderma.* Young specimens of *Amanita* can be recognized be cutting the mushroom lengthwise, revealing an undeveloped pileus and stipe within. Species of *Scleroderma* have a

Fig. 11a. *Inonotus*

Fig. 11b. *Hydnellum*

Fig. 11c. *Ramaria*

Fig. 11d. *Clathrus*

Fig. 11e. *Calvatia*   Fig. 11f. *Helvella*

Fig. 11. Other fleshy fungi and Mushroom look-alikes: (a) *Inonotus*, (b) *Hydnellum*, (c) *Ramaria*, (d) *Clathrus*, (e) *Calvatia*, (f) *Helvella*.

very tough, leathery peridium and black spore mass within. True puffballs like *Calvatia* and several other genera have thin, membranous peridia and, in young specimens, firm, spongy and white within. There are several large, fleshy fungi found among the Ascomycota, those fungi that form their spores in sacs. Most belong to the cup-fungi or Discomycetes, so named because in most their ascomata are cupulate or discoid. An exception to this is the "saddle mushroom," *Helvella* (fig. 11f), which has a number of species known to have the toxin monomethylhydrazine. Species of *Gyromitra* and the choice edible *Morchella* have not been found in Florida. These and other of the fleshly Discomycetes are only distantly related to true mushrooms.

A key to the families of mushrooms is provided in which essential features are noted and figures are cited. Following the diagnosis of a family, a key to common genera is provided, each, in turn, with a key to common Florida species.

A Key to Orders
of Mushrooms and Allied Groups

1. Tissues of the basidiomata with both clusters of globose cells, sphaerocysts, and filamentous hyphae (heteromerous); spores with ornaments or a reticulum that turns blue when mounted in iodine .... **Russulales** (p. 35)

1 Tissues of the basidiomata not containing sphaerocysts; spores if ornamented, not turning blue in iodine 2

    2. Tissues of the basidiomata of basically filamentous cells (homoiomerous) 3

    2. Tissues monomitic, dimitic, or trimitic, with non inflated generative hyphae, and usually firm fleshy to leathery, indeterment growth .... **Aphyllophorales** (p. 18)

3. Basidiomata not truly gilled; hymenium continuous, in ridges, folds, or smooth .... **Cantharellales** (p. 26)

3. Basidiomata either gilled or tubular 4

    4. Hymenium gilled; gill edge sterile; spores globose, subglobose, ellipsoid, rarely cylindric, variable in color ... **Agaricales** (p. 75)

    4. Hymenium usually tubular, if gilled, radial lamellae with cross veins; spores mostly fusoid, sometimes ribbed, colors range from pinkish-brown, smokey-brown, to blackish .... **Boletales** (p. 256)

Aphyllophorales

There are two families of bracket fungi (Aphyllophorales) that have gilled basidiomata, the Schizophyllaceae and Polyporaceae. The following key will help to distinguish mushroom-like members.

1. Hymenium becoming falsely gilled, with lamellae appearing longitudinally split .... *Schizophyllum* (p. 19)

1. Hymenium truly gilled, centrally or laterally attached, often firm fibrous and leathery 2

    2. Tissue monomitic, fleshy, soon decaying .... *Pleurotus* (p. 24)

    3. Tissue dimitic, tough, leathery .... *Lentinus* (p. 20)

Schizophyllum

The basidiomata are sessile, growing singly or in clusters on wood, white to brownish, thin and leathery, with split lamellae. One species is common in Florida.

Schizophyllum commune Fr.:Fr.   **12**

(inedible)

- The white to brownish pileus is 1.0-5.0 cm in diameter, laterally attached with a constricted base and covered with fine hairs. The false gills are split with recurved margins. The pileus is attached directly to the substrate.

- The spores are white in deposit, allantoid, cylindric, 3.0-6.0 x 1.2-2.0 µm, thin-walled and smooth. Basidia narrowly clavate 15.0-20.0 x 4.0-6.0 µm, with four sterigmata.

- This species is worldwide in distribution, growing mainly on decaying hardwood. It is easily recognized by its clustered, fibrous, basidiomata with split lamellae. Cooke (1961) has monographed this genus.

Fig. 12. *Schizophyllum commune* (x 0.5)

Aphyllophorales

Lentinus

The basidiomata are tough, leathery, persistent, convex to depressed and often funnel-form, and the surface covered with fibrillar hairs or scales. The lamellae are always decurrent, crowded, mostly with a denticulate (toothed) edge. The stipe is either central, eccentric, or rarely laterally attached. Spores are white to cream in deposit and do not turn blue in iodine. Many of the species currently placed in *Lentinus* were once placed in *Panus*, whereas, others once placed in *Lentinus* are now in *Lentinula.*

A Key to Common *Lentinus* in Florida

1. Basidiomata large, fleshy, glabrous, growing in clusters from trunks and roots of pines and other conifers .... *Lentinus lepidus* (p. 21)
1. Basidiomata not as above 2

> 2. Pileus finely velutinus, dark brown and deeply depressed with enrolled margins, stipe long, arising from a basal ....
> pseudosclerotium .... *Lentinus velutinus* (p. 23)
>
> 2. Not dark brown or with pseudosclerotium 3

3. Pileus 1-4 cm in diameter, yellowish to reddish-brown, strongly striate, stipe without fibrillar annulus .... *Lentinus crinitus* (p. 20)
3. Pileus 1-10 cm in diameter, grayish-brown to blackish, only margins striate, stipe with fibrillar annulus
    .... *Lentinus tigrinus* (p.23)

I 3   *Lentinus crinitus* (Linn.:Fr.)Fr.

(inedible)

■ The pale yellowish-brown to reddish-brown pileus often with a purplish tint is 1.0-4.0 cm in diameter, and covered with loose brown fascicles of brown hairs with free ends. The lamellae are deeply decurrent, slightly fusing or appearing almost poroid near the stipe, and with dentate edges. The stipe is 1.0-4.0 x 0.2-0.6 cm, scurfy, and slightly lighter in color than the pileus.

■ The spores are white in deposit, narrowly cylindric to allantoid, 5.5-7.0 x 1.8-2.7 μm, not turning blue in iodine. Basidia are narrowly clavate, 12.0-14.0 x4.0-5.0 μm, with four sterigmata.

■ This species can be recognized from others by its pale stipe, crowded lamellae, and cap margins that are only slightly enrolled. This species is very common on decaying logs throughout Florida.

Fig. 13. *Lentinus crinitus* (x 1.0)   (Robert Williams)

Lentinus lepideus (Fr.:Fr.)Fr.   **14**

(edible)

- The pileus is 3.0-15.0 or more cm in diameter, firm fleshy convex to slightly depressed, white to pale yellowish-brown, cuticle disrupted, forming rings of large scales. The white to pale-yellowish lamellae are decurrent with strongly dentate to lacerated edges. The stipe is central to eccentric, 2.0-11 x 1.0-3.0 cm, tapering towards the base, or rarely with a bulbous base.

- The spores are white in deposit, cylindric, 8.5-12.5 x 4.7-5.0 µm, not turning blue in iodine. Basidia long, narrowly clavate, 35.0-46.0 x 5.0-7.0 µm, with four sterigmata.

- This species is easy to recognize by its robust size and growth habit mainly on conifers. In Florida it is found commonly in clusters growing from the base of pine trees with heart or root rot. It is well known as the cause of brown rot in conifer timbers.

Fig. 14. *Lentinus lepidus* (x 1.0)

Fig. 15. *Lentinus tigrinus* (x 1.0)   (Robert Williams)

Lentinus tigrinus (Bull.:Fr.)Fr.   **15**

(inedible)

■ The pileus is 1.5-10.0 cm in diameter, depressed to funnel-shaped, initially enrolled surface, at first greyish-brown to blackish due to closely appressed fibrillar, radially arranged scales. The lamellae are decurrent, crowded, white to whitish-yellow with ragged margins. The greyish brown to fawn colored stipe is 2.0-6.0 x 0.4-1.0 cm, central to eccentric, tapering downward.

■ The spores are white in deposit, narrowly cylindric, 6.0-9.5 x 2.5-3.5 µm, not turning blue in iodine. The basidia are elongate, clavate, 24.0-30.0 x 4.0-6.0 µm, with four slender sterigmata.

■ This species is usually found growing in clusters on decaying hardwoods. It resembles *L. crinitis* but differs in having dark brown fibrils on the cap and a cob-webby inner veil in youth.

Lentinus velutinus Fr.   **16**

(inedible)

■ The pileus is 2.0-8.0 cm in diameter, thin, leathery, broadly funnel-shaped, thickly covered with fine, greyish-cinnamon to chestnut-brown hairs. Gills are arcuate to short decurrent, pale buff to cinnamon-brown, closely crowded, and with entire margins. The stipe is slender, elongate, 2.0-25.0 x 0.2-1.0 cm, thickly covered with fine hairs as the color of the pileus, and often attached to a large, 2.0-30.0 cm pseudosclerotium composed of wood impregnated with the fungus.

■ The spores are buff to creamy in deposit, oblong to cylindric, 5.0-7.0 x 3.0-3.7 µm, not turning blue in iodine. The basidia are narrowly cylindric, 18.0-22.0 x 4.0-5.0 µm, with four sterigmata.

■ This is a remarkable species in that it sclerotizes the wood on which it grows, and basidiomata will emerge from these pseudosclerotia year after year. The basidiomata are recognized by the thick coverage of fine, very dark hairs and long slender stipes.

Aphyllophorales

Fig. 16. *Lentinus velutinus* (x 0.3)

Pleurotus

These fungi are what we commonly refer to as the "oyster mushrooms" because of the shape and color of the pileus. They have eccentric stipes and are laterally attached to the wood on which they grow. They have white to off-white, decurrent lamellae, and a white to creamy or faintly lilac spore print. They are choice, edible mushrooms which are currently being grown commercially on hardwood sawdust,

Fig. 17. *Pleurotus djamor* (x 0.5)   (Robert Williams)

pulverized straw, cottonseed hulls, and a variety of other crude cellulosic compost. More than 50 species are recognized worldwide, and
several of them occur in Florida. Because of their complex tissue
structure, firm flesh, and eccentric, laterally attached basidiomata,
many current workers, such as Pegler (1983), place *Pleurotus* in the
Aphyllophorales, an order commonly referred to as the bracket fungi.

A Key to Common Florida species:

1. Pileus 2.0-7.0 cm in diameter, white to whitish, mostly glabrous;
   stipe absent or highly reduced .... *Pleurotus djamor* (p. 24)

1. Pileus 6.0-14.0 cm in diameter, grayish-buff when young, buff
   brown with age, stipe variable, up to 2.0 cm
   .... *Pleurotus ostreatus* (p. 25)

Pleurotus djamor (Fr.) Boedijn   17

(edible)

■ Pileus 2.0-7.0 cm wide, laterally attached, spatulate to bell-shaped,
often in clusters; surface white, creamy with brownish to greyish
tints; smooth, often with a silvery sheen. Gills deeply decurrent
white to creamy; somewhat crowded. Stipe absent or extremely
short, if present, always lateral; surface white and tomentose.

■ Spores white in deposit, cylindric, 6.0-9.0 x 3.0-3.7 µm; smooth,
not turning blue in iodine. Basidia, clavate, 14.0-2.0 x 5.0-6.0 µm;
bearing four sterigmata.

■ This is the most common species of *Pleurotus* in Southeast Asia.
This species was found in Southwest Florida (Williams, *personal
communication*) and perhaps represents the first report of its
occurrence in the U.S.

Pleurotus ostreatus (Jacq.:Fr.) Kumm   18

(edible)

■ Pileus 5.0-20.0 cm wide, oyster-shaped, hygrophanous; white to
greyish-buff. Gills decurrent, crowded, white to greyish-white to
buff.

- Stipe absent or very short, 0.5-1.0 x 0.5-1.0 cm, fibrous to hairy; whitish-grey to buff.

- Spores white to pale lilac in deposit, ellipsoid, 7.0-9.0 x 3.0-3.5 µm; not turning blue in iodine. Basidia clavate, 14.0-17.5 x 3.5-4.5 µm; bearing four sterigmata.

- This is a highly variable species that might assume various sizes and shapes, depending on its orientation on the substrate on which it is growing. There are several color variants that are currently being grown commercially on different cellulosic substates.

Fig. 18. *Pleurotus ostreatus* (x 0.4)

Cantharellales

Pileus normally with a central stipe in which the hymenium is smooth or in folds or ridges, the latter appearing as lamellae but with fertile edges, often depressed or funnel-shaped; spores smooth, hyaline, not turning blue in iodine; on soil or plant debris. Twelve families have been placed in the Cantharellales. Only one, the Cantharellaceae, is agaricoid and will be considered among the mushrooms.

The Cantharellaceae

Basidiomata have a gymnohymenial development, range from pileate, tubular, to funnel-shaped, and the decurrent hymenium may be smooth or in folds or gill-like ridges. Spores are white to pale ochraceous to salmon pink, subglobose to ellipsoid, hyaline, smooth, and unchanged in iodine. Members of this family are found on the soil and most are assumed to be ectomycorrhizal. Most are recognized as choice edible species. Species of *Gomphus, Polyozellus, Cantharellus,* and *Craterellus* are placed here. Only species of *Cantharellus* and *Craterellus* are represented in Florida.

A Key to the Florida Cantharellaceae

1. Pileus cream to yellow, grayish-yellow, pinkish to reddish-yellow; hymenium smooth, ridged, or gilled, of similar color as the pileus; hyphae with clamp connections .... (*Cantharellus*)....2

1. Pileus purplish, dark gray, grayish-brown or blackish; hymenium smooth or faintly veined, of similar color to the pileus; hyphae without clamp connections ....*Craterellus fallax* (p. 27)

   2. Mature pileus usually less than 4 cm wide 3

   2. Mature pileus much larger 4

3. Basidiomata yellow to yellow-orange....*Cantharellus minor* (p. 34)

3. Basidiomata cinnabar-red .... *Cantharellus cinnabarinus* (p. 29)

   4. Multiple pilei arising from the same stipe..............................5

   4. Stipe with a single pileus 6

5. Flesh thin, bright orange-yellow to ochraceous, each hymenophore tubular, stipe highly branched .... *Cantharellus odoratus* (p. 33)

5. Flesh thicker, egg-yoke yellow, stipe strongly inflated upward, forming confluent pilei .... *Cantharellus confluens* (p. 31)

   6. Pileus with well-formed lamellae, bright yellow in color, fading to a whitish-yellow .... *Cantharellus cibarius* (p. 28)

   6. Pileus hymenium smooth or with shallow folds, yellow-orange in color .... *Cantharellus lateritius* (p. 32)

Craterellus fallax Smith   **19**

(edible)

■ The pileus is 2.5-7.5 cm wide, brownish-black to grayish-brown, funnel-shaped with a hollow tubular depression; the margin is decurved, and slightly scaly. The hymenium is smooth to slightly folded, deeply decurrent to a very short stipe, and slightly lighter in color than the pileus.

Fig. 19. *Craterellus fallax* (x 0.4)

■ The spores are broadly ellipsoid, 12.0-15.0 x 7.0-l0.0 μm, ochraceous to buff in deposit. Basidia approaching 75 μm in length, usually two-spored.

■ Numerous collections labeled *Craterellus cornucopioides* in the Mycology Herbarium at the University of Florida have been confirmed to be *C. fallax*. It occurs during the rainy summer season throughout the state.

---

20   *Cantharellus cibarius* Fr.:Fr

(edible)

■ The pileus is from 2.5-15.0 cm in diameter, deeply depressed at first but becoming flattened by maturity, bright egg-yoke yellow, sometimes fading whitish. Most specimens have well-formed decurrent lamellae that may become blunt folds with interconnecting veins. The stipe is more or less cylindric, 1.5-7.5 cm long, 6.0-12.0 mm wide, tapering gradually towards the base and basically the same color as the pileus. The flesh within is whitish to pale yellow, fibrous to fleshy, often with an apricot-like odor.

- Spores are ovoid to elliptical, smooth, pale buff to faintly yellow in deposit, 7.5-10.0 x 5.0-6.5 µm. The basidia are long, cylindric to clavate reaching amost 100 µm with usually four sterigmata.

- This species occurs in abundance from mid-June through mid-September in Florida. They are common under oaks and pines, but especially abundant beneath water, laurel, and live oaks, growing individually or more often in clusters or rings beneath their mycorrhizal hosts. *Cantharellus cibarius* is one of the most highly prized edible mushrooms worldwide. Because it is widely sought after, collectors should beware of look-alikes; especially *Omphalotus olearius* (DC: Fr.) Singer, the "jack-o-lantern" fungus, which is similar in size and color, but has sharp-edged lamellae and grows in clusters on rotting wood.

Fig. 20. *Cantharellus cibarius* (x 0.5)

Cantharellus cinnabarinus Schw.   **21**

(edible)

- The pileus is 1.2-4.0 cm in diameter, at first convexed, becoming flat with incurved, wavy margins, cinnabar-red, fading to pinkish-red with age. The hymenium has well developed, thick, decurrent lamellae, with cross veins, and pinkish-red in color. The stipe is

1.2-5.0 cm high, 0.6-1.2 cm wide, often tapering downward, and similar in color to the pileus.

■ Spores are broadly ellipsoid, 6.0-10.0 x 4.0-6.0 μm, smooth, and pinkish-cream in deposit. Basidia are 50-65 μm long, slightly clavate, and with six to eight sterigmata.

■ Like most species of *Cantharellus, C. cinnabarinus* occurs throughout the summer months in mixed oak/pine forests. However, whenever other species of chantharelles begin to dwindle during fall months, this species will continue to appear with frequency in October if rainfall is adequate. Because of its small size and cinnabar-red color, it is not easily confused with other species. While other chantharelles are choice, edible species, there have been reports from Floridians that large servings of *C. cinnabarinus* cause digestive irritation.

Fig. 21. *Cantharellus cinnabarinus* (x 2.0)

(edible)

■ The pileus is 2.5-12.0 cm in diameter, yellow to yellow-orange, forming several confluent hymenophores from a broadly clavate stipe, smooth, neither funnel-shaped or perforated. The stipe is 2.5-12.0 cm high, inflating greatly as it approaches the hymenophore. The hymenium is smooth, faintly lighter in color from the pileus, and extends a distance down the stipe. The flesh is creamy-white and emits a faint apricot odor when broken.

■ Spores are subglobose to broadly ellipsoid, 6.0-7.5 x 5.0-6.0 μm, pale buff to pinkish-yellow in deposit. The basidia exceed 100 μm in length, are cylindric to slightly clavate and have four to six sterigmata.

■ Like the other cantharelles, *C. confluens* occurs in the mixed hardwood-conifer forests in Florida, appearing frequently from mid-July into October. It has been confused most often with *C. odoratus* but differs in its thicker flesh, less tubular hymenophore, and the lack of ochraceous pigments in the stipe and pileus. According to Weber and Smith (1988), *C. lateritius* also has a smooth and slightly wrinkled hymenophore but it differs in having only one pileus per basidiomata and in being light salmon orange to apricot pink.

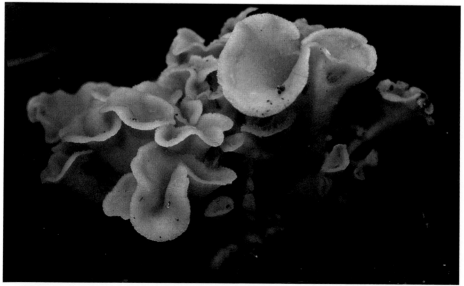

Fig. 22. *Cantharellus confluens* (x 0.8)

Cantharellales

(edible)

■ The pileus is 2.5-10.0 cm wide, slightly depressed, with a wavy, decurved margin, yellow-orange at the center, fading towards the margins. The hymenium is smooth to shallowly veined, with a tinted pinkish color. The stipe is 2.5-10.0 cm high and 0.5-2.0 cm wide, often off-center and yellowish-orange in color. The flesh is somewhat fibrous and emits a fruity odor when broken.

■ Spores are ellipsoid, 7.5-12.5 x 4.5-6.5 µm, smooth, and pinkish-yellow in deposit. The basidia approach 125 µm in length, are cylindric to slightly clavate, and have from four to six sterigmata.

■ This species occurs from June through August in mixed hardwood-conifer forests in Florida. It is the mushroom traditionally known as *Cantharellus craterellus* (Schw.) Fr. in North America. It is most similar to *C. cibarius* in size and shape, with the exception of having a basically smooth hymenium and more of a yellow-orange to ochraceous pigmentation. While the margin of the pileus becomes wavy, it does not become divided into distinct hymenophores.

Cantharellales

Fig. 23. *Cantharellus lateritius* (x 0.5)

Fig. 24. *Cantharellus odoratus*   (x 0.3)

Cantharellus odoratus (Schw.) Fr.   **24**

(edible)

■ This species grows as clusters of bright egg-yoke yellow to ochraceous-yellow, trumpet-shaped caps originating from a common base. The individual pileus may reach almost 10 cm in height and 12-15 cm in diameter. The hymenium is smooth or only minutely veined, similar in color to the pileus. The flesh is thin and emits a strong apricot-like odor when broken.

■ Spores are 5.5-10.3 x 3.5-6.0 µm, smooth, and pale pinkish-yellow to salmon in deposit. The basidia are cylindric and slightly clavate, reaching to 120 µm in length, and with three to six sterigmata.

■ This species occurs within mixed forests of mostly oaks and pines, is abundant from mid-July to late August, but has rarely been found in January. They appear to prefer rolling, well drained hillsides as opposed to *C. cibarius,* which grows more commonly in flat woods. Because of its basically smooth hymenium, earlier workers place this species in *Craterellus.* It has been confused with *C. confluens* (Berk. & Curt.) Petersen, but the latter has a thicker flesh, is less tubular, without an ochraceous color, and the spores are more broadly ellipsoid.

---

25   *Cantharellus minor* Pk.

(edible)

- The pileus is 0.7-4.0 cm in diameter, convexed at first but becoming slightly depressed with an incurved margin, smooth, and dull yellow to orange. The stipe is 2.5-5.0 cm high and approx. 0.7 cm wide, slender, cylindrical, hollow, and similar in color to the pileus. The hymenial area has narrow, decurrent, forked lamellae with interspersed veins, and light yellowish-orange in color.

- Spores are broadly ellipsoid to oblong, 6.0-12.0 x 4.0-6.0 µm, and pale, yellowish-orange in deposit. Basidia approaching 75 µm in length, slightly clavate with four sterigmata.

- This small chantharelle has been infrequently collected in Florida, but when found, it is always in mossy areas in hardwood hammocks during the rainy summer months. Because of its small size and color, it is not easily confused with other cantharelles. It is most like *C. cinnabarinus* in size and shape, but the latter is distinguished by its bright cinnabar-red color.

Fig. 25. *Cantharellus minor* (x 0.5)

Cantharellales

Russulales

Tissues of the basidiomata of the Russulales are heteromerous, i.e. clusters of globose cells called sphaerocysts are interspersed with filamentous hyphae. The spore surface has blunt spines, verrucose ridges, or reticulations that become blue when mounted in iodine. Since fungi do not have starch, such ornaments have been erroneously referred to as amyloid. Basidiomata of this order are highly variable in shape because both epigeous (above ground) and hypogeous (subterranean) groups are currently placed here. Epigeous members are agaricoid (with lamellae), and basidia forcibly eject their spores to become airborne (ballistosporic), whereas, hypogeous members are gasteroid, i.e. like a puffball, and the hymenium is within locules or labyrinthoid cavities in which the spores are not discharged (statismosporic).

There are two families, the Elasmomycetaceae which are hypogeous and gasteroid and the Russulaceae which are epigeous with stipes, caps, and lamellae. Only the Russulaceae will be treated here.

The Russulaceae

Basidiomata of the Russulaceae are more brittle than other mushrooms. They are medium to large, usually with a central stipe, and often brightly pigmented. Development is either gymnohymenial or hemiangiohymenial, leaving them without a volva and very rarely with a fragile annulus. The lamellae are free to occasionally decurrent, crowded to broadly spaced. Spore prints are white to deep ochrayellow. Microscopically, spores are globose to short ellipsoid, always with warts, spines, ridges, or reticula that turn blue in iodine. All species are assumed to be ectomycorrhizal, growing around both hardwood and conifer species.

A Key to the Agaricoid Genera of Florida Russulaceae

1. Basidiomata exuding latex when broken, sphaerocysts scant or missing, lamellae often decurrent .... *Lactarius* (p. 36)
1. Basidiomata not exuding latex, sphaerocysts present, and the lamellae are rarely decurrent .... *Russula* (p. 49)

Lactarius

This is the only genus of gilled mushroom in which all species may exude milk when broken or cut. The color and taste of the milk is very important for the separation of species. These characters are very deceptive in that milk will often change in color after it is exposed to air, in many species the taste of the milk is slow in developing, and older specimens may fail to exude milk. Species of *Lactarius* are usually short and stocky, many with a saucer-shaped pileus and brightly colored. Spores of all species have some type of ornamentation that stains blue when mounted in iodine. They are one of the most abundant groups of summer mushrooms in Florida. Several species are edible, but those with strongly acrid or peppery milk, or those in which the milk turns yellow or purple soon after exposure should be avoided since they can cause digestive irritation. Detailed descriptions of Florida species can be found in Hesler and Smith's (1983) *North American Species of Lactarius*.

A Key to Common species of *Lactarius* in Florida

1. Basidiomata blue, becoming grayish-blue, the latex is brilliant blue ....*Lactarius indigo* (p. 42)
1. Basidiomata and latex not blue 2
   2. Basidiomata white to grayish-white 3
   2. Basidiomata some shade of brown or yellow-brown 5
3. Pileus large, 5.0-10.0 cm, white to creamy, latex copius, white and promptly peppery .... *Lactarius piperatus* var. *piperatus* (p. 45)
3. Pileus smaller, latex mild to slightly acrid 4
   4. Pileus white to grayish-white, latex white, becoming yellow and faintly acrid ....*Lactarius chrysorheus* (p. 39)
   4. Pileus whitish-buff, slightly umbonate, latex mild, milky to whey-like .... *Lactarius luteolus* (p. 44)
5. Pileus up to 15.0 cm, drab cinnamon-gray, very viscid, latex clay to creamy, slowly becoming very acrid ......*Lactarius argillaceifolius* ....var. *argillaceifolius* (p. 37)
5. Pileus and latex not as above 6
   6. Pileus deep rusty-brown, undulate, latex mild, copius, white ... but staining tissues brown .... *Lactarius corrugis* (p. 39)
   6. Pileus lighter in color, surface not undulated 7

Lactarius argillaceifolius var. *argillaceifolius* Hesl. & Smith   **26**

(inedible)

■ A medium-sized mushroom, 4.0-15.0 cm broad, with a broadly convex to depressed pileus with enrolled margins. It is cinnamon-drab to grayish in color and quite viscid when moist. The dull cream-colored latex tastes mild at first but slowly becomes a burning-acrid, and on drying turns the lamellae a grayish-brown. The lamellae are decurrent, close, pale cream when young but becoming a dull clay color with age. The stipe is 6.0-9.0 cm long, 1.5-3.5 cm thick, and slightly tapering downward.

■ Spores are pinkish-buff in deposit, subglobose to broadly ellipsoid, 8.0-10.0 x 7.0-8.0 µm, with isolated warts or ridges that sometimes form a reticulum. The basidia are 45.0-52.0 x 9.0-10.5 µm interspersed with long, pointed fusoid pleurocystidia measuring 60.0-105.0 x 6.0-12.0 µm.

■ This species is found commonly in mixed forest in northern Florida during the summer rainy season. It has been most commonly identified as *Lactarius trivialis*; a species, according to Hesler and Smith (1983), that is restricted to the conifer forest of the Pacific Northwest. Because of its distinct color, viscid cap, and delayed milk reaction, *L. argillaceifolius* is an easy species to recognize.

Russulales

Fig. 26. *Lactarius argillaceifolius* var. *argillaceifolius* (x 0.5)

Fig. 27. *Lactarius chrysorheus* (x 1.0)

Russulales

Lactarius chrysorheus Fr.   **27**

(poisonous)

■ A small to medium-sized species with a 3.0-7.0 cm pileus that is convex to slightly depressed, becoming funnel-form with incurved margins. The surface is moist to subviscid, becoming whitish or grayish to a pale yellowish-cinnamon color. The flesh when broken exudes a white copious milk that soon becomes yellow and tastes distinctly acrid. The pallid to pale orange lamellae are decurrent, and often fork towards the stipe. The stipe is 3.0-4.0 cm long and 1.0-1.5 cm thick and a buff-orange in color.

■ The spores are pale yellow in deposit, broadly ellipsoid, 6.0-8.0 x 5.5-6.5 µm, the surface with many isolated warts that may form an indistinct reticulum. Basidia are 37.0-45.0 x 8.0-10.0 µm interspersed with pointed, fusoid, 45.0-75.0-7.0-11.0 µm pleurocystidia.

■ This species is commonly found in mixed forests of Florida during the summer rainy season. Its acrid milk that changes quickly from white to yellow, along with the pale color of the cap, helps to separate this from other species of *Lactarius,* having yellow milk.

Lactarius corrugis Peck   **28**

(edible)

■ This is a medium to large mushroom with a 5.0-12.0 cm pileus that is convex to depressed, with a dark cinnamon-brown to rusty color, and an undulated or corrugated surface. It has a mild tasting, copious, white latex that stains the flesh brown when broken or cut. The lamellae are adnate to decurrent, pale cinnamon-buff to ochraceous, and are closely arranged. The stipe is 5.0-11.0 cm long and 1.5-2.5 cm thick, grayish to reddish-brown, but usually paler than the pileus.

■ Spores are white in deposit, globose to subglobose, 9.0-12.0 x 9.0-11.0 µm, with a prominent surface reticulum that stains blue in iodine. Basidia are 44.0-68.0 x 9.0-12.0 µm interspersed with subfusoid to lance-shaped pleurocystidia that measure 35.0-78.0 x 4.0-8.0 µm.

■ This species is very common in mixed forest throughout Florida during the rainy summer months. It is easily recognized by its deep

Russulales

Fig. 28. *Lactarius corrugis* (x 0.8)

rusty-brown, corrugated pileus and copious white milk. It may be confused with *L. volemus* (Fr.) Fr., which is lighter in color and has a smooth cap.

---

29 *Lactarius gerardii* var. *gerardii* Peck

(edible)

■ This is a medium-sized mushroom with a 5.0-10.0 cm pileus that is convex with a small umbo, but later expands and may become slightly depressed and wavy towards the margins. Its color varies from dark yellowish-brown to snuff brown, but often fades to a golden brown. The mild-tasting latex is white, unchanged on drying, and does not stain the tissues. The lamellae are adnate early but become decurrent, widely spaced, white becoming cream, and with numerous interconnecting veins. The stipe is 3.5-8.0 cm long and 0.8-1.5 cm thick, cylindric, and similar in color to the pileus.

- The spores are white in deposit, subglobose to broadly ellipsoid, 8.0-10.0 x 7.5-9.0 µm, with broad surface bands forming a reticulum. The basidia are 52.0-58.0 x 7.0-9.0 µm interspersed with clavate to cylindric, 38.0-63.0 x 6.0-11.0 µm pleurocystidia.

- This species is fairly common in mixed forest of Florida during the summer months. The white, widely spaced lamellae which exude white latex that does not stain the mushroom tissues tends to set this species apart from other species of *Lactarius*.

Lactarius hygrophoroides Berk. & Curt.   **30**

(edible)

- This is a small to medium-sized mushroom with a 3.0-10.0 cm pileus that is convex at first but expands and becomes depressed, sometimes slightly funnel-shaped, and has a dry, reddish to orange-cinnamon surface. The lamellae are somewhat distant, cream colored or yellowish-buff, adnate-decurrent, and with interconnecting veins. The mild tasting latex is white and does not stain the flesh on drying. The stipe is 3.0-5.0 cm long, 0.5-1.5 cm thick, cylindric, and of similar color to the pileus.

Fig. 29. *Lactarius gerardii* var. *gerardii* (x 0.6)

- The spores are white in deposit, ellipsoid, 7.5-9.5 x 6.0-7.5 μm, with isolated surface warts that seldom interconnect to form a reticulum that stains blue in iodine. The basidia are 37.0-66.0 x 7.0-9.0 μm, but pleurocystidia are not present.

- This is a common species in mixed forests and woody lawns throughout most of Florida. It is somewhat similar to *L. volemus*, but may be distinguished from the latter by lighter colored and more distant lamellae, and in the absence of pleurocystidia.

Fig. 30. *Lactarius hygrophoroides* (x 0.4)   (Terry Hinkel)

---

3 I   *Lactarius indigo* (Schw.) Fr.

(edible)

- This is a medium-sized mushroom with a 5.0-15.0 cm pileus that is at first convex but becomes depressed or funnel-form with enrolled margins. It is at first indigo blue and somewhat moist, but fades to a grayish to silvery lustre with age, often appearing greenish and zonate. The mild to slightly bitter latex is indigo blue on freshly cut surfaces, becoming a dark green on exposure to the air. The lamellae are broadly adnate, becoming decurrent, and are of similar color to the cap but may become green when bruised. The stipe is 2.0-8.0 cm long and 1.0-2.5 cm thick, cylindric but sometimes tapering downward.

■ The spores are cream colored in deposit, broadly ellipsoid to subglobose, 7.0-9.0 x 5.5-7.5 μm, and with an incomplete surface reticulum. The basidia are 37.0-45.0 x 8.0-10.0 μm with ventricose, 37.0-62.0 x 5.0-8.0 μm pleurocystidia.

■ This bright blue species is found throughout mixed forests in Florida. It usually appears in the late summer, and is a common species in the autumn months when there is sufficient rainfall. With age and drying, it may be confused with *L. paradoxa* Beardsl. & Burl., which has a bluish-gray color.

Fig. 31. *Lactarius indigo* (x 0.75)   (Henry Aldrich)

(edible)

- This is a rather small mushroom with a 2.5-6.0 cm pileus that is convex to plane, with a slight umbo, azonate, and white to whitish-buff in color. The flesh has a strong fetid odor, mild taste, and a copious white to whey-like milk that stains brownish on drying. The lamellae are adnate to subdecurrent, close, white and becoming yellowish-brown when bruised. The stipe is 2.5-6.0 cm long, 0.5-1.2 cm thick, cylindric, and of similar color to the cap.

- The spores are white to cream colored in deposit, ellipsoid, 7.0-8.5 x 5.5-6.0 µm, with prominent isolated warts. Basidia are 32.0-43.0 x 6.0-8.0 µm interspersed with flexuous to subcylindric, 47.0-70.0 x 3.0-6.0 µm pleurocystidia.

- This species is found commonly in mixed forests of northern Florida during rainy summer months. It is somewhat related to *L. volemus* but is smaller, lighter colored, and has less copious milk.

Fig. 32. *Lactarius luteolus* (x 1.0)

Fig. 33. *Lactarius piperatus* var. *piperatus* (x 0.5)

Lacterius piperatus var. *piperatus* (Fr.) Gray   **33**

(inedible)

■ This is a medium to large mushroom with a 5.0-15.0 cm pileus that is initially convex, but later becomes depressed or funnel-shaped. It is white at first, but often stains tan or creamy-white and remains azonate. The extremely acrid (peppery) latex is white when exuded but may become creamy on drying. The lamellae are white to creamy, crowded, and branched extensively. The white stipe is 2.0-8.0 cm long, 1.0-2.5 cm thick, and cylindric.

■ The spores are white in deposit, ellipsoid, 5.0-7.0 x 5.0-5.4 μm, with isolated surface warts that do not form a reticulum and stain blue in iodine. The basidia are 38.0-46.0 x 6.0-8.0 μm interspersed with large, 38.0-67.0 x 5.0-9.0 μm, subclavate, pleurocystidia.

■ This is one of the most common species of *Lactarius* in the mixed forests of Florida. It appears throughout the rainy summer months, and will occasionally appear in the late fall when there is adequate rainfall. A second variety, *L. piperatus* var. *glaucescens* (Crossl.) Hesl. & Smith, also occurs here and is recognized by its slightly more crowded lamellae, and copious white milk that turns olive-green on drying.

Russulales

(inedible)

■ This is a rather small mushroom with a 2.0-7.5 cm pileus that is convex, but becomes depressed with encurved margins. It is slightly moist, rusty to orange-cinnamon with faint apricot-orange zones. The slightly acrid latex is white to pale vinaceous, but soon becomes yellow when exposed. The lamellae are close to crowded, decurrent, pinkish-buff in color, and with numerous shorter veins. The stipe is 4.0-6.0 cm long, 1.0-1.5 cm thick, cylindric to slightly broader below, and of similar color to the pileus.

■ The spores are white or yellowish in heavy deposits, subglobose to broadly ellipsoid, 7.0-9.0 x 6.0-7.5 μm, and with blunt warts or ridges that may be interconnected and stain blue in iodine. The

Fig. 34. *Lactarius thejogalus* (x 1.0)

Russulales

basidia are 2;8.0-37.0 x 7.0-10.0 µm interspersed with fusoid, 48.0-85.0 x 7.0-11.0 µm pleurocystidia.

■ This species is found in moist, mossy areas of mixed forests during the summer months in Florida. It has been found most commonly associated with evergreen oaks. It is distinguished from other orange to pinkish-orange species of *Lactarius* by its generally smaller size, pileus with a faint apricot-orange zonation, and white milk that slowly turns yellow on exposure.

Fig. 35. *Lactatius volemus* var. *volemus* (x 0.5)   (Henry Aldrich)

Lactarius volemus (Fr.) Fr. var. *volemus*   **35**

(edible)

■ This is a medium-sized mushroom with a 5.0-10.0 cm pileus that is initially convex, but becomes depressed to funnelform. Most have a rich Kaiser brown, reddish-cinnamon to rusty color, which in some varieties may be paler yellow-brown or tawny. The mild-tasting latex is white to whey-like, but can become cream-colored on exposure, and turns the tissue a dark brown to grayish-brown. The lamellae are adnate to decurrent, often forked, at first white but becomes cream-colored or dark brown when bruised. The stipe is 5.0-10.0 cm long, 0.8-1.2 cm thick, cylindric or tapering toward the base, and similar in color to the pileus.

The spores are white in deposit, globose to subglobose, 7.5-9.0 x 7.5-8.5 µm, with a prominent surface reticulation that turns blue in iodine. The basidia are clavate, 42.0-60.0 x 9.0-12.0 µm, interspersed with large, 48.0-145.0 x 5.0-13.0 µm, ventricose to subfusoid pleurocystidia.

This is one of the most abundant yellow-brown species of *Lactarius* in mixed forest in Florida. It has been most often identified as *L. lactiflua* (L.) Burl., and is often confused with *L. corrugis*. It differs, however, from *L. corrugis* in having a smooth, lighter pigmented pileus. Another variety, *L. volemus* var. *flavus*, remains yellow throughout development. All of these yellowish to rusty-brown species with copious white milk are widely collected for food.

---

36   *Lactarius volemus* var. *flavus* Hesler & Smith

(edible)

The pileus is 5.0-9.0 cm in diameter, convex to plane, ivory to Naples yellow, becoming brownish when bruised, and with a mild, white latex that stains all parts brown. The lamellae are adnate, whitish to cream colored, and frequently forked. The stipe is 5.0-10.0 x 0.8-1.6 cm, equal, cream color, and dry.

The spores are creamy in deposit, globose to subglobose, 7.0-8.5 x 6.0-7.5 µm, ornaments up to 0.5 µm high, and forming an incom-

Fig. 36. *Lactarius volemus* var. *flavus* (x 0.5)

plete reticulum that stains blue in iodine. Basidia are narrowly clavate, 36.0-40.0 x 7.0-8.0 µm.

■ This yellow variant of *L. volemus* is found throughout the Gulf coastal region, and is common beneath laurel and live oaks in northern Florida.

Russula

Species of *Russula* and *Lactarius* appear similar in the field because of their short, stout stature and the usual lack of membranes or veils on the basidiomata. Unlike *Lactarius,* species of *Russula* will not exude milk when broken or cut. In most cases the pileus is glabrous and brightly colored, and the degree to which the cuticle of the pileus will peel away is important. The spores are white, pale yellow to ochraceous in deposit, and under the microscope they all have various types of surface ornamentation that turn blue when mounted in iodine. Since basidial size and morphology are of little taxonomic value, they will be excluded here. Nearly 300 species of *Russula* are recognized, and the genus is plentiful in Florida. Several species are edible, yet others cause distressing digestive disorders. Thus, it is important to know the species. Avoid those that stain red, brownish, or black. *Keys to the Species of Russula in Northeastern North America* by Kibby and Fatto (1990) also has keys and descriptions of most Florida species.

A Key to Common species of *Russula* in Florida

1. Pileus brown, gray, black or mixture of colors 2
1. Pileus another color 3
   2. Pileus dark sepia to grayish-brown   *Russula amoenolens* (p. 51)
   2. Pileus whitish at first but becomming dark brownish to eventually black .... *Russula nigricans* (p. 61)
3. Pileus white to cream-colored 4
3. Pileus not white or cream-colored 6
   4. Pileus creamy white, 7.0-15.0 cm ...... *Russula compacta* (p. 53)
   4. Pileus smaller, whiter 5
5. Pileus white to yellowish, spore print yellowish
   .... *Russula anomala* (p. 52)
5. Pileus milk white, spore print white. .... *Russula perlactea* (p. 63)
   6. Pileus yellow, ochre or orange 7

Russula amoenolens Romag.   **37**

(inedible)

■ The pileus of this species is 4.0-10.0 cm in diameter, dark grayish to yellow-brown, slightly viscid, with a striate margin and the cuticle peeling half way. The lamellae are adnate, creamy-buff but darken with age. The stipe is whitish to grayish-brown, 3.0-6.5 x 1.5-2.0 cm. Tissues taste umpleasant and slowly become hot.

Fig. 37. *Russula amoenolens* (x 0.4)   (Sherri Angels)

Russulales

The spores are cream in deposit, subglobose, 6.0-9.0 x 5.0-7.0 µm, with isolated warts that turn blue in iodine.

This species has been previously called *Russula pectinata,* and has been found thus far in mixed forests of the northeastern U.S.

---

38   *Russula anomala* **Peck**

(?edibility)

■ The pileus is 3.0-10.0 cm wide, convex to depressed, white to slightly yellowish, dry, margins slightly striate, and peels 1/4 the width. The lamellae are crowded, adnexed, white but become yellowish with age. The stipe is white, 4.0-4.5 x 1.5-2.0 cm, often tapering upward. The tissue is moderately acrid and odorless.

The spores are cream-colored in deposit, broadly ellipsoid, 8.0-10. x 7.0-8.0 µm, with isolated warts and a few interconnections that stain blue in iodine.

This species was first collected in Florida beneath laurel oaks on lawns, and described as a new species *Russula subalbidula* Murrill. Several collections of this species have been made in the area of Gainesville.

Fig. 38. *Russula anomala* (x 0.8)

Russulales

Fig. 39. *Russula compacta* (x 1.0)

Russula compacta Frost   **39**

(edible)

- The pileus is 3.0-18.0 cm in diameter, convex, becoming plane and depressed, firm, whitish to cream or pale yellowish-brown, with a smooth margin and a cuticle that peels half way to the center. The lamellae are adnate, somewhat crowded, white to pale cream and bruising brownish. The stipe is 2.0-10.0 x 1.2-3.0 cm, whitish to cream, and bruising brownish.

- The spores are white in deposit, subglobose, 7.0-10.0 x 6.0-8.0 µm, with isolated warts that are interconnected and turn blue in iodine.

- This is a very common species of *Russula* in Florida, and is frequently found associated with evergreen oaks in various areas of the state. It is one of the larger, compact species found locally.

---

40   *Russula cremeirosea* Murr.

(?edibility)

- This is a small rosy-pink mushroom 4.0-8.0 cm in diameter, with creamy areas over the surface which peel up to 1/3 of the disc. The lamellae are adnate, creamy and subdistant. The stipe is stout, 3.0-5.5 x 1.0-2.0 cm, white, with a pinkish blush.

- The spores are creamy in deposit, subglobose, 7.5-9.5 x 6.5-8.5 µm, with isolated warts that turn blue in iodine.

- This is a midsummer mushroom found growing beneath oak trees near lake shores. It is apparently ectomycorrhizal on live and laurel oak trees, and is one of the few pink species of *Russula* in the area.

Fig. 40. *Russula cremeirosea* (x 1.0)

Russulales

Fig. 41. *Russula emetica* (x 0.5)

Russula emetica (Schaeff.:Fr.) Gray   **41**

(inedible)

■ The pileus is 5.0-10.0 cm wide, convex but becoming depressed, viscid, bright scarlet to blood-red, the cuticle easily peeling. The brittle flesh is pink beneath the peel with a fruity odor, but very bitter taste. The stipe is cylindric, 5.0-10.0 x 1.0-2.5 cm, white and very fragile. The lamellae are white to creamy, broadly spaced, and free to slightly adnexed.

■ The spores are white in deposit, globose, 8.0-11.0 x 7.0-8.5 μm, with large conical warts that merge to form an incomplete reticulum that turns blue in iodine.

■ This is a common species in Florida, found during summer months in moist, sphagnum areas around pine trees. *Russula silvicola* is slightly larger, more reddish-yellow in color and grows in mixed forest, while *R. subfragiliformis* is similar but has a pinkish stipe and a mild taste.

(inedible)

■ This is a uniformily red species, 2.0-3.0 cm in diameter, that is glabrous, with a slightly striate margin, and a cuticle that peels 1/3 to the disc. The lamellae are adnate, crowded, white to pallid, and very acrid to the taste. The white stipe is 3.0-3.5 x 0.5-0.7 cm, and tapers slightly downward.

■ The spores are white in deposit, subglobose, 7.0-9.0 x 6.5-7.5 μm, with connected warts that form a faint reticulum and stains blue in iodine.

■ This species is found in leaf mulch beneath laurel oaks in northern Florida, but according to Kibby and Fatto (1990), it is also found beneath pines as well. It is distinguished from other red-capped *Russula* by its small size, white stipe, and cuticle that peels much of the radius of the pileus.

Fig. 42. *Russula fragiloides* (x 1.3)

Russulales

Fig. 43. *Russula fragrantissima*   (x 0.3)

Russula fragrantissima Romag.   **43**

(inedible)

■ The pileus is from 7.5-20 cm wide, convex at first but becoming flat to slightly depressed, and with prominent striations. The cuticle is strongly viscid, peeling almost to the center, slightly to moderately acrid with a benzaldehyde or fetid odor, yellow, yellowish-orange to yellowish-brown or chestnut-brown with age. The lamellae are adnexed to adnate, close to subdistant, occasionally forked, yellowish-white when young, becoming pale yellowish-orange with age. The stipe is 7.0-15.0 cm long, 1.5-6.0 cm thick, cylindric or tapering towards the base, yellow-brown overall, but becoming darker towards the base.

■ The spores are pale yellow in deposit, broadly ellipsoid, 6.3-9.0 x 5.7-7.7 μm, with conic to cylindric warts and short to long ridges that turn blue in iodine.

■ According to Shaffer (1972), this species is the common mushroom with large basidiomata and strong odor, usually called *Russula foetens* in this country. A related species, *R. pectinatoides* Pk. is similar in color and appearance, but is smaller and has a very different spore ornamentation. *Russula amoenolens* is similar but is usually smaller and has a more yellow-brown color.

Russulales

(edible)

- This is a medium-sized species, with a 5.0-11.0 cm wide pileus that is greenish-olive to purplish-gray, and a cuticle that peels 1/4 to 1/2 to the disc. The lamellae are adnate, close, and cream in color. The stipe is white with a pinkish to lilaceous tint, 4.5-6.0 x 1.4-2.0 cm, and tapers downwards. The tissues are mild to the taste.

- The spores are deep cream in deposit, subglobose, 6.5-8.0 x 5.5-6.5 µm, with warts, some interconnected, that turn blue in iodine.

- This species is found under various hardwood species, and has been found in Florida beneath evergreen oaks.

Fig. 44. *Russula grisea*   (x 0.7)

Russulales

Fig. 45. *Russula heterophylla*   (× 0.7)

Russula heterophylla Fr.   **45**

(edible)

■ The pileus is 5.0-10.0 cm wide, convex at first becoming flat to depressed, varying from green, yellow-green to ochre in color, and with a cuticle that peels about halfway. The lamellae are adnate, crowded, white to pale cream, and forked near the stipe. The stipe is 50-100 cm long, 1.0-2.0 cm thick, often tapering downward, white but browning on handling. It has a mild taste and no odor.

■ The spores are white in deposit, subglobose, 5.0-7.0 x 4.0-6.0 µm, with isolated warts that are rarely connected and stain blue in iodine.

■ This species is found in mixed forests in northern Florida. It is often confused with *R. aeruginea,* which has yellowish spores, and *R. virescens* which has larger spores and a pileus with greenish patches.

(edible)

- The pileus is 3.0-8.0 cm wide, convex but soon depressed, varying in color from wine-red to purple or violet, and the cuticle peels to the center. The pale yellow lamellae are adnate and crowded. The stipe is 2.0-6.0 cm long, 0.5-2.0 cm thick, often tapering downward, and white to pinkish in color. The taste is mild to slightly acrid and there is no odor.

- The spores are pale yellow in deposit, subglobose, 6.5-8.5 x 5.5-7.5 μm, with prominent reticulations that turn blue in iodine.

- This species is fairly common throughout the wooded areas of Florida. Murrill (1938) recognized *R. alachuana* for another purplish *Russula* that seems to differ by its lighter spore print, and *R. subcyanoxantha* and *R. rubripurpurea* that are smaller and with white lamellae and spores. Kirby and Fatto (1990) place all but *R. rubripurpurea* in synonymy with *R. mariae*.

Fig. 46. *Russula mariae*   (x 0.6)

Russulales

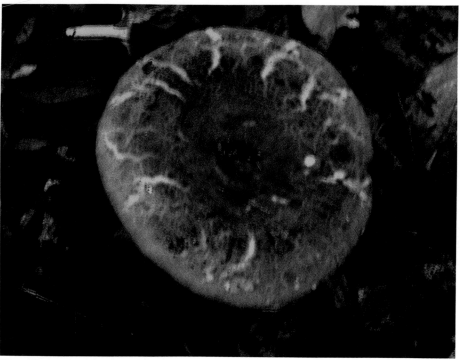

Fig. 47. *Russula nigricans*   (x 0.6)

Russula nigricans Fr.   **47**

(?edibility)

- The pileus is 5.0-15.0 cm wide, convex but soon becoming depressed, slightly viscid when young, dirty white but becoming burnt-brown to blackish, and peeling almost to the center. The lamellae are widely spaced, adnate, and pallid to straw colored, and bruising bright red then brownish. The stipe is 3.0-8.0 x 1.0-4.0 cm, and white, then staining dark like the cap. It has a fruity to unpleasant odor and a mild taste.

- The spores are white in deposit, broadly ellipsoid, 6.3-8.0 x 5.5-7.0 µm, and with warts that merge to become reticulate and turn blue in iodine.

- This species is found under live oaks and pines throughout much of Florida, occurring during summer months. It is the only *Russula* in this area that is blackish and wounds reddish when handled. Not recommended for food since species related to *R. nigricans* cause digestive disorders.

Fig. 48. *Russula pectintoides* (x 0.5)

---

48   *Russula pectinatoides* Pk.

(inedible)

- ■ The pileus is 3.0-8.0 cm wide, convex to centrally depressed, yellowish to dull brown in color, and prominently striate on the margins. The lamellae are thin, adnate and white to pale cream colored. The stipe is 2.5-5.0 x 0.5-1.0 cm, cylindric or slightly bulbous below, and white to pale yellowish or brownish when bruised. It has a slightly foetid odor and somewhat acrid taste.

- ■ The spores are cream in deposit, subglobose to broadly ellipsoid, 5.5-9.0 x 4.6-70 µm, with mostly isolated warts and a few connections that turn blue in iodine.

- ■ This species is often collected under evergreen oaks, especially in lawns throughout Florida. It is similar to two other straw-colored to grayish-brown mushrooms with a foetid odor. They are *R. fragrantissima* (traditionally identified as *R. foetens)* which has larger basidiomata and spores with a more pronounced ornamentation, and *R. amoenolens* that has a grayish-brown, faintly striate pileus.

Russulales

Russula perlactea Murr.   **49**

(?edibility)

■ The pileus is 4.0-7.0 cm wide, convex to slightly depressed, white to cream-colored, somewhat viscid in youth, and with a cuticle that peels to near the center. The lamellae are adnate, rather distant, white and unchanging, and with a few branches. The stipe is cylindric, 5.0 x 1.8 cm, white, and unchanging on bruising. The flesh is odorless but distinctly acrid.

■ The spores are white in deposit, broadly ellipsoid, 9.0-11.5 x 7.5-9.0 µm, with isolated warts and a few interconnections that turn blue in iodine.

■ This species is found under both oaks and pines throughout north Florida. It is distinguished from other white species of *Russula* by its unchanging white lamellae, sharply acrid taste, and chalk-white spores. There are a number of other white species such as *R. albidula, R. albida,* and *R. westii* that have a mild taste and yellowish spores.

Fig. 49. *Russula perlactea*   (x 0.7)

Russulales

(?edibility)

■ The pileus is approximately 5.0-5.5 cm wide, convex to slightly depressed, uniformly red or pinkish-red, somewhat viscid, margin striate, and peels readily. The lamellae are adnate, white but soon become yellow, and frequently branch towards the stipe. The stipe is 4.0-5.0 x 1.0-1.3 cm, cylindric, white and unchanging when bruised. The flesh is odorless and tastes mild.

■ The spores are cream-ochre in deposit, ellipsoid, 8.0-9.5 x 7.2-8.0 μm, with isolated warts that turn blue in iodine.

■ This species has been collected only in the mixed forests of high hammock areas around Gainesville, Florida. According to Murrill (1945), it occurs under laurel oaks from April to July.

Fig. 50. *Russula pusilliformis* (x 1.2)   (Sherri Angels)

Russulales

Fig. 51. *Russula rosietincta* (x 0.4)

Russula roseitincta Murr. **51**

(?edibility)

- The pileus is 6.0-8.0 cm wide, convex to depressed, viscid when wet, yellowish-pink to pale yellowish-orange, with an even margin, and cuticle that peels readily. The lamellae are cream-colored, adnate, rather close, and frequently forked. The stipe is white with a flush of pink, 5.0-6.0 x 1.0-1.4 cm, and more or less cylindric. The taste is mild and there is no odor.

- The spores are cream in deposit, subglobose to broadly ellipsoid, 6.0-10.5 x 5.0-7.2 μm, with isolated warts and a few fine lines that turn blue in iodine.

- This species is found in deep, mixed forests of northern Florida, and occurs most often under laurel and live oaks during rainy summer months.

Russulales

(?edibility)

■ This is a fairly small mushroom, 4.5-6.0 cm in diameter, with a grayish-rosy or yellow-blotched and slightly moist pileus in which the cuticle scarcely peels away from the striate margin. The lamellae are adnate, narrow, close, initially white but becoming yellowish. The stipe is 4.0-6.0 x 1.0-1.5 cm, tapering downward, white, but turning brown when bruised.

■ The spores are white in deposit, subglobose, 6.0-7.0 x 5.5-6.2 µm, with distinct ornaments that turn blue in iodine.

■ This species of *Russula* has been found in a number of habitats around Gainesville and, according to Murrill (1943), prefers limy soil. In such habitats it is associated with evergreen oaks, and is distinguished by its drab rosy-isabelline pileus with yellowish blotches.

Fig. 52. *Russula rosei-isabellina* (x 1.0)

Russulales

Fig. 53. *Russula roseipes*   (x 0.6)

Russula roseipes (Secr.) Bres.   **53**

(edible)

- This is a small, 3.0-5.0 cm, fragile species in which the rosy-pink cuticle becomes whitish towards the striate margin. The lamellae are adnate, broadly spaced and creamy-yellow. The stipe is 5.0-6.0 x 0.5-1.0 cm, white with a rosy-pink tint and tapers upwards.

- The spores are deep yellow in deposit, subglobose, 7.0-9.5 x 6.0-7.5 μm, with warts that have a few interconnections and turn blue in iodine.

- This species is found in conifer and mixed forests throughout eastern North America. It is very similar to *R. cremeirosea* in the field, but differs in having a darker spore deposit and a more pigmented stipe.

(?edibility)

■ The pileus is 5.0-9.0 cm in diameter, convex to plane, scarlet red with darker disc, cuticle viscid when wet, peeling 1/3 away from the striate margin. The lamellae are adnate, widely spaced, and deep yellowish-brown. The stipe is 3.0-8.0 x 0.5-1.0 cm, more or less equal, and turning brownish then black when bruised.

■ The spores are pale yellow in deposit, subglobose, 7.0-10.0 x 6.8-8.0 µm, with warts that are scarcely connected and turn blue in iodine.

■ This species is one of the many red *Russulas* found in Florida. Its most distinctive feature is the brownish, then black staining of the stipe when bruised. It is found in low, poorly drained areas near evergreen oaks.

Fig. 54. *Russula rubescens* (x 1.0)   (Sherri Angels)

Russulales

Fig. 55. *Russula rubripurpurea* (× 1.0)   (Sherri Angels)

Russula rubripurpurea Murr.   **55**

(?edibility)

■ The pileus is 3.0-5.0 cm, convex to depressed, glabrous, moist, with a red to purplish disc, margin even, and not peeling easily. The lamellae are adnate, white, unchanging with age, and fairly crowded. The stipe is cylindric, 2.5-3.5 x 0.8-1.2 cm, white, and smooth.

■ The spores are white to cream colored in deposit, subglobose to broadly ellipsoid, 6.3-8.0 x 5.0-7.5 μm, with warts that may form a fine reticulum on areas of the spore and turn blue in iodine.

■ This species has been collected several times in northern Florida, growing in oak woods. It is the smallest of the species of purplish species of *Russula* found in this area, the most common of which is *R. mariae.*

Russulales

Fig. 56. *Russula sanguinea* (x 0.6)   (Sherri Angels)

56   *Russula sanguinea* (Bull.:St. Amans) Fr.

(inedible)

- ■ The pileus is 5.0-10.0 cm in diameter, convex to plane, often upturned; cuticle blood to cherry-red, with lighter blotches, and without striations. The lamellae are adnate to slightly decurrent, crowded and pale to cream colored. The stipe is 4.0-10.0 x 1.0-3.0 cm, tinted pinkish to red, and tapers downward.

- ■ The spores are pale to deep creamy-yellow in deposit, subglobose, 7.0-10.0 x 6.0-8.0 µm, with slightly interconnected warts that turn blue in iodine.

- ■ This species is found under pines and is widely distributed through North America. It is distinguished from other local *Russulas* by its somewhat robust, pinkish to red stipe.

(?edibility)

- The pileus is 4.0-6.0 cm in diameter, deep violet-purple to reddish-purple, moist, smooth, and the cuticle peels 3/4 to the middle. The lamellae are adnate, distant, and white. The stipe is 3.0-7.0 x 1.0-1.5 cm, white, and more or less equal.

- The spores are white in deposit, subglobose, 7.0-8.5 x 5.3-9.0 μm, with isolated warts that turn blue in iodine.

- This species is found in mixed forests throughout North America. It has been found on several occasions in oak forests of central and northern Florida.

Fig. 57. *Russula sericonitens*　(x 0.7)

Russulales

(?edibility)

- The pileus of this species is small, 5.0-6.0 cm, convex to slightly depressed, slightly viscid when moist, rosy isabelline; margin slightly striate, and readily peeling. The flesh is odorless and mild. The lamellae are adnexed, occasionally branched, not crowded, and white to yellow. The stipe is cylindric, 5.0 x 1.5 cm, white and unchanging.

- The spores are creamy in deposit, broadly ellipsoid, 8.0-9.0 x 6.0-7.0 µm, with prominent warts that turn blue in iodine.

- Murrill (1943) found this species growing beneath oak trees in Gainesville. It has subsequently been found in several locations in north Florida, growing under both laurel and live oaks. The pale pink coloration sets this species apart from other species of *Russula*.

Fig. 58, *Russula subpussila* (x 1.2)   (Sherri Angels)

Russulales

Fig. 59. *Russula variata*   (× 0.4)

Russula variata Bann. & Peck   **59**

(?edibility)

■ The pileus is 5.0-15.0 cm wide, convex but becoming depressed, color varying from shades of lavender to green, or intermixed with pink. The cuticle is dry, smooth and without striations. The lamellae are adnate to slightly decurrent, crowded, and white. The stipe is 3.0-10.0 x 1.0-3.0 cm, white to dull cream, and sometimes tapers downward. The brittle flesh is acrid and without odor.

■ The spores are white in deposit, ovoid, 7.0-11.0 x 5.5-9.5 μm, with isolated warts and occasional fine lines that turn blue in iodine.

■ This species occurs frequently under live oaks in lawns throughout northern Florida. It is similar to *R. heterospora*, a species with much more elongate spores, smaller pileus, and a deeper purple color.

Russulales

Fig. 60. *Russula virescens*   (x 0.5)

---

60   *Russula virescens* Fr.

(edible)

- The pileus is 5.0-12.0 cm wide, convex then slightly depressed, dull green to olive, breaking up in patches, with slightly striate margins and a cuticle that peels readily. The lamellae are white to cream, adnate, fairly crowded, and without forks. The stipe is white, sometimes slightly browning, cylindric 4.0-9.0 x 2.0-4.0 cm, and often restricted at the base. The odor is pleasant and the taste is nutty and mild.

- The spores are white in deposit, ellipsoid to subglobose, 6.0-9.0 x 5.5-7.0 µm, with medium warts that form a partial reticulum that turns blue in iodine.

- This species is very common in mixed forests and on lawns throughout northern Florida. It looks similar to *R. subgraminicolor* Murr., which is smaller and has a smooth, striate pileus.

Agaricales

The current concept of the Agaricales restricts the order to those mushrooms with true lamellae, not folds (Cantharellales) or pores (Boletales), and not those with heteromerous tissues and warted spores that turn blue in iodine (Russulales). Development of the basidiomata varies from gymnohymenial, pseudoangiohymenial, hemiangiohymenial, or angiohymenial. As a result, there is a tremendous variation in the presence or absence of a volva, inner veils, marginal veils, structure and attachment of lamellae, pileus size and shape, and many other surface features.

Paramount to an accurate identification of families and genera of Agaricales is the color of spore deposits. Unfortunately for those without a microscope, some of the most critical characteristics are those of spore shape and ornamentation, cellular arrangement of the gill trama, presence and kinds of cystidia, and chemical reactions seen only with a microscope. These characters have not been stressed here in the keys and descriptions.

A Key to the Families of Agaricales

1. Spore deposit white, cream-colored, pale pink, buff, pale lilac, or green to olive 2

1. Spores deposits darker in color 5

    2. Gills thick, truncate, widely spaced, often waxy; basidia 5.3 times longer than spore length ..... **Hygrophoraceae** (p. 109)

    2. Gills and basidia not as above 3

3. Angiohymenial development, remains of universal veil usually present as a volva or scars at the base of stipe; with a bilateral trama, annulus when present, superior .... **Amanitaceae** (p. 76)

3. Not angiohymenial, no volva; gill trama parallel or interwoven 4

    4. Gills free, pileus and stipe readily separating; spores white to green .... **Lepiotaceae** (p. 114)

    4. Gills attached, not readily separating ....
    .... **Tricholomataceae** (p. 136)

5. Spore deposit pink to salmon-pink 6

5. Spores deposit not pink to salmon-pink 7

    6. Spores nodulose or angular, lamellae sinuate (notched), ectomycorrhizal .... **Entolomataceae** (p. 183)

6. Spores subglobose to broadly ellipsoid, lamellae free with a convergent trama, saprobic .... **Plutaceae** (p. 175)

7. Spores hazel, or deep ochraceous with a germ pore, mostly small to medium-sized mushrooms .... **Bolbitiaceae** (p. 195)

7. Not as above 8

   8. Spore deposit gray, purplish-brown or black..........................9

   8. Spore deposit not gray, purplish-brown or black 10

9. Basidiomata fragile, with mottled or deliquescing lamellae, spores black, purplish-brown, or reddish-brown ....**Coprinaceae** (p. 242)

9. Basidiomata fleshy; spores truncate with a germ pore, spores purplish-black..**Strophariaceae** (p.232)

   10. Spores small, deposit chocolate-brown to reddish brown, lamellae free .... **Agaricaceae** (p. 219)

   10. Spore deposit yellow to deep rusty-brown; lamellae adnexed or decurrent .... **Cortinariaceae** (p. 199)

The Amanitaceae

Members of this family are characterized by having a white spore deposit, free lamellae, and an angiohymenial development in which there is a universal (outer) veil, i.e. peridium, and an inner veil that forms in most groups between the lamellae and stipe. In many species, whenever the pileus pushes through the universal veil there is a distinct cup or volva left at the base of the stipe. In others, however, remnants of the outer veil remain on the cap as volval patches. Usually, the inner veil, when present, detaches from the margin of the lamellae and hangs as an apron around the stipe. This apron-like veil is referred to as the superior annulus because, unlike the annulus in other taxa, it is attached at the top of the stipe.

A Key to the Genera of the Amanitaceae

1. Outer veil slimy; no volva formed .... *Limacella* (p. 76)

1. Outer veil membraneous or powdery; a volva present, at least early in development .... *Amanita* (p.78)

Limacella

Species of *Limacella* are small to medium-sized mushrooms with viscid caps and slender stipes. The universal veil or peridium is mucilaginous, leaving no volva but often with a slimy marginal veil. The white lamellae are free or deeply notched. Most have viscid, cylindric stipes that in some become slightly bulbous at the base. Spores are white to cream in deposit, smooth to finely verrucose, and do not turn blue in iodine. They are found in mixed forests or shaded lawns. Only one species will be treated here.

Limacella illinita (Fr.:Fr.) Murr.   **61**

(?edibility)

■ The white to creamy pileus is 2.0-7.0 cm wide, bell-shaped at first but becoming convex to flat with a central umbo, and viscid with a slimy marginal veil. The lamellae are free, white, and moderately crowded. The stipe is 5.0-9.0 x 0.5-1.0 cm, white, sticky or slimy, and tapered upward.

■ The spores are white in deposit, globose to broadly ellipsoid, 4.5-6.5 x 4.0-6.0 μm, smooth, and not turning blue in iodine.

■ It is common on wooded lawns and scattered oak woods in Florida. Without careful observation, it could be confused with species of *Lepiota* or *Tricholoma*.

Fig. 61. *Limacella illinita* (x 0.5)

Amanita

Amanita is the largest genus of mushrooms in Florida. The species are highly variable in size, color, shape, and seasonal distribution. Both edible and deadly poisonous species occur here and many of these look alike. They all have angiohymenial development, and in the young stage will have a universal veil surrounding the embryonic mushroom. In most, this remains as a volva or scars around the base of the stipe. In others, most of the universal veil will remain on the pileus as volval patches or as fragments at the base of the stipe. All have free lamellae with a divergent gill trama and thin-walled, white to creamy spores in deposit. Some of the most toxic species have smooth spores that turn blue in iodine.

Caution: Since the genus *Amanita* contains species of the most deadly mushrooms, while other species in the genus are edible, accurate identification of species is vital. It is very wise to have collections at different stages of development in order to determine if a volva or a superior annulus was initially present, since by maturity they may become fragile or disappear completely. An *Amanita* without a volva or a superior annulus could easily be misidentified as a *Lepiota,* the latter of which has several choice edible species. Those wishing to delve further into species of *Amanita* can refer to Bas (1969), Jenkins (1986), and Tulloss (1998).

A Key to Common Florida Species of *Amanita*

1. Volva cupulate, saccate, and membranous 2
1. Volva not as above 11
    2. Margin of pileus striate; spores not turning blue in iodine 3
    2. Margin of pileus not striate; spores turning blue in iodine 4
3. Pileus bright reddish orange .... *Amanita jacksonii* (p. 93)
3. Pileus grayish with a darker disc .... *Amanita vaginata* (p. 105)
    4. Volval patches on pileus membranous; stipe with a marginate . to submarginate bulb 5
    4. Volval patches floccose or mealy; pileus usually with a marginal veil 10
5. Pileus distinctly pigmented 6
5. Pileus white, disc sometimes whitish 7
    6. Pileus yellow to greenish-yellow
         .... *Amanita citrina* var. *citrina* (p. 85)

6. Pileus brownish; stipe becoming brownish when bruised; annulus white ... *Amanita brunnescens* var. *brunnescens* (p. 83)

7. Gills white, becoming flesh colored ... *Amanita hygroscopica* (p. 91)

7. Gills not changing color 8

    8. Spores ellipsoid to cylindric .... *Amanita verna* (p. 106)

    8. Spores globose to subglobose 9

9. Pileus 3.0-10.0 cm; basidia two-spored ... *Amanita bisporiga* (p. 82)

9. Pileus 6.0-15.0 cm; basidia four-spored ..... *Amanita virosa* (p. 107)

    10. Annulus present; with a rooting bulb
    .... *Amanita cylindrispora* (p. 87)

    10. No annulus; without a rooting bulb
    .... *Amanita volvata* (p. 108)

11. Margin of pileus striate; spores not turning blue in iodine 12

11. Margin of pileus not striate; spores turning blue in iodine 14

    12. Floccose, pinkish volval remnants around the base of the stipe .... *Amanita komarekensis* (p. 94)

    12. Volval remnants not as above 13

13. Pileus pale yellow to amber, with whitish to creamy, floccose, volval patches .... *Amanita gemmata* (p. 90)

13. Pileus scarlet to orange-red; volval remnants remain as whitish patches .... *Amanita muscaria* var. *muscaria* (p. 96)

    14. Pileus distinctly colored; basal bulb usually small 15

    14. Pileus white to creamy, basal bulb relatively large 17

15. Pileus bronze, along with stipe, slowly staining reddish; volva golden brown .... *Amanita rubescens* var. *rubescens* (p. 103)

15. Pileus and volva different 16

    16. Pileus yellowish-brown; with deep yellowish volval patches; bruising red .... *Amanita flavorubescens* (p. 89)

    16. Pileus yellow-orange to orange; volval patches lighter in color; not bruising red .... *Amanita flavoconia* (p. 88)

17. Pileus white, creamy to pale yellow, not staining 18

17. Pileus and volval remnants pigmented or staining when bruised 27

    18. Basal bulb slightly or deeply rooting 19

    18. Basal bulb not rooting 23

19. Annulus membranous, persistent; pyramidal volval warts around the base of the stipe .... *Amanita cokeri* (p. 86)

19. Annulus absent or small and fragile; without warted volval remnants around the base of the stipe. 20

20. Membranous volval patches on the pileus; with torn submembranous remnants on the bulb
.... *Amanita roanokensis* (p. 102)

20. Volval patches more fragile 21

21. Volval remnants on pileus of fragile, conical warts or felted patches; bulb prominent 22

21. Volval remnants powdery; basal bulb slightly larger than base of the stipe; with a strong chlorine odor
.... *Amanita chlorinosma* (p. 84)

22. Felty volval patches; strong garlic odor
.... *Amanita alliacea* (p. 81)

22. Volval patches crusty, floccose, often forming conical warts; with no distinct odor .... *Amanita rhoadsii* var. *rhoadsii* (p. 101)

23. Pileus less than 7.0 cm in diameter 24

23. Pileus usually more than 8.0 cm in diameter 26

24. Powdery volval remnants on the pileus but not on the basal bulb.. *Amanita longipes* (p. 95)

24. Volval remnants on pileus as patches, warts or crust 25

25. Annulus absent or a fragile zone .... *Amanita inodora* (p. 92)

25. Annulus membranous; stipe with an ellipsoid, marginate to submarginate bulb .... *Amanita praelongispora* (p. 100)

26. Pileus pinkish-buff; stipe fibrillose, floccose or scaly; odor very strong and sickening .... *Amanita praegraveolens* (p. 99)

26. Pileus whitish; without an odor *Amanita solitariiformis* (p. 104)

27. Pileus whitish-gray with darker gray disc and with darker gray warts; flesh not bruising red .... *Amanita onusta* (p. 98)

27. Pileus whitish, cream to pinkish-yellow; with thin volval remnants; flesh turning red when bruised .... *Amanita mutabilis* (p. 97)

(?edibility)

- The pileus is 6.0-8.0 cm wide, white, smooth with small, white volval patches, convex, and with non-striate margins. The lamellae are crowded, and free to slightly adnexed. The white stipe is 10.0-11.0 x 1.5-2.0 cm, tapering towards the apex, with a broadly fusoid and rooting basal bulb, and a submembraneous to fragile annulus. Fresh basidiomata have a distinct smell of galic.

- The spores are white in deposit, bacilliform,12.0-15.0 x 4.0-4.5 μm, smooth or with extremely fine punctations, and turn blue in iodine. The basidia are 40.0-55.0 x 3.0-11.0 μm, with four sterigmata and without clamps.

- This species is found in mixed forests throughout much of Florida. It is very similar to *A. roanokensis, A. cokeri, A. rhopalopus, A. rhoadsii,* and *A. chlorinosoma* in having a deeply rooting base. The strong smell of garlic, felted volval patches, and spore size distinguish it from other similar species.

Fig. 62. *Amanita alliacea*   (x 0.5)

63 *Amanita bisporigera* Atkinson

(deadly poisonous)

■ The milk-white pileus is 3.0-10.0 cm wide, convex to almost flat, slightly viscid when moist, and without striations or volval patches. The lamellae are free and crowded with many short lamellulae. The white stipe is 6.0-14.0 x 0.7-1.8 cm, tapering slightly upwards, with a globose basal bulb, and a thin, membranous superior annulus. The volva is a white, membranous sac that may become appressed to the stipe.

■ The spores are white in deposit, globose, 7.8-9.6 x 7.0-9.0 µm, thin-walled, and turn blue in iodine. The basidia are 35.0-45.0 x 4.0-11.0 µm and bear two sterigmata.

■ There are several milk-white species of *Amanita* that grow throughout the mixed forests of Florida. All are assumed to be ectomycorrhizal on pines and oaks. They are commonly referred to as the "death angels" because of their appearance and deadly toxicity. These species are extremely difficult to identify in the field, and most require the use of a microscope and chemical tests for accurate identification.

Fig. 63. *Amanita bisporigera* (x 0.6)

(Robert Williams)

Fig. 64. *Amanita brunnescens* var. *brunnescens* (x 7.5)

Amanita brunnescens var. *brunnescens* Atk.   **64**

(?toxic)

- ■ The pileus is 3.5-10.0 cm wide, convex to plane, grayish-brown with whitish, felted patches. The lamellae are free, white, and crowded. The white stipe is 6.5-14.5 x 0.8-2.1 cm, tapering upwards and with an abrupt, globose basal bulb. It has a dingy white, persistent, membranous superior annulus. The volva disintegrates into floccose patches similar to the felted patches on the pileus. The flesh slowly turns to a brownish color when bruised.

- ■ The spores are white in deposit, globose to subglobose, 7.8-9.4 x 7.8-8.6 μm, smooth, and turn blue in iodine. The basidia are 32.0-41.0 x 4.0-11.0 μm and bear four stigmata.

- ■ This species is common in mixed forests of Florida. The grayish-brown pileus with whitish patches, and the brownish reaction when bruised separates this from other species of *Amanita*.

Amanita chlorinosma (Austin) Lloyd

(toxic)

■ The pileus is very large, 6.0-28.0 cm, convex to plane, white, with non-striate margins, and with a thick powdery layer of volval fragments. The lamellae are free, crowded, and are fairly close to the stipe. The white powdery stipe is cylindric, 9.0-31.0 x 1.0-3.0 cm, slightly tapering toward the apex, and with a bulbous, slightly elongate base. The white annulus is very delicate and usually fragments away as the pileus expands. It has a strong odor of chloride of lime.

■ The spores are white in deposit, 8.0-10.9 x 5.5-6.7 μm, ellipsoid to elongate, smooth, and stains blue in iodine. The basidia are 39.0-53.0 x 4.0-11.0 μm and bear four sterigmata.

■ This species is found frequently in mixed forests and wooded lawns of north central Florida. Because of its odor, it is easily confused with other large white species, especially *A. polypyramis* which has larger spores and more pyramid-like warts on the pileus. *Amanita rhopalopus* is similar in size and shape but has a strong pungent odor, deeply rooting base, and faintly brownish patches on the pileus.

Fig. 65. *Amanita chlorinosma* (x 0.3)   (Sherri Angels)

Agaricales

Fig. 66. *Amanita citrina* var. *citrina*   (x 0.6)

Amanita citrina var. *citrina* (Schaeff) Roques   **66**

(toxic)

- The pileus is 4.0-13.0 cm wide, convex to plane, pale greenish-yellow, somewhat viscid, non-striate, and with pale yellowish volval patches. The lamellae are white to pallid, fairly crowded, and free to barely touching the stipe. The stipe is 6.0-14.0 x 0.6-2.0 cm, tapering upwards, white to pallid, with a marginate to submarginate basal bulb. The superior annulus is persistent, similar in color to the pileus, and often adheres to the stipe.

- The spores are white in deposit, globose to subglobose, 6.3-7.0 x 5.9-6.3 μm, smooth, and turn blue in iodine. The basidia are 26.0-36.0 x 4.0-8.0 μm and bear four sterigmata.

- This species has been found growing under water oaks in northern Florida. It is distinguished from other species of *Amanita* by its greenish-yellow color with pallid volval patches, and a stipe that is abruptly bulbous at the base. It has characteristics of some of our most toxic species of *Amanita* and is assumed to be deadly poisonous.

Amanita cokeri (Gilb. & Kuhn.) Gilb.

(?edibility)

■ The pileus is 7.0-15.0 cm in diameter, convex to plane, non-striate, shiny white, with whitish to brownish pyramidal volval patches, and with a powdery to flacky margin. The lamellae are free, crowded, and white to creamy. The stipe is 11.0-20.0 x 1.0-2.0 cm, tapering upwards, white, scaly to lacerate-scaly towards the basal rooting bulb; the superior annulus is membranous, persistent, but becoming floccose below.

■ The spores are white in deposit, ellipsoid, 11.0-14.0 x 6.8-9.3 µm, smooth, thin-walled and turn blue in iodine.

■ This species is found in mixed conifer and hardwood forest throughout the southeastern U.S. It is often found on sandy road embankments near pine forests in north Florida.

Fig. 67. *Amanita cokeri* (x 0.6)   (Ulla Benny)

Agaricales

Fig. 68. *Amanita cylindrispora*   (x 0.8)

Amanita cylindrispora Beards.   **68**

(?edibility)

- The pileus is 4.0-8.0 cm wide, white, convex to plane, viscid when moist, non-striate, and sometimes with scattered volval patches. The lamellae are free to adnate, crowded, and white. The narrowly cylindric stipe is 4.0-10.0 x 0.5-0.8 cm, has a large bulb that is enlarged in the middle and may be deeply rooting in the soil. The superior annulus is persistent, white, and often adheres to the stipe. Fresh specimens have an odor of chloride of lime.

- The spores are white in deposit, cylindric to bacilliform, 11.7-15.0 x 4.0-5.5 µm, smooth, and turn blue in iodine. The basidia are 36.0-46.0 x 4.0-13.0 µm and bear four sterigmata.

- This species in widely distributed in mixed hardwood and pines throughout Florida. Jenkins (1986) considers it to be synonymous with *A. cylindrisporiformis* Murr., which was believed different because of its shallow rooting bulb. It differs from the other smaller, white species of *Amanita* by its chloride of lime odor and narrowly cylindric spores.

Fig. 69. *Amanita flaviconia* (x 0.7) (Robert Williams)

---

69 *Amanita flavoconia* Atkinson

(?toxic)

■ The pileus is 3.0-9.0 cm wide, orange-yellow with yellowish-orange volval patches or warts, convex to plane, non-striate, and viscid when moist. The white lamellae are free and moderately crowded. The stipe is 5.5-11.5 x 0.7-1.4 cm, whitish, with remnants of the volva and an ovoid basal bulb. There is a membranous, yellowish-orange superior annulus. It has no apparent odor when fresh.

■ The spores are white in deposit, ellipsoid, 7.8-8.6 x 5.4-6.5 μm, smooth and do not turn blue in iodine. The basidia are 35.0-43.0 x 4.0-12.0 μm and bear four sterigmata.

■ This species is common in oak-pine forests and on wooded lawns in much of Florida. It is well represented in the Mycological Herbarium of the University of Florida. It resembles *A. frostiana* which differs in having whitish patches on the distinctly striate pileus.

Amanita flavorubescens Atkinson   **70**

(?toxicity)

■ The pileus is 4.5-10.5 cm wide, convex to plane, golden yellow to bronze, viscid when moist, non-striate, and with scattered, yellowish floccose volval patches. The lamellae are free, white, and moderately crowded. The stipe is 7.0-14.5 x 0.8-1.7 cm, whitish, and the flesh on the lower portion becomes reddish when injured. There is an ovoid basal bulb which is usually surrounded by yellowish volval remnants. The superior annulus is thin, yellowish, and sometimes tears into shreds.

■ The spores are white in deposit, ellipsoid, 9.7-10.2 x 6.3-7.0 μm, smooth, and turn blue in iodine. The basidia are 30.0-40.0 x3.0-12.0 μm and bear four sterigmata.

■ This species is common under oaks throughout Florida. Its bright golden-yellow pileus with yellowish volval patches and stout stipe that bruises reddish make this an easy species to recognize.

Fig. 70. *Amanita flavorubescens* (x 0.4)

Amanita gemmata (Fr.) Bert. in DeCham.

(?edibility)

■ The pileus is 2.5-11.0 cm wide, plane to convex, sometimes up-turned, viscid when moist, pale yellow to amber with creamy volval patches, and with a striate margin. The lamellae are white to cream-colored and somewhat crowded. The stipe is 4.0-15.0 x 0.5-1.9 cm, slightly tapered upward, white to cream-colored with an ovoid basal bulb and a persistent, white superior annulus. The volva remains as white floccose remnants around the bulb.

■ The spores are white in deposit, broadly ellipsoid, 8.7-11.0 x 5.5-8.5 µm, smooth, and do not turn blue in iodine. The basidia are 45.0-60.0 x 4.0-11.0 µm and bear four sterigmata.

■ This species is commonly found beneath evergreen oaks in Florida. While it is similar to other small to medium sized, yellowish species of *Amanita,* it differs in having a white univesal veil that leaves white volval patches on the pileus and around the bulb.

Fig. 71. *Amanita gemmata*   (x 0.5)

Fig. 72. *Amanita hygroscopica*   (x 0.4)

Amanita hygroscopica Coker   **72**

(?edibility)

■ The pileus is 4.5-9.0 cm, white to straw colored, viscid, appearing water-soaked, plane to convex with a non-striate margin that is sometimes upturned. The lamellae are crowded, white, but becoming flesh colored. The stipe is 8.0-17.0 x 0.5-1.7 cm, tapering upward, white, with a fairly large ovoid basal bulb. It has a fragile, white, membranous superior annulus that collapses against the stipe. The white, saccate, volva often collapses against the stipe.

■ The spores are white in deposit, ellipsoid, 9.0-12.0 x 6.2-8.1 μm, smooth, and turn blue in iodine. The basidia are 36.0-50.0 x 3.0-11.0 μm and bear four sterigmata.

■ Several collections of this species are in the Mycological Herbarium at the University of Florida. They have been found in mixed forests throughout the area. It is recognized by the water-soaked appearance and white lamellae that become flesh colored.

Amanita inodora (Murr.) Bas

(?edibility)

- The somewhat powdery white pileus is 3.0-6.0 cm wide, convex to plane, dry with a crust of felty volval remnants, and a nonstriate margin. The lamellae are white, free, and usually crowded. The stipe is 3.5-5.5 x 0.8-1.6 cm, tapering upwards, with a broadly ovoid, turnip-shaped bulb surrounded by remnants of the fragile volva. There is a fluffy annular zone on the upper third of the stipe.

- The spores are white in deposit, narrowly cylindric, 11.0-15.5 x 3.5-5.0 µm, smooth and stain blue in iodine. The basidia are 40.0-50.0 x 3.0-11.0 µm and bear four sterigmata.

- This species was considered by Murrill (1946) to be a variety of *A. roanokensis*. It differs, however, in having a broad, turnip-shaped bulb, spores without fine warts, and lacking an odor. It is commonly found under evergreen oaks in Florida.

Fig. 73. *Amanita inodora* (x 1.0)

Agaricales

Fig. 74. *Amanita jacksonii*   (x 0.3)   (Robert Williams)

Amanita jacksonii Pomerl.   **74**

(edible)

■ The pileus is 6.0-22.0 cm in diameter, smooth, moist, convex, becoming plane, initially bright scarlet-red, later yellowish and prominantly striate at the margins. The pale yellowish lamellae are free and crowded. The stipe is 9.0-23.0 x 0.9-3.1 cm, tapering upwards, pale yellow, smooth but often becoming scaly, and without a swollen base. The deep volva is large, white, thick, and membranous. The superior annulus is membranous, yellowish, and persistent.

■ The spores are white in deposit, ellipsoid, 7.8-9.4 x 5.5-6.7 µm, smooth, thin-walled, and not turning blue in iodine. The basidia 31.0-39.0 x 3.0-11.0 µm, and bear four sterigmata.

■ This is one of the best known species of *Amanita* in eastern North America; until recently going under the name *Amanita caesarea*. It is recognized by its large size, brilliant red color, and the fading, striate margin of the pileus. Pomerleau (1980) concluded that this colorful, edible *Amanita* in eastern North America was distinct from the European *A. caesarea,* and named it *Amanita umbonata* Pomerl., only later to name it *A. jacksonii,* the name I chose to use here. *Amanita jacksonii* is very common most years beneath laurel and water oaks, in shaded lawns and sparse woodlands in northern Florida.

Amanita komarekensis Jenkins & Vinopal

(?edibility)

■ The creamy-white to beige pileus is 4.0-7.5 cm wide, plane to convex, sometimes with a small umbo, with pinkish-beige volval patches. The creamy-white lamellae are free and with numerous lamellulae. The dingy white stipe is 6.0-11.0 x 0.5-1.4 cm, tapering upwards, with a globose to ovoid basal bulb surrounded by chunks or patches of pinkish-beige volval remnants. The superior annulus is membranous at first but sometimes becomes powdery and covered with pinkish-beige volval remnants.

■ The spores are white in deposit, broadly ellipsoid, 8.2-10.2 x 5.5-7.8 µm, smooth, and do not turn blue in iodine. The basidia are 38.0-51.0 x 4.0-11.0 µm and bear four sterigmata.

■ This species seems to be restricted to the southeastern U.S., and is found associated with pines and oaks in Florida. It is distinguished by its creamy-white pileus that is covered by powdery, pinkish-beige volval patches.

Fig. 75. *Amanita komarekensis*   (x 0.5)

Fig. 76. *Amanita longipes*   (× 0.6)

Amanita longipes Bas in Tulloss & Jenk.   **76**

(?edibility)

■ The pileus is 2.4-8.1 cm in diameter, hemispheric, becoming broadly convex, white with a pale buff to grayish-brown disc, and remaining more or less smooth with powdery volval remnants. The lamellae are narrowly adnate, close, whitish to creamy or grayish, sometimes with powdery remnants of the inner veil. The stipe is 2.5-14.2 x 0.5-2.0 cm, tapering upwards, floccose above; the slightly rooting basal bulb is 2.2-7.2 cm in diameter, flattened or doglegged, often with rusty spots and volval floccules.

■ The spores are white in deposit, ellipsoid to cylindric, 8.4-17.5 x 4.2-7.0 μm, smooth, thin-walled and do not blue in iodine.

■ Jenkins (1986) did not indicate that this species occurred in Florida. However, several collections have been found beneath evergreen oaks around Gainesville.

(poisonous)

- This species is known as the "fly agaric", because it is reported to exude droplets on the cap that kills flies. It is a striking mushroom because of its robust size, 5.0-22.0 cm pileus, 5.0-16.0 cm stipe, and a bright red to orange-red cap covered with pale whitish to yellowish volval patches or warts. The stipe and lamellae are white, and a persistent, whitish inner veil or superior annulus occurs. Concentric rings of the universal veil remain around the bulbous base of the stipe.

- The spores are white in deposit, broadly elliptic, 9.4-13.0 x 6.3-8.7 µm and does not turn blue in iodine. The basidia are 40.0-63.0 x 3.0-11.0 µm and bears four sterigmata.

- *Amanita muscaria* occurs from November to March throughout northern Florida, and appears to be ectomycorrhizal on a number of species of pines throughout the area. It is only rarely found in mixed forests of oaks and pines, and seems to prefer well drained areas.

- This species is both toxic and hallucinogenic. Lincoff and Mitchel (1977) report very low levels of toxic quaternary ammonium compounds called muscarine in *A. muscaria*. To die from muscarine, it would be necessary for a person to consume more than 250 lbs. of this mushroom. Poisoning results, however, from the presence of three isoxazole derivatives, ibotenic acid;, muscimol, and muscazone which are found at high levels in this species.

Fig. 77. *Amanita muscaria* var. *muscaria*   (x 0.3)

Fig. 78. *Amanita mutabilis* (x 0.4)   (Robert Williams)

Amanita mutabilis Beards.   **78**

(?edibility)

- The whitish to cream-colored pileus is 6.0-11.0 cm wide, plane to convex, with a non-striate margin, and slightly viscid when moist. The white to cream-colored lamellae are crowded and, like the flesh of other tissues, turn pink when bruised. The whitish stipe is 5.0-16.0 x 1.0-2.2 cm, tapering upward and has a globose, marginate basal bulb. The superior annulus is whitish to pale yellowish, membranous, and sometimes disintegrates. The volva is also fragile often remains as free membranous lobes.

- The spores are white in deposit, ellipsoid to cylindric, 10.0-14.5 x 5.5-9.0 μm, smooth, and do not turn blue in iodine. The basidia are 50.0-75.0 x 4.0-14.0 μm and bear two to four sterigmata.

- This species is found in pine-oak forests of Florida. It is easily recognized from other white, medium-sized species of *Amanita* by the prominent pink staining of tissues when bruised. Jenkins (1986) concluded that *A. anisata, A. submutabilis, and A. abruptiformis* are synonymous with this species.

Fig. 79. *Amanita onusta* (x 0.4)

---

79   *Amanita onusta* (Howe) Sacc.

(?edibility)

■ The pileus is 2.5-10.5 cm in diameter, convex to plane, sometimes becoming slightly depressed and umbonate, with an appendaged margin; the surface is dingy white to pale gray with brownish-gray, floccose, volval patches or warts. The lamellae are crowded, free, and whitish to creamy yellow. The stipe is 3.5-15.5 x 0.6-1.5 cm, slightly tapering upwards, grayish above, brownish-gray towards the base where there is a slightly rooting bulb covered with brownish-gray warts or scales. The very delicate, whitish to creamy annulus quickly disintegrates.

■ The spores are white in deposit, broadly ellipsoid, 8.1-11.0 x 5.2-8.4 μm, smooth, thin-walled, and turn blue in iodine. The basidia are 40.0-59.0 x 3.0-12.0 μm and bear four sterigmata.

■ This is a very characteristic species due to its size and bluish-gray pileus. It has been found in parts of eastern North America and occurs beneath pines in Florida during the summer months.

Amanita praegraveolens (Murr.) Sing.　　**80**

(?edibility)

- The pileus is 6.0-12.5 cm in diameter, convex, becoming plane, whitish to pinkish-buff, subfelted, with scaly floccules or volval patches, and an appendaged margin. The lamellae are crowded, free, and slightly pinkish. The stipe is 10.0-15.0 x 0.7-2.0 cm, whitish, covered with pinkish-buff scales or fibrils, tapering slightly towards the base where there is a small, ellipsoid bulb covered with volval remnants. There is a membranous, felty superior annulus similar in color to the stipe. The mushroom has a strong sickening smell.

- The spores are white in deposit, broadly ellipsoid, 7.0-9.5 x 6.5-9.0 μm, with smooth walls that turn blue in iodine. The basidia are 35.0-45.0 x 3.0-13.0 μm and bear four sterigmata.

- This is a remarkable species of *Amanita* because of its pinkish-buff color, floccose pileus, and an extremely unpleasant odor. It has the most penetrating mushroom odor that I have ever experienced. It is ectomycorrhizal in north Florida with both oaks and pines, found beneath isolated stands of pines and oaks. Murrill (1939a) first described this species as *Lepiota praegraveolens;* later he (Murrill, 1951) transferred it to *Amanita*. In 1945 he described other collections of the species as *A. maladora*, noting the extremely unpleasant odor.

Fig. 80. *Amanita praegravoelens*　(x 0.5)

81   *Amanita praelongispora* (Murr.) Murr.

(?edibility)

■ The pileus is 4.0-7.0 cm in diameter, convex to plane, white with white powdery volval patches, margins fragmented and non-striate. The lamellae are crowded, free, whitish to slightly pinkish, and browning slightly with age. The stipe is 5.0-8.0 x 0.6-1.2 cm, even, white with yellowish tints, powdery, with an abrupt, ellipsoid, marginate basal bulb. The superior annulus is membranous, white, and sometimes clings to the expanding pileus.

■ The spores are white in deposit, narrowly cylindric, 10.0-13.5 x 4.0-5.0 µm, smooth, thin-wall, and turning blue in iodine. The basidia are 35.0-40.0 x 4.0-11.0 µm and bear four sterigmata.

■ This species is found beneath oaks and pines in northern Florida. Bas (1969) notes that it is similar to *A. parva*, but the latter is smaller and has a smooth pileus margin.

Fig. 81. *Amanita praelongispora*   (x 0.8)

Fig. 82. *Amanita rhoadsii* var. *rhoadsii* (x 0.5)

Amanita rhoadsii var. *rhoadsii* (Murr.) Murr.　　**82**

(?edibility)

■ The white non-striate pileus is 4.0-11.0 cm wide, dry, covered with powdery patches or warts of volval remnants and a shaggy marginal veil. The white to creamy-white lamellae are free and crowded. The stipe is white, 6.5-19.0 x 0.8-2.2 cm, tapering upwards, and with an oblong to ellipsoid slightly rooting bulb. The annulus and volval remnants disintegrate into powdery remnants by maturity.

■ The spores are white in deposit, cylindrical to elongate, 10.8-14.9 x 3.6-4.8 µm, smooth, and turn blue in iodine. The basidia are 45.0-55.0 x 0.3-1.1 µm and bear four sterigmata.

■ This species is found commonly under live and laurel oaks in northern Florida. It is recognized from other species of *Amanita* by the shaggy marginal veil, fusiform, rooting bulb, and cylindric spores that turn blue in iodine.

(?edibility)

■ This species has a large whitish to creamy pileus, 7.5-13.0 cm wide, convex to plane, slightly viscid when fresh, with whitish membranous volval patches, and a nonstriate margin. The lamellae are moderately crowded, white, and free to almost adnexed. The stipe is white, 9.0-13.5 x 1.0-2.2 cm, tapering upwards and covered with the powdery remains of an annulus, with a slightly rooting, ellipsoid basal bulb surrounded by membraneous fragments of the volva. It has a faint odor of chlorine of lime.

■ The spores are white in deposit, narrowly cylindric, 11.2-15.1 x 3.5-5.2 µm, smooth or with very fine warts on the polar areas that turn blue in iodine. The basidia are 40.0-50.0 x 4.0-12.0 µm and bear four sterigmata.

■ This species appears to be widespread throughout the southeastern U.S. Bas (1969) concluded that *A. watsoniana* Murr. represents the same species, which differs only in the powdery nature of volval remnants. *Amanita inodora* Murr. differs in having a more turbinate bulb and spores without the small iodine positive warts. It is most common in the dry pine-oak forest of northern Florida.

Fig. 83. *Amanita roanokensis*   (x 0.5)

Agaricales

Fig. 84. *Amanita rubescens* var. *rubescens* (x 0.4)

Amanita rubescens var. *rubescens* (Pers:Fr.) Gray   **84**

(toxic)

■ The bronze to reddish-brown pileus is 4.0-22.0 cm wide, convex to plane, with scattered volval patches and a nonstriate margin. The lamellae are white, crowded, and free. The stipe is 7.0-24.0 x 0.7-4.0 cm, tapering upwards, whitish to pale tan, and with a slighly inflated basal bulb surrounded by irregular or warted volval remnants.

■ The spores are white in deposit, ellipsoid, 6.8-9.2 x 5.2-6.8 µm, smooth, and turn blue in iodine. The basidia are 32.0-40.0 x 4.0-12.0 µm and bear four sterigmata.

■ This species is easily recognized by its bronze to reddish-brown color. It is very widespread in the eastern U.S., and is commonly found in pine and mixed forests around northern Florida.

Fig. 85. *Amanita solitariiformis* (× 0.7)

---

85 *Amanita solitariiformis* (Murr.) Murr.

(?edibility)

■ The white to creamy-white pileus is 6.0-8.0 cm wide, convex to plane, with sharp, pyramid-like volval warts, and a non-striate margin. The lamellae are white to creamy-pink, free, and crowded. The stipe is 3.0-5.0 x 0.8-1.6 cm, tapering upwards, white to creamy-white, with an ovoid, rooting bulb, and lacking distinct volval remnants.

■ The spores are white in deposit, narrowly cylindric, 12.0-14.8 x 4.7-5.5 μm, smooth, and do not turn blue in iodine. The basidia are 45.0-60.0 x 4.0-12.0 μm and bear four sterigmata.

■ This species is found in mixed forests, but appears to be most common under pines. It is similar to *A. subsolitaria* but differs in being a smaller, more compact mushroom, with less distinct warts, and slightly less pigmented lamellae.

Amanita vaginata (Bull.: Fr.) Vitt.   **86**

(?edibility)

■ The grayish, striate pileus is 4.0-9.5 cm wide, convex to plane or slightly umbonate, viscid when moist, and usually with a darker center and lighter towards the margins, some varying in color from yellowish-gray to almost blackish. The lamellae are free, white to sometimes grayish, and fairly crowded. The stipe is 6.5-12.0 x 0.4-1.3 cm, white, slightly tapering upwards, and without a basal bulb or annulus. The base is surrounded by a deep membraneous, white volva.

■ The spores are white in deposit, globose to subglobose, 7.9-10.2 x 7.0-10.2 µm, smooth, and do not turn blue in iodine. The basidia are 35.0-52.0 x 4.0-13.0 µm and bear four sterigmata.

■ This species is abundant and widespread throughout mixed forests of eastern North America. It is especially abundant in north Florida, and has been associated with a number of hardwood and conifer species.

Fig. 86. *Amanita vaginata*   (x 0.5)   (Terry Hinkel)

Agaricales

(poisonous)

- The pileus is 6.0-14.0 cm wide, convex to plane, white or rarely with a faintly yellowish center, viscid when moist, and non-striate. The lamellae are free, white and crowded. The stipe is 8.0-15.0 x 0.9-2.5 cm, tapering upwards, white, with a large globose to ovoid basal bulb surrounded by a membranous saccate volva. The superior annulus is persistent, white, and drapes like an apron around the stipe.

- The spores are white in deposit, ellipsoid to broadly ellipsoid, 8.1-11.3 x 6.6-8.8 µm, smooth, and turn blue in iodine. The basidia are 45.0-60.0 x 3.0-12.0 µm and bear four sterigmata.

- There are a number of collections from Florida in the Mycological Herbarium at the University of Florida labeled *A. verna*. According to Jenkins (1986), only minor characters separate this species from *A. pseudoverna, A. verniformis, A. suballiacea, A. virosa,* and *A. bisporiga.* All grow in similar habitats of mixed forests of hardwood and conifer species. They are often found on wooded lawns, especially under evergreen oaks and longleaf and loblolly pines.

Fig. 87. *Amanita verna* (x 0.5)

Fig. 88. *Amanita virosa* (x 0.3)

Amanita virosa (Fr.) Bert. & DeCham.   **88**

(poisonous)

■ The pileus is 5.0-15.0 cm wide, convex to plane, white but often with a very pale tan disc, viscid when moist, and smooth with a non-striate margin. The lamellae are free, white, and crowded. The stipe is 7.0-20.0 x 0.8-2.0 cm, tapering upwards, smooth to powdery, with a globose to ovoid basal bulb surrounded by a white, membraneous volva that collapses around the bulb. The white superior annulus is persistent and drapes around the stipe.

■ The spores are white in deposit, globose to subglobose, 8.6-11.7 x 8.6-10.0 μm, smooth, and turn blue in iodine. The basidia are 56.0-70.0 x 4.0-16.0 μm and bear four sterigmata.

■ This species is indistinguishable in the field from a large group of small to medium-sized, white species of *Amanita*. The size of spores and the number of spores per basidium are key microscopic features used to separate members of this group. *Amanita bisporiga* and *A. vernella* have two instead of four spores on the basidium. *Amanita bisporiga*, *A. virosa*, and *A. vernella* have more or less globose spores, whereas the others are broadly ellipsoid to cylindric and elongate. All are found in oak-pine forests of Florida.

Amanita volvata (Pk.) Mar.

(?edibility)

■ The pileus is 5.0-10.0 cm wide, convex to plane, margins striate, smooth with scattered volval patches, white, bruising light reddish-brown and without an obvious odor. The lamellae are white, free, and somewhat crowded. The stipe is 5.0-10.0 cm by 1.0-1.5 cm, white with a powdery surface, and emerging from a fleshy, membranous cup-like volva.

■ The spores are white in deposit, ellipsoid, 9.0-11.0 x 6.0-7.0 μm, and turn blue in iodine. Basidia are clavate, 35.0-46.0 x 4.0-11 μm and bear four sterigmata.

■ This species was traditionally placed in *Amanitopsis* because of the lack of an annulus. Although it has been listed as occurring southward into Tennessee and the Carolinas, collections have been made in mixed pine/hardwood forests in Florida.

Fig. 89. *Amanita volvata* (x 0.4)

Agaricales

The Hygrophoraceae

The Hygrophoraceae are small to medium-sized mushrooms that stand apart somewhat from other white-spored families by their widely spaced waxy lamellae that are truncate on their edges. Many species have brightly colored, viscid, cone-shaped caps. Their spores are white, smooth, and do not turn blue in iodine. Five genera have been considered in the family, the best known is *Hygrophorus*. Largent and Baroni (1988) distinguish *Hygrophorus* with a divergent gill trama from *Hygrocybe,* in which the trama is of parallel hyphae. An extensive treatment of the genus may be found in Hesler and Smith's (1963) North American species of *Hygrophorus,* in which *Hygrocybe* is merged with *Hygrophorus*. Only a few species occur in Florida and all are retained in *Hygrophorus*.

A Key to the species of Florida *Hygrophorus*

1. Pileus sharply conical, viscid, and bright orange to red 2
1. Pileus not as above 3
    2. Pileus blackening when bruised ... *Hygrophorus conicus* (p. 111)
    2. Pileus not blackening when bruised *Hygrophorus ruber* (p. 114)
3. Pileus deep blood-red, with a striate margin
           .... *Hygrophorus punicus* (p. 113)
3. Pileus not as above 4
    4. Pileus broadly conical to umbonate, glabrous; lamellae red to yellow-orange .... *Hygrophorus coccineus* (p. 110)
    4. Pileus bone to olive-brown ...... *Hygrophorus hypothejus* (p. 112)

Fig. 90. *Hygrophorus coccineus* (x 1.1)   (Sherri Angels)

90   *Hygrophorus coccineus* (Fr.) Fr. sensu Ricken

(edible)

■ The pileus is 2.0-5.0 cm wide, obtusely conical with incurved margins and often with distinct umbo, deep scarlet-red, and viscid when moist. The lamellae are adnate to adnexed, somewhat distant, and orange-red to yellow-orange. The stipe is 3.0-7.0 cm long and 0.3-0.8 cm thick, slightly swollen toward the base, and similar in color to the pileus.

■ The spores are white in deposit, ellipsoid, 7.0-10.5 x 4.0-5.0 µm, smooth and unchanged in iodine. The basidia are 43.0-54.0 x 6.0-8.0 µm and bear four sterigmata.

■ This species is found occasionally during winter months in hardwood forests in north Florida. Its deep scarlet, umbonate pileus with incurved margins separate it from other species.

Agaricales

(?edibility)

- The pileus is 2.0-7.0 cm wide, conical, reddish to scarlet-orange, slightly viscid when moist, and quickly becoming black when bruised. The lamellae are almost free, white to pale yellowish or olive-yellow. The stipe is 6.0-11.0 cm long and 0.5-1.0 cm thick, cylindric, whitish at the base but the upper portion is dark red, orange or yellow.

- The spores are white in deposit, subellipsoid, 9.0-12.0 x 5.5-6.5 µm, smooth. Basidia 30.0-49.0 x 5.5-6.5 µm and bear four sterigmata.

- This species is common in mixed forests throughout Florida during the wet summer months. It is easily distinguished from other species of *Hygrophorus* by its bright red to orange conical pileus that blackens when bruised.

Fig. 91. *Hygrophorus conicus* (x 0.5)   (Henry Aldrich)

Hygrophorus hypothejus (Fr.) Fr.

(?edibility)

- The pileus is 2.0-8.0 cm wide, slightly umbonate, becoming convex, bone to olive-brown towards the center, and dull greenish-yellow to brownish towards the edge. The lamellae are decurrent, distant, whitish but becoming pale yellow or darker like the pileus. The stipe is 8.0-16.0 x 0.6-1.2 cm, tapering downward, whitish to yellowish below but becoming the color of the pileus upwards.

- The spores are white in deposit, ellipsoid, 7.0-9.0 x 4.0-5.0 µm, smooth and do not turn blue in iodine. Basidia 42.0-60.0 x 6.0-7.0 µm, and bear four sterigmata.

- This species has been associated with conifers throughout North America. I suspect that it is ectomycorrhizal with pines, under which it is found in Florida. Its large size and olive-brown to blackish color separate it from other species found in the state.

Fig. 92. *Hygrophorus hypothejus* (x 0.5)　　　(Sherri Angels)

Fig. 93. *Hygrophorus puniceus* (x 0.8)

(Sherri Angels)

Hygrophorus puniceus (Fr.) Fr. **93**

(?edibility)

- ◾ The pileus is 2.0-7.0 cm wide, broadly conical, becoming um-bonate with incurved margins, somewhat viscid, deep blood-red, fading with streaks of red-orange. The lamellae are adnate with a decurrent tooth, subdistant, and becoming pale yellow to orange-yellow. The stipe is 2.0-7.0 x 1.0-1.5 cm, cylindric, reddish, but fading to orange or yellow.

- ◾ The spores are white in deposit, subellipsoid, 8.0-11.0 x 4.0-6.0 µm, smooth, and unstained in iodine. Basidia are 32.0-65.0 x 6.0-11.0 µm, and bear four sterigmata.

- ◾ This species is found in mixed forest in northern Florida. Its deep blood-red color, viscid pileus, and somewhat striate margins distinguish this from other species.

Agaricales

(?edibility)

■ The pileus is 1.5-5.0 cm wide, usually remaining acutely conical, bright red, and viscid to glutinous. The lamellae are adnexed, yellow to yellow-brown, and not crowded. The stipe is approximately 2.0 cm long and 0.2 cm thick viscid, and of similar color to the pileus.

■ The spores are white in deposit, ellipsoid, 7.0-9.0 x 4.5-6.0 µm, smooth and not turning blue in iodine. The basidia are 31.0-44.0 x 6.0-8.0 µm and bear four sterigmata.

■ This species is common in mixed woods, usually in moist mossy areas. It resembles *H. conicus,* but differs in not becoming black when bruised and in having a more viscid stipe.

Fig. 94. *Hygrophorus ruber* (x 0.6)

The Lepiotaceae

The Lepiotaceae is a family of saprobic species commonly referred to as the "parasol mushrooms." They have a central stipe with free lamellae, a partial veil that normally leaves a loose annulus. Spores are white to pale greenish in deposit, ellipsoid to subglobose, sometimes thick-walled, with or without a germ pore, and become dextrinoid when mounted in Melzer's reagent. Lepiotaceae are mostly terrestrial, but also occur on grassy pastures and lawns. Some are well-known edible species while others cause severe intestinal irritation. While there are a number of treatments of the Lepiotaceae, I have relied heavily on Akers' (1997) dissertation, *A Systematic Study of Lepiotaceae of Florida.*

A Key to Common Genera of Lepiotaceae in Florida

1. Spore wall simple, thin, hyaline, dextrinoid, and lacking a germ pore ....*Lepiota* (p. 115)
1. Spore wall more complex and with a germ pore..........................2
   2. Spore print olive-green to green........... *Chlorophyllum* (p. 120)
   2. Spore print white, cream to pinkish 3
3. Basidioma large, annulus complex .... *Macrolepiota* (p. 121)
3. Basidioma small, annulus simple 4
   4. Thick stocky mushrooms with a non-striate margin .... *Leucoagaricus* (p. 125)
   4. Slender mushroom with striate margins *Leucocoprinus* (p. 131)

Lepiota

The pileus is usually squamulose, but often smooth or glabrous towards the margins which bear a marginal veil in some. The lamellae are free, thin and lightly colored. The stipes are central, mostly with a loose annulus. The spore print is white to buff or pinkish and the spores are thin-walled, hyaline and without a germ pore.

A Key to Common Species of *Lepiota* in Florida

1. Pileus small, dark gray to almost black .... *Lepiota phaeostictiformis* (p. 118)
1. Pileus not gray to black 2
   2. Pileus light cinnamon-brown.......... *Lepiota clypeolaria* (p. 116)
   2. Pileus brick to ochraceous-brown 3
3. Pileus 2.0-3.0 cm in diameter, convex to plane, brick to yellow-brown, stipe not bruising saffron ...... *Lepiota cristatiformis* (p. 117)
3. Pileus 3.0-6.0 cm in diameter, umbonate with an incurved margin, stipe bruising saffron to pinkish ... *Lepiota subcristatiformis* (p. 119)

(poisonous)

- The pileus is 1.0-2.4 cm wide, convex to plane, with slight umbo and faintly striate margins, light cinnamon-brown with fibrillar squamules. The lamellae are free, somewhat crowded and white. The stipe is cylindric, 4.0-5.0 cm x 1.0-2.0 mm, with a white to slightly yellowish fribrillar annulus.

- The spores are whitish in deposit, fusoid, 11.0-15.5 x 4.0-6.0 µm, smooth, with a slight dextrinoid reaction in iodine. Basidia clavate, 20.0-30.0 x 5.7-10.0 µm, with four sterigmata.

- This species is widely distributed throughout the mixed hardwood/ pine forests of northern Florida, and can be distinguished from other small species of *Lepiota* by its fusoid spores. It is reported by Phillips (1991) to be poisonous.

Fig. 95. *Lepiota clypeolaria*   (x 2.0)

Fig. 96. *Lepiota cristatiformis* (x 1.3)   (Ulla Benny)

Lepiota cristatiformis Murr.   **96**

(?edibility)

■ The pileus is 2.0-3.0 cm, convex to plane, white with brick-red scales, darker towards the disc. The gills are free, whitish, crowded and slightly fimbriated. The stipe is up to 4.0 cm long, 2.0-3.0 mm wide, tapering towards the apex, with inconspicuous brownish scales around the base. The annulus is apical to medium, somewhat brick-red and fragile.

■ The spores are whitish in mass, ellipsoid, 8.6-11.0 x 5.5-6.8 µm, dextrinoid, and with a germ pore. The basidia are clavate, 29.0-35.0 x 9.5-11.0 µm, with two sterigmata.

■ This species was found in high hammocks and under tung-oil trees around Gainesville, Florida.

Fig. 97. *Lepiota phaeostictiformis* (x 2.0) (Walter Sundberg)

---

97   *Lepiota phaeostictiformis* Murr.

(?edibility)

■ The pileus is 1.0-1.1 cm wide, convex to plane or slightly um-bonate, dark gray to blackish, with concentric rings of small squamules. Gills free, cream to pale ochraceous, and somewhat crowded. The stipe is up to 3.0 cm long, 1.0-2.0 mm wide, with a white membranous annulus bearing remnants of dark fibrils.

■ The spores are whitish in deposit, narrowly ellipsoid, 5.0-7.7 x 3.1-4.0 μm, slightly dextrinoid, and without a germ pore. Basidia are clavate, 15.0-18.0 x 7.5-8.0 μm, with four sterigmata.

■ This small species has been consistently found on old decaying pine or oak logs or stumps in Florida. It occurs during both summer and winter seasons.

Agaricales

(?edibility)

- The pileus is 1.5-5.0 cm broad, globose at first, becoming convex with incurved margins, surface cinnamon-buff to brick-red, breaking up into large, arched to rectangular scales against a whitish background. The lamellae are dull white to cream, later bearing brownish blotches. The whitish to cream-colored stipe is cylindric, 2.4-9.0 x 0.1-1.0 cm, tapering upward with a bulbous base, easily bruising to a dull pinkish to reddish brown color, and bears a membranous annulus fringed with scales similar in color to the pileus scales.

- The spores are titanium white in mass, ellipsoid to oblong, 8.0-11.6 x 4.1-5.8 µm, wall thick, dextrinoid and without a germ pore. Basidia are clavate, 26.0-29.0 x 8.6-11.0 µm, with two sterigmata.

- This species resembles a large *Lepiota crispa*, but differs in having a prominent annulus with colorful cuticular remnants. It has been found beneath oaks in wooded pasture areas.

Fig. 98. *Lepiota subcristatiformis* (x 1.0)

Chlorophyllum

This genus differs from *Lepiota* in having spores with a germ pore, a more complex spore wall, and spores that are greenish in mass. The basidiomata are large, with free lamellae and a central stipe bearing a mobile ring. Most recognize *Chlorophyllum* as a monotypic genus, containing *C. molybdites*, which is found extensively in lawns, golf courses, and pastures throughout Florida.

---

99   *Chlorophyllum molybdites* (Meyer: Fr.) Massee

(poisonous)

■   The pileus is 5.0-24.0 cm wide, at first globose but becoming convex to plane with a slight umbo. The pileus is initially covered by a brownish cuticle that disappears or remains as squamules towards the margins but remains on the umbo. The lamellae are free, remote from the pileus, pale whitish-buff when young, becoming greenish to olive-green when mature. The stipe is 11.0-28.0 x 1.3-2.5 cm, whitish to pale greenish, with a more or less bulbous base.

Fig. 99. *Chlorophyllum molybdites*   (x 0.3)

- Spores are pea-green in deposit when fresh but fade, obovoid to broadly ellipsoid, 8.0-11.0 x 6.2-8.0 µm, truncate, with a distinct germ pore and a 3-layered dextrinoid wall. Basidia are broadly clavate, 24.0-28.0 x 8.0-10.0 µm, with four short sterigmata.

- This is a very cosmopolitan species, found abundantly in tropical and subtropical regions, and easily recognized by its green spore deposit. For many years it was called *Lepiota morgani* (Pk.) Sacc., or Morgan's *Lepiota,* and recognized for causing severe intestinal irriatation when eaten. It is the most frequently reported cause of mushroom poisoning in Florida and the United States. This species is easily confused in the field with a choice edible species, *Macrolepiota procera.*

Macrolepoita

Members of this genus have very large basidiomata with free, detached lamellae and a complex, often double annulus, and spores that are white in deposit and have a prominent germ pore.

A Key to Florida species of *Macrolepiota*

1. Spores ellipsoid, usually more than 12.0 µm long; flesh not bruising orange to red .... *M. procera* (p. 121)
1. Spores almond shaped, usually less than 12.0 µm long, flesh bruising orange to red 2
    2. Pileus with large, appressed scales; spores 7.2-10.6 x 5.1-7.6 µm .... *M. subrhacodes* (p. 124)
    2. Pileus with prominent upright scales; spores 9.0-12.0 x 7.0-9.0 µm .... *M. rhacodes* (p. 123)

Macrolepiota procera (Scop.: Fr.) Sing.   **100**

(edible)

- The pileus is 7.0-10.0 cm wide, initially broadly globose, becoming convex, with a beige to tan or chocolate-brown cuticle that becomes fragmented into rings of scales. The lamellae are free, crowded and cream colored. The stipe is 18.0-23.0 x 1.0 cm, slightly tapering upwards with a basal bulb up to 2.5 cm and a movable, double edged annulus.

■ The spores are white to buff in mass, ellipsoid, 14.5-22.4 x 10.6-15.0 µm, strongly dextrinoid in iodine. Basidia are narrowly clavate, 40.0-48.0 x 14.5-16.3 µm, with four sterigmata.

■ This species is widespread on several continents and is recognized as a choice edible mushroom. It is found on wooded lawns, around clearings in forests, and in open pastures throughout northern Florida. As noted above, it is easily confused with the toxic *Chlorophyllum molybdites.*

Fig. 100. *Macrolepiota procera*   (x 0.8)   (Walter Sundberg)

Macrolepiota rhacodes (Vittad.) Sing.   **101**

(choice, edible)

- The pileus is 7.0-10.0 cm wide, convex to plane, brown, becoming very coarsely scaly except at the disc. The lamellae are free, white to beige, and somewhat crowded. The stipe is stout, 8.0-10.0 x 1.0-2.0 cm, smooth, white, strongly bulbous at the base, and becoming brownish-orange when bruised.

- The spores are white in deposit, ovoid to ellipsoid, 9.0-12.0 x 7.0-9.0 µm, smooth, with a thin wall and prominent germ pore. The basidia are 27.0-4.0 x 10.0-12.5 µm, with four sterigmata.

- This species is normally found in clusters and often forms fairy rings in open lawns and pastures. Along with *M. subrhacodes*, it has often been confused with *Chlorophyllum molybdites*, but the latter has greenish spores when mature and the basidiomata do not bruish brownish-orange when bruised. It has larger squamules than *M. subrhacodes*.

Fig. 101. *Macrolepiota rachodes* (x 0.7)

102   *Macrolepiota subrhacodes* (Murr.) Akers

(choice, edible)

■ The pileus is 8.0-10.0 cm wide, globose, becoming campanulate to plane with a slight umbo; white to pale brownish, becoming darker with rows of flat scales. The lamellae are free, white to brownish when dry, and somewhat crowded. The stipe is 9.0-10.0 x 0.3-1.0 cm, tapering upwards, pale brownish with a basal bulb up to 2.0 cm broad and a white to brownish membraneous, double-edged movable annulus.

■ The spores are white in mass, ovoid to almond-shaped, 7.2-10.6 x 5.1-6.3 µm smooth, dextrinoid, and with a prominent germ pore. Basidia are clavate, 28.5-44.5 x 9.0-15.0 µm, with four sterigmata.

■ This species is similar to *M. rachodes* in that the flesh becomes orange to red when bruised. Untrained collectors might easily confuse this species with *Chlorophyllum molybdites*, both of which may be found in similar habitats in Florida, although *M. subrachodes* is most often found near wooded areas.

Fig. 102. *Macrolepiota subrachodes*   (x 0.3)   (Brian Akers)

Leucoagaricus

This genus is characterized by small to medium-sized stocky mushrooms with a smooth or squamulose non-striate pileus. They have white to pinkish lamellae reflective of their spore color. The spores have germ pores which are often indistinct, their walls are somewhat thick and dextrinoid, and may sometimes have small ornaments.

A Key to Florida Species of *Leucoagaricus*

1. Pileus dark brown to blackish ... *Leucoagaricus sanguifluss* (p. 129)
1. Pileus not as above 2
    2. Pileus pale cinnamon to pinkish 3
    2. Pileus not pale cinnamon or pinkish 4
3. Pileus minutely squamulose .... *Leucoagaricus tinctorius* (p. 131)
3. Pileus with large squamules ..... *Leucoagaricus americanus* (p. 125)
    4. Pileus cuticle dark smoky-brown but drying to a deep
       chocolate-brown .... *Leucoagaricus brunnescens* (p. 126)
    4. Pileus of different colors 5
5. Pileus dull yellow to yellowish-buff*Leucoagaricus hortensis* (p. 127)
5. Pileus rosy-red to brick-red .... *Leucoagaricus rubrotincta* (p. 128)

Leucoagaricus americanus (Peck) Singer   103

(choice, edible)

- The pileus is 3.0-15.0 cm wide, globose, becoming convex then flattened with a slight umbo; whitish with reddish-brown scales which are especially concentrated on the center of the disc. The lamellae are free, white to pinkish-buff, and somewhat crowded. The stipe is 7.0-13.0 x 0.5-2.2 cm, swollen below and tapering downward; white at first but staining pinkish to reddish-brown with age.

- The spores are white in deposit, ellipsoid, 9.0-10.5 x 7.0-8.5 µm, smooth, and dextrinoid. Basidia are clavate, 20.0-26.0 x 8.0-1.0 µm, with four sterigmata.

- This species is found widely distributed in eastern North America. It is most commonly found around wooded roadways, the edge of clearings, or in sparsely wooded areas.

Fig. 103. *Leucoagaricus americanus* (x 0.3)   (Walter Sundberg)

104	*Leucoagaricus brunnescens* (Peck) Bon

(edible)

■ The pileus is 2.0-2.7 cm wide, convex but becoming plane with raised margins and a broad umbo, dark brown with concentrically arranged fibrils. The lamellae are brown and some fairly crowded. The stipe is up to 4.0 cm long, 1.0-3.5 cm thick, cylindric to slightly tapering upward, with a chocolate-brown, membranous annulus, and a slightly bulbous base.

■ The spores are whitish in deposit, ellipsoid to ovoid, 5.0-7.0 x 3.1-4.7 μm, with a hyaline, dextrinoid wall that has a germ pore. The basidia are clavate, 16.8-21.0 x 6.2-8.6 μm, with four sterigmata.

■ This is a very common species in northern Florida. It has been found most often on leaf mulch in wooded areas, and may be recognized from other species of *Leucoagaricus* by its small size and dark brown fibrils on the pileus. A similar species, *L. floridanus* (Murr.) Akers, has been found occasionally. It differs in having a lighter colored pileus and stipe and more broadly ellipsoid spores.

Fig. 104. *Leucoagaricus brunnescens* (x 2.0)   (Walter Sundberg)

Leucoagaricus hortensis (Murr.) Pegler   **105**

(?edibility)

- The pileus is 2.0-5.9 cm broad, convex to plane, umbonate, dull yellow-ochraceous, with small darker scales towards the margins. The stipe is 2.0-5.0 cm long, 0.2-0.3 cm thick, with a slightly bulbous base, and a persistent, membranous, double-edged annulus.

- The spores are whitish in mass, elliptical to ovoid, 7.3-11.3 x 5.9-7.8 µm, dextrinoid, and with a small germ pore. Basidia are clavate, 16.2-25.0 x 6.6-9.2 µm, with two sterigmata.

- This species is found extensively throughout the eastern and midwestern U.S. It is found in Florida on open lawns, pastures, and sparsely wooded areas during the summer rainy season. According to Akers and Sundberg (1997), *Lepiota humei* Murr., *L. subfulvidisca* Murr., and *L. mammillata* Murr. are synonyms of *L. hortensis*.

Fig. 105. *Leucoagaricus hortensis* (x 1.0)   (Brian Akers)

---

106   *Leucoagaricus rubrotincta* (Peck) Singer

(?edibility)

■ The pileus is 1.5-5.0 cm wide, convex with a slight umbo, surface with appressed fibrils, rosy, red to brick-red or reddish-orange, and the disc purplish-red or darker. The lamellae are free, white, and with a fringed edge. The stipe is white to pale in color, 3.0-7.5 x 0.2-0.6 cm, tapering upward, with a bulbous base and a membranous annulus.

■ Spores are white in deposit, ellipsoid to almond-shaped, 6.3-9.2 x 3.9-5.0 µm, wall dextrinoid, and without a germ pore. Basidia are clavate, 12.0-23.0 x 7.0-10.0 µm, with four sterigmata.

■ This species is common throughout much of the U.S., and is especially common in Florida. It belongs to a group of species in which the spores are without germ pores. It is set apart from others of the group by its red to brick-red color and medium size. Most of the collections have been made in wooded areas throughout Alachua County.

Fig. 106 *Leucoagaricus rubrotincta*   (x 0.8)

Leucoagaricus sanguifluus (Murr.) Akers   **107**

(?edibility)

■ The pileus is 5.0-8.5 cm wide, convex with a broad umbo, dark brown on the disc with concentric scales towards the margins. The lamellae are dull brown, crowded, with a fringed margin. The stipe is cylindric to slight swollen but tapering below, 10.0 x 0.3-1.0 cm, with a thin, brown, membranous annulus.

■ The spores are whitish in deposit, broadly ellipsoid, 7.6-9.9 x 5.2-7.4 µm, wall moderately dextrinoid, with a prominent germ pore. Basidia are clavate, 28.0-32.0 x 9.0-9.9 µm, with four sterigmata.

■ Although originally described from under live oaks in Gainesville, Florida by Murrill (1945), this species appears to occur also throughout the midwestern U.S. In many respects it is similar to *L. americanus* and *L. tinctorius,* but differs in color and in having scaly remnants on the stipe.

Fig. 107. *Leucoagaricus sanguifluus*
(× 6.0)

Fig. 108. *Leucoagaricus tinctorius*   (× 0.4)

(?edibility)

■ The pileus is 7.0-9.0 cm wide, convex with a small umbo; cuticle dark brown on a lighter brown background, breaking up into rows of fibrillar scales. Gills are brown, somewhat close, and with fringed margins. The stipe is cylindrical, 6.0-7.0 x 0.5-1.5 cm, tapering above with a persistent, membranous, white to pale chestnut annulus.

■ The spores are whitish in mass, ellipsoid to subglobose, 7.3-10.2 x 5.0-7.9 µm, moderately dextrinoid, and thick-walled with a germ pore. Basidia are clavate, 30.0-35.0 x 9.3-10.5 µm, with four sterigmata.

■ This species has been found on shaded lawns of the University of Florida campus and adjacent residential areas. In many respects, this species is similar to *L. americanus,* but has finer cuticular scales and the stipe is not as strongly fusoid.

Leucocoprinus

This is a genus of small, slender mushrooms that have a striate cap and a simple, membranous annulus. Many are white or yellowish and often have small, dark scales.

A Key to Florida species of *Leucocoprinus*

1. Stipe with copious, floccose, circular remnants below 2
1. Stipe not as above 3
   2. Pileus sulfur to lemon-yellow ...... *Leucocoprinus luteus* (p. 135)
   2. Pileus white to whitish .... *Leucocoprinus breviramus* (p. 132)
3. Pileus cuticle yellow to yellowish
                 .... *Leucocoprinus fragilissimus* (p. 133)
3. Pileus a dull yellow-brown ...... *Leucocoprinus longistriatus* (p. 134)

Agaricales

- The pileus is 1.4-6.5 cm wide, convex to broadly bell-shaped, with a cuticle bearing white, scattered floccules. The lamellae are free, thin, widely spaced, and white. The stipe is 10.0-12.0 x 0.8 cm, slightly tapering upward, with a swollen base, white in color but bruising a dull yellowish brown. There is a white, fixed, membranous but fragile annulus.

- Spores are white in mass, ovoid to lemon-shaped, 8.0-11.0 x 5.0-7.2 μm, with a thick dextrinoid wall bearing a prominent germ pore. Basidia are clavate, 19.5-20.0 x 8.8-11.0 μm, with four sterigmata.

- This is a fairly small, white mushroom found on lawns throughout northern Florida. It is similar to *L. cepaestipes* (Sowerby: Fr.) Pat., but the latter has a pale tan, mealy pileus.

Fig. 109. *Leucocoprinus breviramus* (x 1.0)

Fig. 110. *Leucocoprinus fragillisimus* (x 1.0)

Leucocoprinus fragillisimus (Rav.:Berk. & Curt.) Pat.   **110**

(?edibility)

- The pileus is 2.0-5.0 cm wide, very thin and fragile, covered with yellow granules, with a deep yellow central disc and radiating yellow bands onto a whitish surface. The lamellae are white and fairly crowded. The stipe is 7.0-12.0 x 1.5-3.0 cm, yellowish, tapering upward with a fragile yellowish annulus.

- The spores are white in deposit, broadly ellipsoid, 9.0-12.5 x 6.0-8.5 μm, with a thick, dextrinoid wall bearing a prominent germ pore. Basidia are clavate, 38.0-42.0 x 8.0-10.5 μm, with four sterigmata.

- This small, delicate, almost translucent, yellow mushroom is easily distinguished from other Lepiotaceae by its size, color, and shape. It is found in abundance during the rainy summer months on wooded lawns and sparse forested areas. It is too small and fragile to collect for food.

Fig. 111. *Leucocoprinus longistriatus* (x 1.2)

---

111   *Leucocoprinus longistriatus* (Pk.) H.V. Smith & Weber

(?edibility)

■ The pileus is 3.0-4.0 cm wide, bell-shaped but becoming convex, beige with a tan disc, covered with darker granules, and striations that lead to the margins. The lamellae are free, whitish, and moderately crowded. The stipe is 6.0-7.0 x 0.1- 0.4 cm, white to light beige, tapering upwards, with a bulbous base and a whitish, membranous annulus.

■ Spores are white in deposit, ellipsoid to ovoid, 6.0-9.5 x 4.0-5.0 µm, with a thick, dextrinoid wall bearing a prominent germ pore. Basidia are clavate, 15.0-37.5 x 7.0-12.0 µm, with four, or in rare cases, two sterigmata.

■ This small, beige mushroom with a striated cap is one of the most abundant members of the Lepiotaceae on leaf mulch in forests throughout Florida. It is most common during the summer rainy season, but has been found occasionally during winter months.

Leucocoprinus luteus (Bolton) Locq.   **112**

(?edibility)

- The pileus is 3.0-7.0 cm wide, conical but expanding to become convex, sulfur to lemon-yellow, with a granular, striate cuticle. The lamellae are free, sulfur-yellow, thin and moderately crowded. The stipe is 4.0-8.0 x 0.2-0.4 cm, with a prominently swollen base and a fragile, membranous, yellow annulus.

- Spores are white in deposit, ellipsoid to ovoid, 7.0-12.5 x 4,7-7.0 μm, with a complex, dextrinod wall bearing an inconspicuous germ pore. Basidia are clavate, 18.0-20.0 x 7.3-9.0 μm, with four strongly curved sterigmata.

- This bright yellow species of *Leucocoprinus* has most frequently been found on decaying grass clippings and mulch piles. It is found most often during late summer and early fall. It can be confused with *L. fragillisimus,* but the latter is smaller and more fragile. It is poisonous to dogs.

Fig. 112. *Leucocoprinus luteus*   (x 1.0)   (Robert Williams)

The Tricholomataceae

The Tricholomataceae is a large and extremely diverse family of mushrooms. The stipe may be central, lateral or missing. An inner veil or annulus may or not be present, depending if they have a gymnohymenial or hemiangiohymenial development. Spores are white, cream to faintly pink in deposit, thin-walled and without a germ pore, and may or may not be dextrinoid or blue in iodine. They are terrestrial or wood inhabiting. The Tricholomataceae has often been referred to as the "waste basket" family of white-spored agarics. "If it doesn't fit anywhere else, toss it in here!"

A Key to Genera of Florida Tricholomataceae

1. Stipe eccentric .... *Lentinula* (p. 150)
1. Stipe central 2
    2. Spores turn blue in Melzer's iodine; basidiomata fleshy to brittle .... *Melanoleuca* (p. 162)
    2. Spores usually not turning blue in iodine; if so, basidiomata tough and leathery 3
3. Spores spinose, verrucose or punctate. 4
3. Spores smooth 5
    4. Spores coarsely spinose; ectomycorrhizal ....*Laccaria* (p. 148)
    4. Spores finely verrucose; on plant debris ....*Lepista* (p. 153)
5. Dry basidiomata reviving after moistening; stipe usually small and cartilaginous ....*Marasmius* (p. 156)
5. Basidiomata and stipe otherwise. 6
    6. Stipe deeply rooting; cap like wet leather .... *Xerula* (p. 174)
    6. Stipe not deeply rooting, cap otherwise 7
7. Spores large (> 20 μm), globose, with large refractile globules .... *Oudemansiella* (p. 170)
7. Not as above 8
    8. Growing on decaying mushrooms............ *Asterophora* (p. 140)
    8. Not growing on decaying mushrooms 9

9. Gills broadly adnate to deeply decurrent 10

9. Gills adnexed to sinuate 13

    10. Large (10-20 cm), bright orange mushrooms growing in tight clusters on stumps, base of trees, and logs .... ***Omphalotus*** (p. 168)

    10. Not as above 11

11. Small (< 2.5 cm) orange-brown mushrooms found commonly on decaying, moss-covered conifers .... ***Xeromphalina*** (p. 173)

11. Note as above 12

    12. Moderate to large honey or straw-colored muhsrooms; often with fibrils on the young pileus; annulus membranous to fragile and indistinct .... ***Armillaria*** (p. 137)

    12. Basidiomata variable; usually on leaf litter, soil, or occasionally on decaying logs .... ***Clitocybe*** (p. 141)

13. Pileus fleshy to fibrous 14

13. Pileus fragile, conical to campanulate .... ***Mycena*** (p. 164)

    14. Pileus hygrophanous, convex to plane, with enrolled margins; lamellae adnate .... ***Collybia*** (p. 143)

    14. Pileus not hygrophanous; lamellae sinuate 15

15. Basidiomata usually single or scattered; hyphae without clamp connections; ectomycorrhizal .... ***Tricholoma*** (p. 172)

15. Basidiomata large, usually clustered; hyphae with clamp connections; not ectomycorrhizal .... ***Macrocybe*** (p. 155)

Armillaria

More than 50 species have been described in this genus. Most are caespitose, i.e., they grow in clusters, and are honey, straw, to yellow-brown in color. Some have a persistent annulus, while in others it is fragile and disappears as the mushroom matures. They cause wood decay and root rot of many hardwood species. Two species are common in Florida: *A. tabescens,* which occurs in the fall and winter months and causes severe root rot in many living trees and shrubby ornamentals, and *A. mellea,* which occurs less frequently in the spring and causes "shoestring root rot" of many trees. *Armillaria mellea* has a persistent, membranous annulus, while in *A. tabescens* it is fragile and often disappears.

113   *Armillaria mellea* (Vahl:Fr.) Kummer

(edible)

- The pileus is 2.5-10.0 cm, ovoid at first, becoming convex to plane; yellow to rusty-brown with darker scales. The lamellae are slightly decurrent, distant, whitish but staining yellow to reddish. The stipe is 5.0-15.0 cm long, 0.5-2.0 cm wide, fibrous, whitish but discoloring yellow to reddish, with a membranous persistent annulus.

- Spores are white in deposit, broadly ellipsoid, 7.0-9.0 x 5.0-6.7 μm, smooth, and not turning blue in iodine. Basidia clavate, 27.0-33.0 x 5.0-11.0 μm, with four sterigmata.

- This species is known as the "honey agaric", and is a choice edible species that occurs throughout North America, but is most common in the southeastern states. Although it appears occasionally in the summer and fall months, it appears most often in the months of December and January. It causes what forest pathologists refer to as the "shoestring root rot" because of the very distinct, black rhizomorphs in the wood on which they grow.

Fig. 113 *Armillaria mellea*   (x 0.6)

Fig. 114. *Armillaria tabescens* (x 0.2)

Armillaria tabescens (Scop.:Fr.) Dennis **114**

(edible)

- The pileus is 2.5-10.0 cm, convex to plane, sometimes sunken at the disc with uplifted margins; yellow-brown to reddish-brown with flat to erect scales. The lamellae are decurrent, somewhat distant, staining pinkish to brownish with age. Stipes are 7.5-20.0 cm long, 0.5-1.5 cm wide, tapering towards the base; off-white to brownish in color, lacking an annulus.

- Spores are white in deposit, broadly ellipsoid, 6.0-10.0 x 5.0-7.0 µm, not turning blue in iodine. Basidia are clavate, 30.0-35.0 x 7.0-10.0 µm, with four sterigmata.

- This is the most common late fall-early winter mushroom in Florida. It causes mushroom root-rot of numerous tree and shrub species, and is especially critical in the dieback of oaks. It is seldom found in summer months, but appears in striking numbers as soon as late fall rains commence. It is a choice edible species, but because of its toughness, must be cooked longer than the average mushroom.

Asterophora

This is a small group of mushrooms that belongs to the Lyophylleae tribe of the Tricholomataceae, a tribe characterized by dense granules in the basidia that stain with acetocarmine. *Asterophora* differs from other genera in the tribe by being parasitic on members of the Russulaceae, and the presence of chlamydospores on the pileus which gives them a powdery appearance. There is controversy over the proper generic name; some have placed the species in the genus *Nyctalis* (Pegler, 1983). Only one species has been found in Florida.

---

115   *Asterophora lycoperdoides* (Bull.:Maret) Gray

(inedible)

- The pileus is 0.5-2.0 cm, globose, scarcely expanding, white, becoming covered with dense brown powder. Lamellae are adnate, distant, often malformed and whitish. The stipe is 2.0-3.0 cm long, 0.3-1.0 cm wide, stout, silky, white at first becoming brownish.

- Spores are white in mass, ovoid, 5.0-6.0 x 3.5-4.0 µm, thin-walled, and do not turn blue in iodine. Large, 13.0-16.0 µm, buff-colored chlamydospores result in a powdery surface on mature mushrooms.

Fig. 115. *Asterophora lycoperdoides*   (x 0.5)   (Ulla Benny)

■ This small species is found growing on other mushrooms, commonly on species of *Russula* and *Lactarius* in Florida. It is widely distributed in North America, but according to Murrill (1972) it is rarely found around north Florida.

Clitocybe

Species of *Clitocybe* are characterized by distinctly decurrent lamellae and a fleshy-fibrous stipe, without an annulus or volva. They are found mostly on the soil or leaf litter, in rare cases on decaying logs. A number of species are choice, edible mushrooms; others are toxic. Therefore, one should proceed with caution when collecting these for food. More than 40 species have been reported in Florida. The most common species are provided in the key below (see Bigelow 1982, 1985). *Clitocybe* was once a very large genus, but most species have been transferred to *Omphalotus, Armillaria, Gerronema,* and *Trogia.*

A Key to Common Species of *Clitocybe*

1. Pileus hygrophanus, creamy-white .... *Clitocybe gibba* (p. 141)
1. Pileus umber, becoming pale gray-buff
   .... *Clitocybe hydrogramma* (p. 142)

Clitocybe gibba (Fr.) Kumm — 116

(edible)

■ The pileus is 3.0-9.0 cm in diameter, initially plane but becoming deeply depressed, smooth, moist, pinkish-tan to flesh-colored. The lamellae are decurrent, white to pale buff, and somewhat crowded. The stipe is 3.0-7.0 x 0.4-1.2 cm, equal or sometimes with a swollen base, white, and tomentose towards the base.

■ The spores are white in deposit, ellipsoid, 5.0-10.0 x 3.5-5.5 μm, smooth and not turning blue in iodine. Basidia are 22.0-36.0 x 5.0-8.5 μm, usually with four sterigmata, sometimes less.

■ This species has also gone under the name *C. infundibuliformis* (Fr.) Quel. and it is distinct by its pinkish-buff, deeply depressed pileus. It is common in sparcely wooded areas around lakeshores and pastures.

Fig. 116. *Clitocybe gibba*   (× 0.5)

---

117   *Clitocybe hydrogramma* (Fr.) Kummer

(inedible)

■ The pileus is 1.5-6.0 cm wide, thin, convex then plane and often becoming funnel-shaped, somewhat hygrophanous, pale gray to buff, fading to white. The lamellae are deeply decurrent, buff to whitish, and somewhat crowded. Stipes are 2.0-7.0 x 0.2-0.7 cm, cylindric, and of similar colors to the pileus.

■ Spores are white to dingy pink in deposit, ellipsoid, 4.5-6.5 x 3.0-4.0 μm, with a smooth wall that does not turn blue in iodine. Basidia are narrowly clavate, 16.0-24.0 x 3.0-7.0 μm, with four sterigmata.

■ This species grows solitarily, or more commonly in clusters under hardwoods on the soil and leaf litter. It is widespread in North America and has been found extensively in north Florida. Most of the herbarium collections are filed under an older name, *C. adirondakensis*.

Fig. 117. *Clitocybe hydrogramma* (× 0.5)

Collybia

These are small to medium-sized mushrooms with attached lamellae, cartilaginous or brittle stipes that have no annulus or volva, and a convex pileus with incurved margins. Many have a pileus cuticle that feels of "wet leather." They are found on soil, humus, or decaying wood. More than 70 species have been described worldwide, with almost 25 occurring in Florida. Some common species are provided in the following key.

A Key to Common Species of *Collybia* in Florida

1. Pileus 5.0-7.0 cm in diameter, dark reddish brown, convex to umbonate .... *Collybia luxurians* (p. 146)
1. Pileus smaller and not umbonate 2
    2. Pileus violet to pinkish violet .. .. *Collybia iocephala* (p. 145)
    2. Pileus another color 3
3. Pileus rusty-brown, deeply depressed ... *Collybia spongiosa* (p. 147)
3. Pileus ochre to reddish-tan, not depressed
                     .... *Collybia dryophila* (p. 144)

Collybia dryophila (Bull.:Fr.) Kummer

(edible)

■ The pileus is 2.0-5.0 cm wide, convex, becoming plane and finally depressed; surface hygrophanus, buff to whitish, and finely striated when moist. The lamellae are adnexed to adnate, whitish to yellowish, and crowded. Stipes are 3.0-7.0 x 0.2-0.3 cm, cylindric, whitish, becoming yellowish to buff, without an annulus or volva.

■ The spores are white to pale cream in deposit, ellipsoid, 4.5-7.5 x 3.0-4.0 μm, not turning blue in iodine. Basidia narrowly clavate, 15.0-18.0 x 4.0-6.0 μm, bearing four sterigmata.

■ This species is found scattered on plant debris in oak and pine forests, and occasionally on wooded lawns throughout northern Florida during all seasons of the year. It is somewhat similar to certain species of *Marasmius,* but may be distinguished by its more fibrous/fleshy stipe and an array of microscopic features.

Fig. 118. *Collybia dryophila*   (x 0.6)

Fig. 119. *Collybia iocephala* (x 0.5)   (Terry Hinkel)

Collybia iocephala (Berk. & Curt.) Singer   **119**

(edibile)

- The pileus is 3.0-5.0 cm wide, convex to plane, with margins incurved at first; violet fading to faintly lilac; and with a very unpleasant odor. The lamellae are broadly spaced and similar in color to the pileus. The stipe is 2.5-5.0 x 0.15-0.3 cm, lilac to whitish, somewhat enlarged at the base; and without a volva or annulus.

- The spores are white in deposit, ellipsoid, 7.0-8.5 x 3.0-4.0 µm, smooth; not turning blue in iodine. Basidia are clavate, 32.0-40.0 x 8.0-12.0 µm, bearing four sterigmata.

- This species of *Collybia* is easy to recognize because of its thin, almost translucent, lilac-colored pileus, and its strong, offensive odor. Some describe the odor as "garlic-like," others, like gunpowder. It is found in mixed forests throughout Florida. Because of their odor, clusters of *C. iocephala* can be detected at a great distance in the forest.

(?edibility)

- The pileus is 5.0-7.5 cm wide, convex to plane; pinkish-cinnamon but with a reddish-brown disc. The lamellae are adnexed, narrow, crowded; and of similar color to the pileus. The stipe is 5.0-7.0 x 0.5-0.8 cm, tapering upwards, somewhat twisted; reddish-brown, with whitish mycelium at the base.

- Spores are white in deposit, ovoid, 7.0-8.0 x 5.0-6.0 µm, not turning blue in iodine. Basidia are narrowly clavate, 22.0-28.0 x 7.5-8.6 µm, with four sterigmata.

- This species has been found most often on mulch in shaded lawns, but it has also been found in open lawns. Murrill (1945) first described this species as *Gymnopus subluxurians*, but according to Halling (1986), it is Peck's *C. luxurians*.

Fig. 120. *Collybia luxurians* (x 1.0)

Fig. 121. *Collybia spongiosa* (× 1.0)   (Sherri Angels)

Collybia spongiosa (Berk. & Curt.) Singer   **121**

(?edibility)

■ The pileus is 1.0-3.0 cm wide, convex to plane or depressed, margins incurved at first but expanding; reddish-brown but becoming buff colored. The lamellae are adnexed to adnate, moderately spaced, and off-white to buff. Stipes are 2.5-7.5 x 0.1-0.2 cm, with a swollen, spongy base, reddish-brown, and covered with reddish-brown hairs.

■ Spores are white in deposit, ellipsoid, 6.0-8.5 x 3.0-4.0 µm, smooth, not turning blue in iodine. Basidia are clavate, 25.0-30.0 x 5.0-6.5 µm, with four sterigmata.

■ This species has been found growing on decaying oak leaves in forests from Quebec to Florida. It is especially common on leaves of laurel and water oaks around Gainesville. It is recognized from other species of *Collybia* by its hairy, reddish-brown stipe with a bulbous base.

Laccaria

The genus *Laccaria* encompasses a number of small mushrooms with waxy, violet to purple or rosy lamellae. They appear to be the only members of the Tricholomataceae with globose, spiny to verrucose spores that do not turn blue in iodine. Three species are common in Florida

A Key to Common species of *Laccaria*

1. Most of the stipe buried in sand; basidiomata reddish flesh-colored, covered with sand particles.....*Laccaria trullissata* (p. 150)

1. Not as above 2

   2. Pileus and lamellae a dull violet to purplish-gray; spore deposit violaceous .... *Laccaria amethystina* (p. 149)

   2. Pileus orange brown; lamellae flesh-colored; spore deposit white .... *Laccaria laccata* (p. 149)

Fig. 122. *Laccaria amethystina* (x 1.0)

Laccaria amethystina (Bolt.: Hooker) Cooke   **122**

(?edibility)

- The pileus is 0.5-4.7 cm in diameter, convex to plane, becoming depressed, dry, sometimes faintly striate, grayish-purple to dark purple-gray, but fading yellowish. The lamellae are sinuate to somewhat decurrent, thick, waxy, and similar in color to the pileus. The stipe is 1.2-5.8 x 0.1-0.7 cm, equal or slightly tapering below, striate, and similar in color to the pileus.

- The spores are violaceous in deposit, globose to subglobose, 8.3-12.2 x 8.3-11.7 µm, and with spines up to 1.7 mm Basidia are 29.6-63.0 x 6.0-13.6 µm, with four, sometimes fewer, sterigmata.

- This species is found in pine or mixed hardwood forests, often in poorly drained areas and associated with *Sphagnum*. It is easily recognized from other species by its small size and purplish color.

Laccaria laccata (Scop.: Fr.) Cooke   **123**

(edible)

- The pileus is 1.0-5.0 cm wide, convex to plane with a central depression and sometimes with an upturned margin; pinkish to reddish-brown, fading to ochra-white. The lamellae are adnate to slightly decurrent, distant, waxy, pink to pinkish-brown. The stipe is 2.5-7.5 x 0.3-0.5 cm, tough, fibrous, and similar in color to the pileus.

- The spores are white in deposit, globose to broadly ellipsoid, 8.5-10.5 x 7.5-9.0 µm, not turning blue in iodine, and with spines up to 2.0 mm. Basidia clavate, 28.0-35.0 x 8.0-10.0 µm, with four sterigmata.

- This species is often found clustered in poor soil and waste places. It is very common in Florida in marshy areas where plantation pines are being established.

Fig. 123. *Laccaria laccata* (x 1.0)

(?edibility)

- The pileus is 3.0-10.0 cm in diameter, convex to plane, moist, reddish flesh-colored fading to dusky pink, and often becoming scaly with age. The lamellae are distant, and are initially violaceous, becoming a reddish flesh color. The stipe is 3.0-10.0 x 1.0-2.0 cm, dull violaceous, often buried in sand, clavate at the base, and usually covered with sand particles.

- The spores are white in deposit, strongly elongate, 14.7-21.0 x 6.0-7.8 μm, and very finely roughened. The basidia are 30.0- 53.0 x 9.2-12.4 μm, with four sterigmata.

- This species is found in open forests and wooded lawns, or along roadsides. According to Mueller (*per. comm*), this species is in the central states as well as along the Gulf coastal plain.

Fig. 124. *Laccaria trullissata* (x 0.5)   (Greg Mueller)

Lentinula

This genus is recognized for a number of species of wood-inhabiting mushrooms, with slightly eccentric stipes and with lamellae that are adnexed to sinuate and soon separated from the stipe. They have a pseudoangiohymenial development in which there is an inner veil, which in most species will leave a fragile marginal veil or indistinct annulus. Two species occur in Florida, *Lentinula boryana* (Berk. & Mont.) Pegler and *L. edodes* (Berk.) Pegler, the popular "shiitake" mushroom was introduced for cultivation. These species have been traditionally placed in *Lentinus*, a group of tough, leathery mushroom-like species that belong in the Aphyllophorales (see Pegler, 1983).

A Key to Common Species of *Lentinula* in Florida

1. Pileus 2.0-5.0 cm in diameter, yellowish-brown to pale chocolate brown; stipe smooth, yellowish-brown .. *Lentinula boryana* (p. 151)
1. Pileus 5.0-15.0 cm in diameter, brown to purplish brown, with whitish-buff scales; stipe scaly .... *Lentinus edodes* (p. 152)

Lentinula boryana (Berk. & Mont.) Pegler   **125**

(edible)

■ The pileus is 2.0-5.0 cm wide, soft, fleshy, convex but becoming plane with a central depression, and with a whitish to pale yellow-brown cuticle. The lamellae are adnate to adnexed, soon pulling away from the stipe, very crowded; cream-colored but becoming brownish. Stipes are 1.0-6.0 x 0.2-0.5 cm, slightly eccentric, fibrous to woody, often curved; pale rusty-brown, often with a very fragile annulus.

■ The spores are creamy in deposit, oblong to ellipsoid, 5.0-6.0 x 2.0-3.5 μm, thin-walled and smooth. Basidia are narrowly clavate, 15.0-17.0 x 3.0-4.0 μm, bearing four sterigmata.

Fig. 125. *Lentinula boryana* (x 0.6)   (Brian Akers)

■ This species is found in abundance during the rainy season on decaying logs, especially those of oak species, throughout Florida. Structurally it is very similar to the commercially grown shiitake, *L. edodes*. Shiitake differs, however, in being larger, more purple-brown in color and more scaly.

---

126   *Lentinula edodes* (Berk.) Pegler

(edible)

■ The pileus is 5.0-12.0 cm, sometimes up to 20 cm wide, globose at first becoming convexed to plane with incurved margins; yellowish-brown to reddish or purplish-brown; usually adorned with large whitish to buff-colored scales in circular bands around the margins. The lamellae are rather close, adnexed but detaching from the stipe; whitish with purplish-brown spots. The stipe is stout and fibrous, usually eccentric, 3.0-5.0 x .8-1.3 cm; whitish-brown above, becoming yellowish-buff to reddish-brown below; sometimes with a scant fibrillar annulus in youth, with darker brown scales.

■ The spores are white in deposit, ellipsoid, 5.8-6.4 x 2.8-3.3 µm, not turning blue in iodine. Basidia are clavate 30.0-32.0 x 5.0-6.5 µm, with four sterigmata.

■ *Lentinula edodes*, the popular "shiitake" mushroom, is a native of Asia but is being actively grown commercially throughout North America, including Florida. It is grown outdoors on freshly cut bolts of hardwood logs, and indoors on artificial hardwood sawdust logs.

Fig. 126. *Lentinula edodes* (x 0.2)

Lepista

Basidiomata of *Lepista* are medium sized, with sinuate to decurrent, lamellae, hygrophanous, and often with lilaceous or violaceous pigments. In many respects they look like *Tricholoma*. They differ, however, in having warted to verrucose spores that are pinkish to salmon in deposit, and do not turn blue in iodine. Four species have been found in Florida; two of these will be described.

A Key to Common species of *Lepista* in Florida

1. Pileus creamy-white to pale reddish-brown *Lepista inversa* (p. 153)
1. Pileus violet-blue to violet-buff .... *Lepista nuda* (p. 154)

Lepista inversa (Scop.:Fr.) Pat.   **127**

(inedible)

- The pileus is 3.0-8.0 cm in diameter, convex with a depressed center early but becoming infundibuliform when mature; reddish-brown and somewhat hygrophanous. The lamellae are initially cream-colored, but become reddish-buff. The stipe is 6.0-10.0 x 0.9-2.0 cm, tapering downward; pinkish-brown, but bruising brown when touched.

Fig. 127. *Lepista inversa* (× 1.1)

- The spores are creamy-white in deposit, subglobose, 4.0-5.3 x 3.5-4.3 µm, and finely verrucose. The basidia are narrowly clavate, 22.0-32.0 x 4.0-6.0 µm; with four sterigmata

- This species is found mostly in leaf litter of conifers, or occasionally mixed hardwood forests.

---

128   _Lepista nuda_ (Bull.:Fr.) Cooke

(choice)

- The pileus is 4.0-12.0 cm wide, broadly convex with inrolled margins, becoming plane, later uplifting; shades of violet, light vinaceous, becoming vinaceous-buff; smooth, hygrophanous to appearing subviscid. Lamellae are pale violet at first becoming vinaceous-buff, strongly adnate to decurrent, and somewhat narrow. The stipe is fairly stout, 3.0-6.0 x 1.0-2.5 cm, sometimes bulbous at the base, and of similar color to the lamellae.

- The spores are pinkish in deposit, ellipsoid 5.5-8.0 x 3.5-5.0 µm, smooth to slightly verruculose, not turning blue in iodine. Basidia are narrowly clavate, 21.0-33.0 x 5.5-7.5 µm, with four sterigmata.

Fig. 128. _Lepista nuda_ (x 1.0)   (Ulla Benny)

■ This species is commonly referred to as "blewits" and is highly prized for food. Like other species of *Clitocybe,* it is found on humus along trails under hardwoods, rarely conifers, and occasionally on lawns and pastures. It is somewhat set apart from others species by its blue to violet coloration.

Macrocybe

This is one of the most recent genera of mushrooms to be recognized. Morphological and ecological data, and rDNA sequence comparison led Pegler et al. (1998) to remove seven related tropical species from *Tricholoma* and place them in a new genus, *Macrocybe.* Species of *Macrocybe* are characterized by having large (up to 80 or 100 cm), fleshy, and often clustered basidiomata, which grow saprobically on submerged wood or other decaying plant debris. The lamellae are sinuate or become detached from the stipe, and in most species the stipes are swollen at the base. Of the seven tropical to sub-tropical species, only one, *Macrocybe titans* (Bigelow & Kimbr.) Pegler, Lodge & Nakasone, has been discovered in Florida.

Macrocybe titans
(Bigelow & Kimbr.) Pegl., Lodge & Nakas.   129

(edible)

■ The pileus is 8.0-80.0 cm, in rare cases up to 100 cm wide, convex to plane, becoming upturned and undulating at the margins; warm buff to buff-yellow but darker at the disc; growing in dense clusters; odor of cyanide. The lamellae are strongly sinuate, densely crowded, grayish-buff to pale brown. The stipe is 6.0-25.0 x 1.5-12.0 cm, or swollen to 15.0 cm at the base; tough, fibrous, surface breaking into small scales; color similar to pileus.

■ The spores are creamy in deposit, subglobose to ovoid, 5.5-7.0 x 4.0-5.0 µm, not turning blue in iodine. Basidia are clavate, 25.0-38.0 x 6.5-10.0 µm; with four sterigmata.

■ This is a remarkable species with its robust basidiomata that grow in clusters. The first collection was observed in Florida in 1969, and later in 1973. Numerous specimens have been found throughout the area larger than 60 cm in diameter. It appears to prefer disturbed areas, and has most often been collected around fill dirt for buildings, trails, and roads, on agricultural land, or, most extensively, in land reclamation areas of south Florida (see Eilers et al., 1980). Individuals have eaten *M. titans,* but note that because of its toughness, it should be cooked longer than normal in a well vented room and the water poured off.

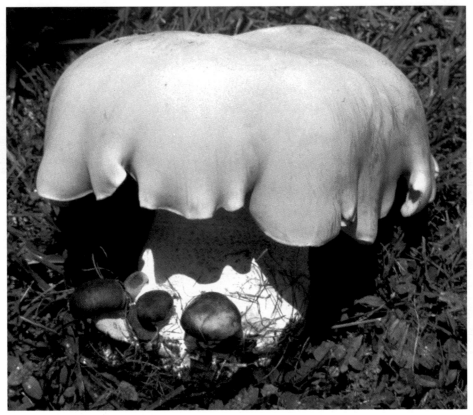

Fig. 129. *Macrocybe titans* (x 0.2)

Marasmius

Species of *Marasmius* are distinguished by their small size, basidiomata that after dying will revive when moistened, and by small, cartilaginous stipes. They have a gymnohymenial or hemiangiohymenial development and do not have an annulus or volva. More than 350 species have been described, many of them difficult to identify and require critical microscopic examination. More than 80 species have been accessioned in the University of Florida Mycological Herbarium.

A Key to Common Species of *Marasmius* in Florida

1. Pileus vinaceous to purple-red
   .... *Marasmius haematocephalus* (p. 160)
1. Pileus another color 2
   2. Pileus tawny, olive-brown .... *Marasmius coniatus* (p. 158)
   2. Pileus not as above 3
3. Pileus dull, brownish to reddish-brown
   ....*Marasmius brunneolus* (p. 157)
3. Pileus another color 4
   4. Pileus conic to umbonate; stipe grayish-buff; slightly
      darker below ....*Marasmius magnisporus* (p. 161)
   4. Pileus convex, becoming depressed 5
5. Pileus whitish to buff; lamellae white to beige, stipe reddish-
   brown, slightly darker below ....*Marasmius rotula* (p. 162)
5. Pileus creamy-white; lamellae few, white and veined; stipe white
   above, yellow-brown below .... *Marasmius epiphyllus* (p. 159)

Marasmius brunneolus (Berk. & Br.) Pegler　　　**130**

(inedible)

■ The pileus is 0.7-1.0 cm in diameter, membranous, convex to
   conical-campanulate, brownish on disc, yellow-brown and

Fig. 130. *Marasmius brunneolus* (x 1.2)

furrowed towards the margin. The lamellae are adnexed, white to pale brown, and very distant. The stipe is 3.0-4.5 cm long, 0.5-1.0 mm in diameter, hyaline with a brownish base.

- The spores are white in deposit, elongate-lanceolate, 20.0-27.0 x 4.0-6.0 µm, smooth and thin-walled. The basidia are 38.0-50.0 x 7.0-8.0 µm, with four sterigmata.

- This species is found on decaying plant debris on the forest floor and appears to be mostly tropical and subtropical. It differs from *M. ferrugineus* (Berk.) Berk. & Curt. in having much larger spores.

---

131   *Marasmius coniatus* Berk. & Br.

(inedible)

- The pileus is 0.3-1.0 cm in diameter, membranous, conic to campanulate; surface tawny-brown to olivaceous brown at the disc and with deep radiating furrows towards the margin. The lamellae are adnexed, somewhat distant, white to pallid, with a reddish-brown edge. The stipe is 1.0-4.0 cm x 0.2-0.4 mm, tawny-brown but becoming blackish towards the base.

- The spores are white in deposit, lanceolate, 13.0 x 18.0 x 3.5-4.5 µm, smooth and thin-walled. The basidia are narrowly clavate, 25.0 x 35.0 x 5.0-6.5 µm, with four sterigmata.

- This species is found on decaying leaves in forests of tropical and subtropical countries.

Fig. 131. *Marasmius coniatus* (x 2.0)
(Sherri Angels)

(inedible)

■ The pileus is 3.0-10.0 mm wide, convex becoming flattened and depressed; white to creamy-white, with radial grooves or wrinkles. The lamellae are few and broadly spaced, adnexed; white, and vein-like. The stipe is hair-like, 15.0-30.0 x 1.0 mm, whitish apically, and reddish-brown below.

■ The spores are white in deposit, narrowly elliptic, 10.0-11.0 x 3.0-4.0 µm, not turning blue in iodine. Basidia are narrowly clavate, 15.0-22.0 x 5.0-6.0 µm; with four sterigmata.

■ This species is in many respects similar to *M. candidus* in having a thin pileus with white, vein-like lamellae. It differs, however, in having much longer stipes and smaller spores.

Fig. 132. *Marasmius epiphyllus* (x 0.5)   (Sherri Angels)

133   *Marasmius haematocephalus* (Mont.) Fr.

(inedible)

- The pileus is 1.0-2.0 cm wide, convex to campanulate, with a strongly purplish-red to vinaceous cuticle, and deep radial striations. The lamellae are free to adnexed, distant, and white to pale purplish-pink. The stipe is 1.5-6.0 cm x 0.2-1.0 mm, dark reddish-brown, glabrous; with well developed basal mycelium.

- The spores are white to creamy in deposit, cylindric to subfusoid, 16.0-20 x 3.0-4.5 µm, not turning blue in iodine. Basidia are clavate, 24.0-28.0 x 6.0-7.5 µm; with four sterigmata.

- This is a common subtropical species found on leaf litter and easily recognized by the deep purplish pileus. It is common in oak/pine forests of Florida.

Fig. 133. *Marasmius haematocephalus* (x 1.0)

Fig. 134. *Marasmius magnisporus* (x 1.2)

Marasmius magnisporus Murrill   **134**

(inedible)

- The pileus is 1.0-1.5 cm in diameter, thin, tough, convex or at times umbonate; white to pale buff with pinkish tint, with a smooth surface, and margins slightly striate. The lamellae are adnate or subdecurrent, widely spaced, and white. The stipe is 1.0-3.0 x 0.2 cm, tapering downward, smooth, tough, grayish-buff below, and lighter in color above.

- The spores are white in deposit, ellipsoid, 10.0-12.0 x 4.0-6.0 µm, smooth and thin-walled. The basidia are 28.0-36.0 x 6.5-7.0 µm; with four sterigmata.

- This species is found on dead wood and appears to be widely distributed throughout temperate regions.

135   *Marasmius rotula* (Scop.: Fr.) Fr.

(inedible)

■ The pileus is 0.5-1.5 cm wide, hemispherical to convex with a sunken umbo; white when young, becoming slightly buff towards the center; with deep radiating furrows. The lamellae are white, becoming beige, broadly spaced and separated from the stipe by a collar. The stipe is 2.0-6.0 cm tall, 0.5-1.5 mm thick, smooth, dark reddish-brown to blackish.

■ The spores are whitish in deposit, ellipsoid 6.8-8.5 x 2.9-4.0 µm, not turning blue in iodine. Basidia are narrowly clavate, 25.0-30.0 x 4.5-6.0 µm; with four sterigmata.

■ This small white species is found commonly growing in clusters on piles of decaying plant material on lawns and forested areas. With their color and deeply straited caps, they resemble small parachutes.

Fig. 135. *Marasmius rotula* (x 1.0)

Melanoleuca

Species of *Melanoleuca* are medium-sized mushrooms with tall, thin stipes without an annulus or volva, and a broad flat cap with an umbo. They resemble species of *Tricholoma* in having sinuate lamellae but differ, however, in having spores that turn blue in iodine. Many resemble certain species of *Collybia* in having a hygrophanous pileus that feels like wet leather. About a dozen species of *Melanoleuca* have been accessioned in the University of Florida Mycological Herbarium. Only one will be treated here.

Fig. 136. *Melanoleuca alboflavida* (× 1.0)

Melanoleuca alboflavida (Pk.) Murr. **136**

(edible)

■ The pileus is 5.0-7.5 cm wide, convex becoming plane and depressed; fleshy, smooth, hygrophanous when moist; and white to slightly yellowish-white. The lamellae are crowded, adnexed, thin, and whitish. The stipe is slender, solid, cylindrical, 7.5-10.0 x 0.6-0.8 cm, whitish, with a slightly bulbous base.

■ The spores are white in deposit, ellipsoid, 7.5-8.7 x 4.0-5.0 µm, with low ornaments that turn blue in iodine. Basidia are clavate, 18.0-25.0 x 7.0-8.0 µm; with four sterigmata.

■ This species has been found consistently in grass beneath trees on lawns, and along trails in northern Florida. It is assumed to be ectomycorrhizal with the trees under which it is found.

Mycena

Species of *Mycena* are small, fragile mushrooms with narrow, brittle stipes, and small, conical to campanulate caps with striate margins. The lamellae are adnate to adnexed and the stipes are without volva or annulus. They grow singlely, but most often in clusters, on needles, leaves, and other decomposing plant debris. Species of *Mycena, Marasmius, Collybia,* and similar small mushrooms are recognized as being some of our most significant mushrooms in the decomposition of leaf litter. They are especially abundant in tropical and subtropical areas. Almost 200 species have been described in North America, and several occur in Florida. Although there are no reports of toxic species, their small size and texture make them not worth the effort of consuming. For an extensive treatment of species, see Maas Geesteranus (1988) for a citation of numerous papers on *Mycena*.

A Key to Common Species of *Mycena* in Florida

1. Basidiomata usually less than 2.0 cm in diameter 2
1. Basidiomata larger 3
    2. Pileus yellow to yellowish-orange ..... *Mycena flavoalba* (p. 164)
    2. Pileus whitish with darker disc .. *Mycena subepiptergia* (p. 168)
3. Pileus creamy to light brown .... *Mycena galericulata* (p. 165)
3. Pileus reddish-orange .... *Mycena laeiana* (p. 166)

---

137   *Mycena flavoalba* (Fr.) Quel.

(?edibility)

■ The pileus is 1.0-2.0 cm in diameter, conic to campanulate, smooth with radiating fibrils, yellowish to yellowish-orange, with a darker umbo, and the margin is striate. The lamellae are whitish, subdecurrent, and with a smooth edge. The stipe is 2.5-4.5 x 0.1-0.2 cm, cylindric, hollow, smooth, dull yellowish-white, and the apex is somewhat paler.

■ The spores are white in deposit, ellipsoid, 6.0-7.7 x 3.8-4.1 µm, smooth, and with thin walls. Basidia are 23.0-30.0 x 5.5-7.0 µm; with four sterigmata.

■ This species has been found on rotting wood, decaying leaves and other plant debris throughout North America.

Fig. 137. *Mycena flavoalba* (x 0.7)   (Sherri Angels)

Mycena galericulata (Scop.: Fr.) Gray   **138**

(?edibility)

■   The pileus is 2.0-5.5 cm, campanulate when young, becoming convex to plane with a prominent umbo and striate margin; creamy to light brown in color. The lamellae are white to grayish-white, somewhat pinkish with age; and finely adnexed. The stipe is cylindric, 4.0-6.0 x 0.2-0.4 cm, sometimes compressed, and gray-beige to brownish in color.

■   The spores are pale creamy in deposit, ovoid, 9.0-12.0 x 6.3-8.6 µm; not turning blue in iodine. Basidia are clavate, 30.0-35.0 x 7.0-8.0 µm; with two sterigmata.

■   This species is somewhat like *M. epipterygia* but is slightly larger, has a compressed stipe, two-spored basidia and is more often found in clusters. It occurs on rotting stumps and branches of various hardwoods and conifers.

Fig. 138. *Mycena galericulata* (x 1.0)

---

139   *Mycena laeiana* (Berk.) Sacc.

(?edibility)

■ The pileus is 1.0-5.0 cm, hemispherical at first, becoming convex with sunken disc, and with a smooth to scruffy, reddish-orange cuticle, fading to yellowish-orange. The lamellae are adnate, close to crowded; pinkish to yellowish-orange with a bright orange edge. The stipe is cylindric, 3.0-7.0 cm x 0.2-0.3 cm, tough-fibrous, orange to yellow with coarse hairs around the base.

■ The spores are white in deposit, ellipsoid, 7.0-10.0 x 5.0-6.0 μm, turning blue in iodine. Basidia are narrowly clavate, 20.0-25.0 x 6.0-8.0 μm; with four sterigmata.

■ This *Mycena* is easily spotted as orange clusters on decaying wood.

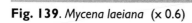

Fig. 139. *Mycena laeiana* (× 0.6)   (Ulla Benny)

Fig. 140. *Mycena subepipterygia* (× 1.4)   (Ulla Benny)

Mycena subepipterygia (Murr.) Murr.

(?edibility)

■ The pileus is 1.0-2.0 cm wide, convex to plane, slightly depressed at disc, which is darker, smooth and somewhat viscid. The lamellae are adnexed, white to buff-white. The stipe is cylindric, 1.5-3.0 x 0.1-0.2 cm, smooth, moist, and white.

■ The spores are white in deposit, ellipsoid, 5.0-6.0 x 3.0-4.0 μm, turning blue in iodine. Basidia are clavate, 20.0-25.0 x 7.0-8.0 μm; with four sterigmata.

■ This small whitish to buff-colored *Mycena* is found in clusters on decaying hardwood logs and limbs. It is similar to *M. epipterygia* but has shorter stipes and smaller spores.

Omphalotus

Species of *Omphalotus* have bright orange, fleshy basidiomata with strongly decurrent lamellae and grow in clusters around the base of rotting trees, on decaying wood, or growing in soil from submerged decaying roots. Their stipes are fibrous, central to slightly eccentric. For many years species of *Omphalotus* were placed in *Clitocybe* because of similar basidiomata, or in *Monodelphus* characterized by basidiomata that grow in tight clusters. Species of *Omphalotus* cause severe gastrointestinal irritation and should be avoided. Two species occur in Florida.

A Key to Species of *Omphalotus* in Florida
1. Spores globose to subglobose, 3.5-5.5 x 3.5-5.0 μm; pileus 2.5-12.0 cm in diameter, margins even .... *Omphalotus olearius* (p. 168)

1. Spores ellipsoid, 7.0-9.0 x 4.5-5.0 μm, pileus 10.0-15.0 cm in diameter, margins undulated.... *Omphalotus subilludens* (p. 170)

Omphalotus olearius (DC:Fr.) Singer

(toxic)

■ The pileus is 2.5 -12.0 cm wide, convex becoming plane, then depressed; surface orange-buff to darker reddish-orange; silky fibrillose or with small squamules, margins incurved. The lamellae

are deeply decurrent, pale orange-yellow to orange; usually bioluminescent. The stipe is central to sometimes slightly eccentric,
cylindric, 2.0-10.0 x 0.5-2.5 cm, tapering towards the base, and
orange-buff to amber-brown in color.

■ The spores are white in deposit, globose to subglobose, 3.5-5.5 x
3.5-5.0 µm; turning blue in iodine. Basidia are clavate, 22.0-32.0 x
4.0-5.5 µm; with four sterigmata.

■ This bright-orange mushroom has been known traditionally in
North America as *Clitocybe illudens*, the "jack-o-lantern" fungus,
or the "false chanterelle." It is well known for its bioluminescence.
All species of *Omphalotus* are poisonous, causing servere
gasterointestinal irritation. Because of its funnel-like shape, decurrent lamellae and bright yellow to orange color, it has been confused with *Cantharellus cibarius*, a choice edible species. Species
of *Cantharellus*, however, do not grow in tight clusters on rotting
stumps or buried wood, the lamellae are deep folds, not "knife
blade like" lamellae as in *Omphalotus*. If you plan to eat such
mushrooms, know these differences!

Fig. 141. *Omphalotus olearius* (x 0.5)

Fig. 142. *Omphalotus subilludens* (× 0.5)

---

142 *Omphalotus subilludens* (Murr.) Bigelow

(toxic)

■ The pileus is 10.0-15.0 cm wide, convex to plane, becoming depressed, with undulated margins and a smooth, orange, rusty-orange to brick-red surface. The lamellae are deeply decurrent, yellowish-orange, and crowded towards the margins. The stipe is central to slightly eccentric, with fine longitudinal lines; 3.0-6.0 x 1.5-2.5 cm, and orange to brownish-orange.

■ The spores are whitish in deposit, ellipsoid, 7.0-9.0 x 4.5-5.0 µm; not turning blue in iodine. Basidia are clavate, 28.0-35.0 x 5.0-6.5 µm; with four sterigmata.

■ This species is indistinguishable from *Omphalotus olearius* when observed in the field. Aside from the spores which are obviously different, *O. subilludens* often has slightly larger basidiomata, the lamellae are deeper, basidia are somewhat larger, and the stipe is generally shorter and broader. To my knowledge, no one has determined if *O. subilludens* is also bioluminescent.

Oudemansiella

Species of *Oudemansiella* are medium-sized, succulent mushrooms with a viscid pileus often covered with squamules. They have large globose spores with conspicuous oil droplets. They are found in abundance throughout tropical and subtropical countries. Only one species, *O. canarii* (Jungh.) Hohn., is found in Florida. It is commonly found growing on branches and trunks of living and decaying trees. For many years the deeply rooting *Collybia radicata* was placed in *Oudemansiella*. It has more recently been placed in *Xerula*, which will be treated later.

Oudemansiella canarii (Jungh.) Hohn.   **143**

- The pileus is 1.0-10.0 cm wide, convex then plane, or even slightly depressed; whitish to gray with a brownish center; viscid when moist and frequently covered with brownish-white squamules. The lamellae are adnexed to adnate, white to pale grayish; and somewhat crowded. The stipe is cylindric, 1.0-6.0 x 0.3-1.5 cm, slightly tapering above; often slightly curved; whitish, and finely striate.

- The spores are white in deposit, globose to subglobose, 15.0-24.0 x 10.0-22.0 µm; smooth, with a somewhat thickened wall. Basidia are long, clavate, 64.0-80.0 x 18.0-24.0 µm; with four sterigmata.

- This is an extremely common species found on dead limbs and trunks of hardwood trees throughout the tropics and subtropics. It has been frequently collected in Florida and has traditionally been identified by Murrill and others as *Armillaria alphitophylla* (Berk. & Curt.) Murr. It is an extremely variable fungus because of the orientation of basidiomata on their substrates varies, and the brownish pileus squamules may disappear in rainy weather. See Pegler (1983) for a lengthy discussion of this species.

Fig. 143. *Oudemansiella canarii* (x 0.4)

Fig. 144. *Tricholoma terreum* (x 0.5)

Tricholoma

Species of *Tricholoma* have a gymnohymenial development, and as such have no volva or annulus. They are soil inhabiting, some at least ectomycorrhizal, and have adnexed or sinuate lamellae which bear small, white, smooth-walled spores that do not turn blue in iodine. There are almost 90 species recognized worldwide, with close to 40 accessioned in the Mycological Herbarium. Only one will be discussed below.

---

144   *Tricholoma terreum* (Schaeff.: Fr.) Kumm

(edible)

- The pileus is 5.0-8.0 cm wide, campanulate at first, expanding to become convex, and with a dull, finely tomentose, mouse to brownish-gray surface. The lamellae are sinuate, gray-white and moderately spaced. The stipe is 4.0-7.0 cm long, 1.0-1.7 cm thick; white to grayish-white, and hollow with age.

- The spores are whitish in deposit, ellipsoid to subglobose, 5.9-7.8 x 4.2-6.0 µm; not turning blue in iodine. Basidia are clavate, 30.0-38.0 x 9.0-10.0 µm; with four sterigmata.

- This species is found worldwide, often on calcareous soil under conifers or rarely in hardwood forests. It is one of the most common species of *Tricholoma* in north central Florida.

Xeromphalina

Species of *Xeromphalina* are usually small, brownish-orange or yellow-brown mushrooms found growing in clusters on old, mossy, decaying conifer stumps or logs, and other decaying plant debris. They have decurrent to broadly adnate lamellae that are often lighter in color than the pileus. There are more than 40 species recognized worldwide; Miller (1968) provided keys and descriptions to 12 North American species. Four species occur in the local herbarium; only one of these, *X. campanella* Fr., will be described.

Xeromphalina campanella (Bat.:Fr.) Kuhn. & Mre. **145**

(inedible)

- The pileus is 1.0-3.0 mm in diameter, convex with a darker depressed center, bright pale yellowish-brown to cinnamon with radial lines. The lamellae are decurrent, widely spaced, pale yellowish to orange. The stipe is 10.0-50.0 x 0.5-3.0 mm, often inflated at the base, and similar in color to the pileus.

- The spores are pale buff in deposit, ellipsoid, 5.0-7.0 x 3.0-4.0 µm, and turn blue in iodine. The basidia are narrowly clavate, 19.0-25.0 x 5.0-6.0 µm, with four sterigmata.

- The most striking aspect of this species is that it is always found in dense clusters, usually on moss-covered, rotten conifer wood. It is common throughout Florida during the rainy season.

Fig. 145. *Xeromphalina campanella* (x 1.0)

Xerula

The genus *Xerula* contains six species of mushrooms that were originally placed in *Collybia* because their compact pileus cuticle feels like wet leather and minor microscopic similarities. They were later placed in *Oudemansiella*, a genus characterized by exceptionally large globose basidiospores with prominent droplets within. Most *Xerula*, however, have clavate to very elongate setae on the stipe and pileus. One species is common in Florida.

---

146   *Xerula radicata (Relh.:Fr.)Dorfelt*

(edible)

- The pileus is 2.5-10.0 cm in diameter, convex to plane, with a broad umbo and incurved margins, smooth to wrinkled, moist; dark brown to smokey-brown. The whitish lamellae are adnate and broadly spaced. The white to brownish stipe is 5.0-20.0 x 0.3-1.0 cm with a deeply rooting base tapering to a point.

- The spores are white in deposit, elliptical, 12.0-16.0 x 9.0-11.0 μm, not turning blue in iodine. The basidia are narrowly clavate, 45.0-55.0 x 10.0-14.0 μm, with four sterigmata.

- This species is usually found near rotting stumps and logs in mixed hardwood forests. It has traditionally gone under the name *Collybia radicata* (Rehl.: Fr.)Kumm, and was later transferred to *Oudemansiella* by Singer (1986).

Fig. 146. *Xerula radicata* (x 0.25)   (Ulla Benny)

The Pluteaceae

This is a small family of mushrooms characterized by free lamellae, rose to dull reddish spores in deposit, and a peculiar convergent gill trama. They are saprobic and may be found growing on all sorts of cellulosic substrates. Species of *Pluteus* are without a volva, whereas those in *Volvariella* have a prominent saccate volva. Members of both genera are edible but species of *Pluteus* are less sought after because of their soft texture when cooked. Both genera are well represented in Florida.

A Key to Common Florida Pluteaceae:

1. Volva present .... *Volvariella bombycina* (p. 176)
1. Volva absent 2
   2. Pileus smaller than 2.0 cm in diameter 3
   2. Pileus larger than 2.0 cm in diameter....................................4
3. Pileus milk-white, non striate ....*Pluteus niveus* (p. 181)
3. Pileus reddish-brown to sooty-black ...... *Pluteus floridanus* (p. 178)
   4. Pileus 2.0-3.0 cm in diameter 5
   4. Pileus larger 6
5. Pileus fawn-colored, smooth, viscid; stipe white with a bulbous base   .... *Pluteus australis* (p. 177)
5. Pileus chestnut-beige with a darker disc; the stipe is grayish to brown, non-bulbous................................. *Pluteus harrisii* (p. 179)
   6. Pileus grayish-brown, glistening; often found growing on submerged wood in lawns .... *Pluteus pellitus* (p. 182)
   6. Pileus not as above 7
7. Pileus 2.0-5.0 cm in diameter, pale ashy-brown and often with minute scales...................................*Pluteus longistriatus* (p. 180)
7. Pileus 4.0-13.0 cm in diameter, smooth, moist, fawn to grayish-brown with a darker disc........................ *Pluteus cervinus* (p. 177)

Fig. 147. *Volvariella bombycina* (x 0.4)   (Henry Aldrich)

---

147   *Volvariella bombycina* (Schff.: Fr.) Sing.

(choice edible)

■ The pileus is 5.0-12.0 cm in diameter, ovoid when young, becoming conical to convex; whitish to cream with fascicles of silky, whitish to creamy hairs. The moderately-spaced lamellae are initially white but soon become pink to rosy. The cylindric stipe is 7.0-15.0 x 1.0-1.5 cm, inflating at the base where it is surrounded by a membranous, saccate volva.

■ The spores are pink to rosy in deposit, broadly ellipsoid, 6.5-9.0 x 4.5-6.5 μm, thin-walled, not turning blue in iodine. The basidia are broadly clavate, 20.0-30.0 x 8.0-11.0 μm, with four sterigmata.

■ This species is so named because it is silky like a bee, hence the name "bombycinus." It is very often found growing on exposed heart rot of hardwoods, on sawdust and other plant debris. It is frequently found in northern Florida.

Pluteus australis Murr.   **148**

(?edibility)

- The pileus is 2.0-3.0 cm in diameter, convex to plane; and a viscid, smooth, dark fawn-colored surface that is darker on the disc. The lamellae are free, narrow, crowded, whitish at first but turning pink. The smooth white stipe is cylindrical, 7.0-7.5 x 0.3-0.4 cm, with a slightly inflated base.

- The spores are pink in deposit, ellipsoid,, 5.0-6.0 x 3.0-3.5 µm, not turning blue in iodine. The basidia are elongate, 25.0-28.0 x 6.5-8.0 µm, with four sterigmata.

- This species was originally found growing on humus in a high hammock near Gainesville. It resembles *P. cervinus* but is smaller, more slender and darker on the disc. Singer (1956) thinks that it may be a form of *P. magnus* McClat.

Fig. 148. *Pluteus australis*   (x 0.8)

Pluteus cervinus (Schaef.) Kumm   **149**

(edible)

- The pileus is 4.0-13.0 cm in diameter, conical at first but becoming convex with an umbo; dark fawn to grayish-brown, viscid when moist. The lamellae are free, somewhat crowded, white at first but becoming salmon-pink. The stipe is cylindric, 5.0-10.0 x 0.7-1.0 cm, white with brownish tinges.

- The spores are salmon-pink in deposit, ellipsoid, 5.0-8.6 x 4.0-6.0 µm, not turning blue in iodine. The basidia are clavate, 25.0-38.0 x 8.0-9.5 µm, with four sterigmata.

Fig. 149. *Pluteus cervinus* (x 0.7)

■ This is one of the most common mushrooms in North America and is found extensively throughout Florida in coniferous, hardwood, and mixed forests.

---

150   *Pluteus floridanus* Murr.

(edible)

■ The pileus is 1.2-2.0 cm in diameter, convex to plane, with a broad umbo, dry, squamulose, sooty black on the disc, fading to reddish-brown on the margins. The lamellae are free, crowded, initially white, but soon become pink. The stipe is 1.8-3.0 x 0.1-0.3 cm, tapering up-wards, white to satiny-gray and smooth.

Fig. 150. *Pluteus floridanus* (x 1.0)   (Sherri Angels)

The spores are pink in deposit, globose, 4.5-5.6 x 4.5-5.6 µm, smooth and thin-walled. The basidia are 24.0-38.0 x 11.0-12.5 µm; with four sterigmata.

This species is found on rotting hardwood throughout the rainy seasons in Florida. It is one of the smaller species of *Pluteus* found in this area.

Pluteus harrisii Murr.   **151**

(edible)

■ The pileus 2.0-3.0 cm in diameter, light beige to buff, becoming dark chestnut-brown. The lamellae are free, somewhat crowded, white early but becoming salmon-pink. The white to pale grayish stipe is 2.5-5.0 x 0.2-0.5 cm, and smooth.

The spores are pink in deposit, broadly ellipsoid, 6.0-9.8 x 5.0-6.5 µm, not turning blue in iodine. The basidia are narrowly clavate, 19.0-24.0 x 7.0-7.7 µm, with four sterigmata.

This species appears to be a subtropical species, occurring in Jamaica, Trinidad, and in Florida. It has been found on burned, woody matter and on decaying wood and plant debris. The microscopic characters are somewhat like those of *P. cervinus,* but it is a distinctly smaller and darker mushroom.

Fig. 151. *Pluteus harrisii* (x 0.5)

Pluteus longistriatus (Pk.) Sacc.

(?edibility)

■ The pileus is 2.0-5.0 cm in diameter, thin, convex then expanding, pale ashy-brown, becoming striate and minutely scaly with age. The lamellae are free, close, white when young, becoming pink. The whitish stipe is cylindric, 3.0-5.0 x 0.2-0.3 cm, and faintly striate.

■ The spores are pale pinkish in deposit, broadly ellipsoid, 6.0-7.0 x 4.5-5.0 μm, not turning blue in iodine. The basidia are narrowly clavate 25.0-35.0 x 8.0-10.0 μm, with four sterigmata.

■ This species is fairly widespread on decaying hardwood throughout northern Florida. With the exception of the smaller, white *Pluteus niveus,* it is lighter in color than other species of *Pluteus* found in this area.

Fig. 152. *Pluteus longistriatus* (x 1.0)

Agaricales

Fig. 153. *Pluteus niveus* (× 1.5)

Pluteus niveus Murr.   **153**

(?edibility)

- The pileus is less than 2.0 cm in diameter, thin, convex to plane, white with a non-striated margin. The lamellae are free, somewhat crowded, initially white, later pale pink. The stipe is 4.0-5.0 x 0.2 cm in diameter, cylindric, glabrose, and white.

- The spores are pink in deposit, broadly ellipsoid, 4.8-5.0 x 6.0-6.2 µm, smooth, and thin-walled. Basidia are cylindric, 25.0-35.0 x 8.0-10.0 µm; with four sterigmata.

- This species is distinguished from other species of *Pluteus* by its small size and milk-white color. It is found on well-decayed hardwood logs.

Fig. 154. *Pluteus pellitus* (x 1.1)

---

154   *Pluteus pellitus* (Per.: Fr.) Kumm

(edible)

- ■ The light grayish-brown pileus is 5.0-7.0 cm in diameter, conical when young, becoming convex to plane with a slight umbo, appearing glistening. The lamellae are free, white then grayish-pink, and somewhat crowded. The whitish stipe is cylindrical, 3.5-7.0 x 0.5-1.0 cm, somewhat dingy white and inflated at the base.

- ■ The spores are grayish-pink in deposit, broadly ellipsoid, 6.6-8.5 x 4.4-6.0 µm, not turning blue in iodine. The basidia are cylindrical, 22.0-35.0 x 7.5-10.0 µm, with four sterigmata.

- ■ This species is recognized by its whitish glistening pileus, often found on lawns in the Southeastern U.S. It likely is growing on buried decaying wood.

The Entolomataceae

Because of its reddish-cinnamon to deep salmon or brick-red spores, this family is superficially similar to the Pluteaceae. They differ, however, in that their lamellae are attached to the stipe, although in many the lamellae are sinuate (knotched) and may appear free, and the spores are angular, grooved and appear knobby. They are also terrestrial, with many shown to be ectomycorrhizal on various tree species. Since many species of *Entoloma* are toxic, one collecting mushrooms for food must learn to differentiate them from the edible *Pluteus* species. Seventeen genera are currently placed in the Entolomataceae (formerly Rhodophyllaceae), and accurate determination of genera often requires microscopic study of spores and hymenial elements. Three genera are well represented in Florida.

A Key to Common Florida Entolomataceae

1. Spore walls undulate, angular only in polar view
   .... ***Rhodocybe*** (p. 193)
1. Spores angular in all views 2
   2. Basidiomata medium to large, stipe central, pileus viscid, stipe fibrous .... ***Entoloma*** (p. 184)
   2. Basidiomata small, stipe lateral or eccentric ***Claudopus*** (p. 183)

Claudopus

These are small, saprobic, laterally-attached mushrooms with a pink to flesh-brown spore deposit, and with spores distinctly angular in all views. Twenty species are recognized worldwide; one of them will be included here.

Claudopus vinaceocontusus Baroni   **155**

(?edibility)

■ The pileus is 2.0-10.0 mm in diameter, white to pale grayish buff, quickly becoming vinaceous when bruised, convex to broadly convex with a shallow depression, and radiating fibrils. The lamellae are pallid at first but become fleshy pink, adnate or becoming somewhat decurrent. The eccentric stipe is 3.0-5.0 x 2.0-3.0 mm, tapering downward, with dense white fibrils, and similar in color to the pileus. A strong garlic odor is present.

Fig. 155. *Claudopus vinaceocontusus* (x 0.3)   (Tim Baroni)

■ The spores are pink in deposit, ellipsoid, 9.5-10.8 x 6.3-7.2 µm, with six to eight rounded or sharp angles, not turning blue in iodine. The basidia are broadly clavate, 26.1-31.4 x 9.0-9.9 µm, filled with vinaceous pigments, and with four sterigmata.

■ This species is distinguished by its small size, strong garlic odor, and purplish coloration. It has been found on moss covered logs in mixed hardwoods and on sandy-loamy embankments.

Entoloma

The genus *Entoloma* contains medium to large fleshy mushrooms with a pinkish, vinaceous or reddish-cinnamon spore print, and usually sinuate lamellae that sometimes become emarginate. The spores are angular in all views and do not turn blue in iodine. Nearly 400 species have been described, but the concept and name of the genus has changed, with many species described as *Rhodophyllus, Nolanea, Leptonia, Claudopus,* or others (Hesler, 1967). *Entoloma* is well represented in Florida, and eight species will be treated below. Most species of *Entoloma* are toxic and species should be avoided by those collecting mushrooms for consumption.

A Key to Common Florida species

1. Pileus lemon to mustard-yellow ....*Entoloma murraii* (p. 189)
1. Pileus another color 2
   2. Pileus conical to umbonate, grayish-brown to olive-buff,
      margin non-striate .... *Entoloma cokeri* (p. 186)
   2. Pileus not conical 3
3. Pileus convex, becoming depressed...4
3. Pileus convex, becoming umbonate or umbilicate 6
   4. Pileus 5.0-8.0 cm in diameter .... *Entoloma felleum* (p. 189)
   4. Pileus smaller...5
5. Pileus hazel to snuff-brown, margin even; stipe whitish to pale
hazel .... *Entoloma commune* (p. 187)
5. Pileus drab brown with a striate margin
.... *Entoloma subgriseum* (p. 191)
   6. Pileus pinkish-cinnamon or yellowish
....*Entoloma unicolor* (p. 192)
   6. Pileus of a different color 7
7. Pileus grayish-brown, smooth, hygrophanous; lamellae white to
flesh colored .... *Entoloma strictus* var. *strictus* (p. 190)
7. Pileus drab, buffy-brown, not hygrophanous, minutely downy;
lamellae pale, grayish-buff................. *Entoloma canescens* (p. 185)

Entoloma canescens Hesler   **156**

(?edibility)

■ The pileus is 1.0-3.0 cm in diameter, convex and becoming umbilicate, buffy-brown, silky, with disc covered by darker, small hairy scales. The lamellae are adnate with a decurrent tooth, pallid at first but becoming cinnamon-pink. The stipe is 3.0-7.0 x 0.2-0.5 cm, brownish or similar to pileus, silky, and slightly inflated below.

■ The spores are orange-cinnamon in deposit, broadly ellipsoid, 8.0-11.0 x 6.0-8.0 µm, grooved, five to six-sided, not turning blue in iodine. The basidia are narrowly clavate, 33.0-40.0 x 7.0-10.0 µm, with four, and in rare cases, two sterigmata.

Fig. 156. *Entoloma canescens* (x 1.0)   (Tim Baroni)

- This species grows on soil in deciduous forests, found initially in several areas of the Great Smoky Mountains National Park, and more recently a number of collections were made in Florida (Baroni, *pers. comm)*.

---

157   *Entoloma cokeri* Murr.

(toxic)

- The pileus is 5.0-8.0 cm in diameter, conic then expanding, strongly umbonate, grayish-brown to deep olive-buff, silky to smooth and somewhat viscid. The lamellae are deeply sinuate, white becoming flesh colored, with eroded edges. The stipe is cylindric, 7.5-11.0 x 1.0-1.5 cm, and with a color similar to the pileus.

■ The spores are salmon to grayish-brown in deposit, subglobose to ovoid, 6.0-8.0 x 5.2-6.5 µm, faintly six to seven-sided. The basidia are narrowly cylindric, 25.0-30.0 x 9.0-10.0 µm, with two to four sterigmata.

■ This species is found on the soil in deciduous forests during rainy summer months. It is recognized by its gray-brown to olive-brown pileus.

Fig. 157. *Entoloma cokeri* (x 0.5)

Entoloma commune Murr.   158

(?edibility)

■ The pileus is 3.0-5.0 cm in diameter, convex, becoming depressed with age, light hazel to chestnut-brown, disc darker, with even margins. The lamellae are sinuate, white but soon become rose colored. The stipe is cylindric, 4.0-5.0 x 0.4-0.6 cm, white to pale hazel, and often twisted.

■ The spores are salmon to cinnamon in deposit, subglobose, 8.0-9.0 x 6.0-7.5 µm, and five-sided. The basidia are narrowly clavate, 32.0-36.0 x 8.0-9.0 µm, with two sterigmata.

Fig. 158. *Entoloma commune* (x 0.6)

■ This species has been found in oak forests throughout eastern North America. In Florida it occurs during rainy summer months and also mild winters. It is somewhat distinct because of its thin, depressed pileus and slender stipe.

Fig. 159. *Entoloma felleum* (x 1.0)

Entoloma felleum Murr.   **159**

(?edibility)

- The pileus is 5.0-8.0 cm in diameter, convex to plane, pale buff-brown, often darker on the disc, and the margins sometimes split with age. The lamellae are adnexed, white to pink, somewhat crowded. The stipe is 7.0-10.0 x 1.5-2.0 cm, white, and slightly tapering upwards.

- The spores are pink in deposit, subglobose to ovoid, 7.0-8.0 x 5.0-6.0 µm, five to six-sided, not turning blue in iodine. The basidia are narrowly cylindric, 33.0-44.0 x 7.0-8.0 µm, with two to four sterigmata.

- This species grows on soil in mixed forests during winter months in northern Florida. Its color and broader stipe distinguish it from other local species of *Entoloma*.

Entoloma murraii (B. & C.) Sacc.   **160**

(?edibility)

- The pileus is 1.0-3.0 cm in diameter, initially conical, becoming campanulate; naples-yellow to mustard-yellow, with slightly lobed margins. The lamellae are adnate, becoming emarginate, with a flesh tint. The stipe is 5.0-12.0 x 0.2-0.4 cm, sometimes with twisted striations.

- The spores are pale cinnamon-pink in deposit, subglobose, 9.0-12.0 x 8.0-10.0 µm, four-sided, not turning blue in iodine. The basidia are narrowly cylindric, 50.0-63.0 x 10.0-12.0 µm, with four sterigmata.

- It is found on damp, marshy soil in deciduous forests and is recognized from other species of *Entoloma* by its bright yellow color.

Fig. 160. *Entoloma murraii* (x 1.1)
(Tim Baroni)

(?edibility)

- The pileus is 2.0-5.0 cm in diameter, convex to plane or campanulate, with a small umbo, hygrophanous, and grayish-brown when moist. The lamellae are emarginate, adnexed to nearly free, and flesh-colored when young. The stipe is 5.0-10.0 x 0.2-0.4 cm, straight, but sometimes twisted, and of similar color to the pileus.

- The spores are light rosy in deposit, ellipsoid, 10.0-13.0 x 7.5-9.0 µm, smooth and thin-walled. Basidia 35.0-45.0 x 10.0-12.0 µm, with four sterigmata.

- This species is found in deep humus in mixed forests. It is distinguished by its gray-brown, convex to campanulate pileus.

Fig. 161. *Entoloma strictus var strictus* (x 1.6)   (Robert Williams)

Agaricales

Fig. 162. *Entoloma subgriseum* (× 0.8)

Entoloma subgriseum Hesler　　　　　**162**

(?edibility)

- The pileus is 2.0-4.0 cm in diameter, convex to plane, becoming depressed, hygrophanous, whitish-gray with yellowish blotches. The lamellae are adnate to seceding, close, pinkish-white becoming salmon to brownish with age. The stipe is 4.0-9.5 x 0.2-0.6 cm, silky-white to ashy in color, and slightly bulbous at the base.

- The spores are rosy-brown in deposit, globose to subglobose, 7.5-9.5 x 7.0-8.0 µm, thin-walled and smooth. Basidia 26.0-30.0 x 8.0-10.0 µm, with four sterigmata.

- This species is found on leaf litter in mixed forests in north Florida. It has a slight odor of chlorine.

Fig. 163. *Entoloma unicolor* (x 1.0)   (Tim Baroni)

---

163   *Entoloma unicolor* (Pk.) Hesler

(?edibility)

■ The pileus is 1.8-4.0 cm in diameter, convex but expanding, light ochra-salmon to pinkish-cinnamon, with a bright umbo when moist. The lamellae are decurrent or sometimes emarginate, pallid to pinkish-cinnamon. The stipe is 4.0-9.0 cm x 1.5-2.5 mm, and similar in color to the pileus.

■ The spores are fawn colored in deposit, ovoid, 8.0-11.0 x 6.0-7.0 µm, five, six, often seven-sided. The basidia are narrowly clavate, 30.0-36.0 x 7.0-9.0 µm, with two to four sterigmata.

■ This species is found on plant debris in deciduous and mixed forests of eastern North America.

Rhodocybe

Species of *Rhodocybe* are highly variable in morphology, and may resemble a number of the Tricholomataceae in the field. Their pinkish to flesh-colored spore deposit easily set them apart from this group. They are distinguished from other Entolomataceae by having angular spores in polar view and warted in side view. For a more thorough study, see Baroni's (1981) revision of the genus. Twenty-five species are recognized, two of these are here.

A Key to Common *Rhodocybe* in Florida

1. Pileus 1.0-4.0 cm in diameter, tawny-ochra to pinkish-cinnamon, hygrophanous .... *Rhodocybe nitellina* (p. 193)

1. Pileus 4.0-7.0 cm in diameter, rosy to hazel-brown; surface smooth, not hygrophanous .... *Rhodocybe roseiavelliana* (p. 194)

Rhodocybe nitellina (Fr.)Sing.   **164**

(?edibility)

■ The pileus is 1.5-5.0 cm in diameter, convex when young, later plane with an indented center; hygrophanous, dark orange-brown when moist, and sometimes slightly zonate. The lamellae are initially whitish to cream colored, becoming reddish-brown, adnate, but sometimes with a slightly decurrent tooth. The stipe is 3.0-7.0 x 0.4-0.9 cm cylindric, sometimes with a swollen base, and similar in color to the pileus.

■ The spores are pink to buff-pink in deposit, elliptical, 6.0-8.9 x 4.0-5.0 µm, not turning blue in iodine. The basidia are narrowly clavate, 28.0-40.0 x 7.0-9.0 µm, with four sterigmata.

Fig. 164. *Rhodocybe nitella* (x 0.4)   (Tim Baroni)

■ This species usually grows in clusters in humus-rich hardwood areas. It occurs during rainy summer months in Florida.

165	*Rhodocybe roseiavellaneus* (Murr.) Sing.

(?edibility)

■ The pileus is 4.0-6.0 cm in diameter, convex, rosy-buff but brownish when bruised, and with a smooth surface. The lamellae are adnate to slightly decurrent, and somewhat distant. The stipe is smooth, glabrous, 5.0-6.0 x 0.8-1.0 cm, and bulbous at the base.

■ The spores are pale pink in deposit, ovoid, 8.0-9.0 x 5.0-6.0 µm, not turning blue in iodine. The basidia are narrowly clavate, 22.0-30.0 x 7.0-8.0 µm, with four sterigmata.

■ Around Gainesville, Florida, this species is found growing under live oaks during the rainy summer months.

Fig. 165. *Rhodocybe roseiavelliana* (x 1.0)   (Tim Baroni)

The Bolbitiaceae

This is a small family of gilled mushrooms with a number of species found on lawns, gardens, and the edges of woodlands. They have a central stipe without an annulus and variable types of gill attachment. The spores are typically rust-colored, hazel-brown, chocolate-brown to blackish-brown, smooth, truncate or with a germ pore. Five genera are recognized in North America, two of them, *Agrocybe* and *Conocybe* are treated here. Species of *Agrocybe* have a thick, fleshy stipe and a dark-brown spore print, whereas, species of *Conocybe* have a slender, fragile to brittle stipe and rusty-brown spores. It should be noted here that certain species of *Conocybe* have high levels of cyclopeptides, the toxins present in the deadly poisonous species of *Amanita*. Since species of *Conocybe* are common in Florida lawns, parents should monitor toddlers when they are outside and tend to "nibble" on things they find in the grass.

A Key to Common Species in Florida

1. Spore deposit dark brown to tobacco-brown; stipe fleshy, 4.0-10.0 mm in diameter .... *Agrocybe praecox* (p. 195)
1. Spore deposit rusty-brown, stipe fragile and brittle, usually less than 3.0 mm in diameter 2
   2. Pileus 1.0-2.0 cm in diameter, hemispherical to convex, yellow brown and hygrophanous .... *Conocybe crispella* (p. 197)
   2. Pileus not as above 3
3. Pileus whitish to creamy .... *Conocybe lactea* (p. 197)
3. Pileus rusty-brown to yellow .... *Conocybe tenera* (p. 198)

Agrocybe praecox (Per.: Fr.) Fay.   **166**

(inedible)

■ The pileus is 2.5-6.0 cm in diameter, ovoid but becoming convex to plane; initially dark brown and somewhat shiny, becoming yellowish-brown with age. The lamellae are whitish when young, later clay colored, adnate to sinuate with a smooth edge. The stipe is 4.0-7.5 x 0.5-1.5 cm, cylindric with a slightly bulbous base, whitish to dingy brown with age.

■ The spores are dark, tobacco-brown in deposit, elliptical, 8.4-10.7 x 5.7-6.7 μm, with a large germ pore, not turning blue in iodine. The basidia are clavate, 25.0-37.0 x 8.0-10.0 μm, with four sterigmata.

■ This species in found on humus, wood chips, and grass in pastures and woodlands. It appears during the summer rainy season in Florida.

Fig. 166. *Agrocybe pracox* (x 0.6)   (Ulla Benny)

Fig. 167. *Conocybe crispella* (x1.5)

Conocybe crispella (Murr.) Sing.   **167**

(inedible)

- The pileus is 1.0-2.0 cm in diameter, hemispherical to convex, yellow-brown on the disc, light brown towards the margin, hygrophanous and finely striate. The lamellae are adnexed to adnate, pale brown to rusty brown. The stipe is 5.0-7.5 x 0.1-0.3 cm, cylindric with a bulbous base, and white with fine hairs.

- The spores are rusty brown in deposit, ellipsoid, 11.0-14.0 x 6.5-8.5 μm, brown, thick-walled, with a truncate germ pore. The basidia are broadly clavate, 26.0-30.0 x 10.0-12.0 μm, with four sterigmata.

- This species grows in clusters of grass, and is distinguished by the fine striations on the cap. It is often found in grass on open lawns around the University of Florida.

Conocybe lactea (Lge.) Mdtr.   **168**

(?edibility)

- The pileus is 1.0-2.5 cm in diameter, conical to hemispheric or convex, whitish to creamy, slightly hygrophanous with a faintly striate margin. The lamellae are nearly free, whitish, becoming cinnamon-tawny. The stipe is slender cylindric, 6.0-8.0 x 0.1-0.2 cm, with a slightly bulbous base, whitish with a powdery blum.

- The spores are cinnamon-brown in deposit, ellipsoid, 4.8-6.9 x 3.4-4.8 μm, rusty brown, thick-walled, with a germ pore. The basidia are short, clavate, 16.0-21.0 x 12.0-14.0 μm, with two to four sterigmata.

Fig. 168. *Conocybe lactea* (x 1.0)

■ The species is scattered or in dense clusters on lawns, and is found frequently throughout the Gulf Coast.

---

169   *Conocybe tenera* (Schaeff.: Fr.) Fay.

(?edibility)

■ The pileus is 1.0-2.0 cm in diameter, initially conical, becoming convex, dull, hygrophanous, rust-brown to yellow-brown, with fine striations. The lamellae are cream-colored when young, becoming rusty brown, finely adnexed, and almost free. The stipe is 5.0-10.0 x 0.1-0.2 cm, cylindric, light brown but darker towards the base.

■ The spores are rusty-brown in deposit, ellipsoid,9.0-14.0 x 5.0-8.0 µm, brown, thick-walled with a germ pore. The basidia are clavate, 19.0-25.0 x 10.0-13.0 µm, with four sterigmata.

■ This species is commonly found in humus rich soil and grass. It is found in similar habitats to *C. lactea,* but is easily distinguished by its darker color.

Fig. 169. *Conocybe tenera* (x 2.0)   (Ulla Benny)

The Cortinariaceae

The Cortinariaceae is a large family containing nearly 30 genera and hundreds of species. The spores are yellow-brown, rusty-orange to rusty brown in deposit, without germ pores, and with ornamentations on almost all species. They display a pseudoangiohymenial development in which there is a fragile membranous or cobwebby inner veil that often remains as an annulus. Most of the species in this family are inedible, some are highly toxic, and the group should be avoided. Species of more than a dozen genera have been found in Florida. The more common ones are treated below.

A Key to Common Genera in Florida

1. Pileus sessile or laterally attached .... *Crepidotus* (p. 211)
1. Pileus not as above 2
    2. Basidiomata routinely growing on wood ... *Gymnopilus* (p. 212)
    2. Basidiomata routinely found on soil 3
3. Young basidiomata with a cortina; lamellae red, violet, yellow, orange or dark brown .... *Cortinarius* (p. 199)
3. Without a cortina; lamellae pale tan, or whitish to grayish 4
    4. Pileus fibrillose to scaly .... *Inocybe* (p. 217)
    4. Pileus glabrous and viscid ....*Heboloma* (p. 216)

Cortinarius

Species of *Cortinarius* are medium to large mushrooms with an inner, fibrillar veil-like cortina, that may leave a cobwebby annulus or marginal veil. The lamellae are often richly colored when young, but become rusty brown as spores mature. Their spores are brownish to rusty-brown and finely wrinkled to distinctly warted. Species appear to be ectomycorrhizal on a large number of tree species. It is probably the largest genus of mushrooms with more than 400 species known worldwide, more than 90 are accessioned in the Mycological Herbarium at the University of Florida.

A Key to Common Species of *Cortinarius*

1. Pileus 5.0 cm or less in diameter 2

1. Pileus larger 4

   2. Pileus yellowish to olive-brown, becoming cinnamon
      brown .... *Cortinarius cinnamomeus* (p. 201)

   2. Pileus another color 3

3. Pileus deep purple, viscid; disc yellowish *Cortinarius iodes* (p. 203)

3. Pileus buff-colored to darker at the disc, shining, with a
   violet tint .... *Cortinarius sublargus* (p. 209)

   4. Pileus ochre to olive buff; slightly darker at the disc; lamellae
      cinnamon to blood-red ..... *Cortinarius semisanguineus* (p. 207)

   4. Not as above 5

5. Pileus predominantly violet, often with tints of other colors 6

5. Pileus beige, cinnamon, or rusty-brown.....................................7

   6. Pileus viscid, violet with a hazel tint; stipe short, 2.0-5.0 cm
      long .... *Cortinarius sublilacinus* (p. 210)

   6. Pileus violet with purplish fibrils; stipe slender, 5.0-10.0 cm
      long .... *Cortinarus lilacinus* (p. 204)

7. Pileus beige, buff, or drab-brown 8

7. Pileus darker brown 9

   8. Pileus beige with a pale violet tint; stipe whitish to beige,
      slender, 5.0-10.0 cm long .... *Cortinarius caninus* (p. 201)

   8. Pileus buff to drab hazel, viscid; stipe short and stout,
      1.8-2.5 cm long .... *Cortinarius praebrevipes* (p. 206)

9. Pileus cinnamon-red with a violet tint
               .... *Cortinarius glaucopus* (p. 202)

9. Pileus rusty to reddish-brown 10

   10. Pileus convex to plane, rusty-brown; stipe bulbous, up to
       3.0 cm at the base .... *Cortinarius perferrugineus* (p. 206)

   10. Pileus convex, becoming depressed, rusty to reddish-brown;
       stipe short and stout .... *Cortinarius straminipes* (p. 208)

Fig. 170. *Cortinarius caninus* (x 0.4)

Cortinarius caninus (Fr.) Fr.   **170**

(inedible)

- The pileus is 3.0-10.0 cm in diameter, convex, at first beige with a tint of violet, later becoming rusty-brown. The lamellae are adnexed, violet when young, rusty-brown with age. The stipe is 6.0-12.0 x 0.8-1.8 cm, inflated below, whitish, with brownish remains of the inner veil.

- The spores are rusty-brown in deposit, subglobose, 7.5-8.5 x 5.5-7.5 μm, with fine ornaments.

- This species has been found on leaf mulch beneath laurel oaks. It has a distinct whitish cortina in youth which darkens and forms fibrillar rings on the stipe.

Cortinarius cinnamomeus Fr.   **171**

(?edibility)

- The pileus 2.0-5.0 cm in diameter, convex but becoming plane, yellow to olive brown, becoming cinnamon-brown. The lamellae are adnate, fairly close, yellowish-olive to cinnamon-buff. The stipe is 3.5-7.0 x 0.3-0.7 cm, yellowish to cinnamon-buff, the fibrillar veil leaving a fragile ring.

- The spores are rusty-brown in deposit, ellipsoid, 6.0-8.0 x 4.0-5.0 μm, distinctly ornamented.

■ This species is commonly found growing in leaf mulch beneath live oak trees. It may be distinguished from other Florida species by its yellowish-olive lamellae and stipe.

Fig. 171. *Cortinarius cinnamomeus* (x 1.0)   (Sherri Angels)

---

172   *Cortinarius glaucopus* (Schaeff.: Fr.) Fr.

(inedible)

■ The pileus is 6.0-10.0 cm in diameter, convex, becoming plane, viscid, cinnamon to reddish-brown with grayish-violet tints. The lamellae are adnate, crowded, initially lavender to grayish-violet, becoming rusty-brown. The stipe is stout, 4.0-8.0 x 1.5-3.0 cm, bulbous at the base, pale lilac to lavender, with a whitish cortina that later darkens with spores.

Fig. 172. *Cortinarius glaucopus* (x 0.4)

- The spores are rusty-brown in deposit, ellipsoid, 7.0-9.0 x 4.0-5.0 µm, with fine ornaments.

- This species can be distinguished by its violet lamellae and stipe, viscid cap, and bulbous stipe. It is found beneath evergreen oaks in Florida, often in late fall and early winter.

Cortinarius iodes Berk. & Curt. **173**

(?edibility)

- The pileus is 2.0-5.0 cm in diameter, convex becoming hemispherical, deep purple-violet with yellowish disc, viscid, and has yellowish spots with age. The lamellae are adnate, somewhat broad, violet, then grayish, and finally rusty. The purplish stipe is slender, 4.0-7.5 x 0.1 to 1.5 cm, with a faint rusty ring, a slightly swollen base, and a light violaceous cortina.

- The spores are rusty-brown in deposit, ellipsoid 7.0-10.0 x 5.0-7.0 µm, and finely ornamented.

- This species is often found in leaf mulch around evergreen oaks in mesic hammock areas of north Florida. It is recognized from other purplish species of *Cortinarius* by its slender stipe and yellowish blotches on the pileus.

Fig. 173. *Cortinarius iodes* (x 1.2)

---

174   *Cortinarius lilacinus* Pk.

(inedible)

■ The pileus is 5.0-10.0 cm in diameter, convex, violet to violet-buff, covered with purplish fibrils. The lamellae are adnexed, moderately spaced, and pale violet. The stipe is stout, 5.0-10.0 x 1.2-2.0 cm, with a broad bulbous base, whitish to faintly violaceous.

■ The spores are rusty-brown in deposit, ellipsoid, 8.5-10.0 x 5.5-6.0 μm, finely ornamented.

- This species may be easily confused with other whitish-violaceous species of *Cortinarius,* but it tends to be more robust with a bulbous base. It is common in mixed forests throughout northern Florida.

Fig. 174. *Cortinarius lilacinus* (× 1.0)   (Henry Aldrich)

175   *Cortinarius perferrugineus* Murr.

(?edibility)

- The pileus is 5.0-7.0 cm in diameter, convex but becoming plane and umbonate, dry rusty-brown with appressed fibrils. The lamellae are sinuate and slightly lighter in color than the pileus. The stipe is stout, 4.0-6.0 x 1.5-2.0 cm with a 3 cm bulbous base, and apically with a scant veil.

- The spores are rusty-brown in deposit, ellipsoid, 11.0-12.0 x 5.0-6.0 µm, with fine low rounded ornaments.

- Several collections of this species have been made in oak-pine forests, and Murrill (1939b) says that it is not rare in woods around Gainesville. Its size and ferruginous color throughout sets it apart from other reddish-brown to cinnamon-colored species.

Fig. 175. *Cortinarius perferrugineus* (x 0.5)

176   *Cortinarius praebrevipes* Murr.

(?edibility)

- The pileus is 5.0-7.5 cm in diameter, convex to plane, clustered, buff to drab hazel-brown, viscid, with an incurved margin. The lamellae are dark violet when young but becoming rusty from the spore color. The stipe is short and very stout, 1.8-2.0 x 2.0-2.5 cm, with a large marginate bulb, and lighter in color from the pileus.

Fig. 176. *Cortinarius praebrevipes* (x 0.5)

- The spores are rusty-brown in deposit, subglobose, 8.5-9.5 x 6.0-7.0 µm, prominently verrucose.

- This species is remarkable because of its short, robust stipe and prominently verrucose spores. It is common under evergreen oaks during summer rainy seasons.

Cortinarius semisanguineus (Fr.) Kauf.   **177**

(?edibility)

- The pileus is 2.0-6.0 cm in diameter, convex to plane with a slight umbo, ochre, olive-buff to reddish, and minutely scaly. The lamellae are adnate, crowded, and cinnamon to blood-red in color. The stipe is 2.0-10.0 x 0.4-1.2 cm, similar in color to the pileus but paler towards the apex.

- The spores are rusty-brown in deposit, ellipsoid, 6.0-8.0 x 4.0-5.0 µm, with a roughened wall.

- This species is found in mixed forest throughout much of North America, and is commonly found in hardwood forests of northern Florida.

Fig. 177. *Cortinarius semisanguineus* (x 1.0)

---

178   *Cortinarius straminipes* Murr.

(?edibility)

■ The pileus is 7.5-8.0 cm in diameter, convex to slightly depressed, smooth and slightly viscid, rusty to reddish-brown. The lamellae are adnexed, crowded, pale reddish-brown, with undulated edges. The short, stout stipe is 2.8-3.0 x 2.0-2.2 cm, with a complete evanescent veil and similar in color to the pileus.

Fig. 178. *Cortinarus straminipes* (x 0.5)

The spores are rusty-brown in deposit, fusiform to ellipsoid, 8.0-10.0 x 4.0-5.0 µm, with punctate markings.

This species is found in winter months beneath oaks in moist, mesic forests.

Cortinarius sublargus Murr.   **179**

(?edibility)

■ The pileus is approximately 5.0 cm in diameter, convex to plane, with a shiny, viscid surface that is buff with a violet tint. The lamellae are adnate, subdistant, and violet to buff. The stipe is 4.5-5.0 x 1.0-1.3 cm, white to pale violaceous, with a persistent, membranous annulus.

The spores are rusty-brown in deposit, ellipsoid, 14.5-15.0 x 6.0-8.0 µm, with fine markings.

This species is found occasionally beneath evergreen oaks around Gainesville, but likely has a broader distribution. Of all of the locally occurring violaceous species of *Cortinarius*, this species is distinguished by having larger spores and a more membranous annulus.

Fig. 179. *Cortinarius sublargus* (x 1.2)

(?edibility)

■ The pileus is 5.0-7.0 cm in diameter, convex to plane, viscid with appressed fibrils, and pale lilac with a hazel-brown tint. The lamellae are sinuate, crowded, and violet in color. The stipe is stout, 2.0-5.0 x 1.5-2.0 cm, violet, with a 3 cm bulb and evanescent cortina.

■ The spores are hazel-brown in deposit, ellipsoid, 9.0-10.0 x 5.0-6.0 µm, with low, rounded punctations.

■ Several collections have been found beneath evergreen oaks on the lawns around the University of Florida. It is likely more widespread wherever laurel and live oaks occur.

Fig. 180. *Cortinarius sublilacinus* (x 1.2)   (Sherri Angels)

Fig. 181. *Crepidotus putrigenus* (x 1.2)   (Sherri Angels)

Crepidotus

The basidiomata of species of *Crepidotus* are sessile, or rarely with a short lateral stipe. They are mostly fan or shell-shaped and vary from whitish, yellowish, brown to reddish-orange. They are typically found on decaying wood or twigs. More than 150 species have been described, but only five or six are found in Florida. One of the most common ones is included here.

Crepidotus putrigenus Berk. & Curt.   **181**

(inedible)

■ The pileus is 1.0-5.0 cm in diameter, lateral, sessile, subreniform, with silky, white to yellowish-white surface, and incurved margins.

The lamellae are close, radiating from a basal cluster, dingy-white becoming rusty brown. There is no stipe present.

■ The spores are rusty-brown in deposit, subglobose 4.5 7.0 µm, and slightly punctate.

■ This species is found growing in clusters on decaying logs and stumps. Its subspherical spores and whitish color sets this species apart from other *Crepidotus*.

Gymnopilus

The characteristics of this genus are its dry, bright-colored pileus, rusty, ornamented spores that lack a germ pore, and its centrally stipitate pileus. Unlike *Cortinarius,* they are wood inhabiting. Hesler (1969) recognized 73 North American species. A number of these are found in Florida.

A Key to Common Species of *Gymnopilus* in Florida

1. Annulus persistent, membranous or densely fibrillose 2
1. Annulus absent or quickly disappearing 3
   2. Pileus yellowish with tawny fibrils, convex with an incurved margin .... *Gymnopilus fulvosquamulosus* (p. 213)
   2. Pileus pale reddish-yellow, convex but becoming depressed, with floccose scales .... *Gymnopilus palmicola* (p. 214)
3. Pileus golden-yellow with minute scales, often growing in clusters .... *Gymnopilus dryophilus* (p. 212)
3. Pileus chrome-yellow, smooth, without scales; stipe 4.0-6.0 cm tall; pallid in color .... *Gymnopilus penetrans* (p. 214)

---

182   *Gymnopilus dryophila* Murr.

(inedible)

■ The pileus is 3.0-5.0 cm in diameter, clustered, convex to plane, pale yellowish to yellowish-buff, with a faintly fibrillar surface. The lamellae are adnate with a decurrent tooth, and pale yellowish in color. The stipe is 5.0-7.0 x 0.8-1.5 cm, pale golden-yellow, slightly fibrillar and tapering upwards.

■ The spores are rusty-brown in deposit, ellipsoid, 6.0-7.5 x 4.0-5.0 µm, verrucose and without a germ pore.

■ This species has been found on decaying logs in Florida and Alabama during both summer and winter months.

Fig. 182. *Gymnopilus dryophila* (x 0.5)

Gymnopilus fulvosquamulosus Hesler 183

(?edibility)

■ The pileus is 4.0-8.0 cm in diameter, convex with recurved margins, with a yellow ochre to bright yellow surface covered by fibrillose, tawny scales. The lamellae are adnate to decurrent, close, dull yellow, becoming rusty with crenulate edges. The stipe is 3.0-6.0 x 0.7-1.2 cm, cylindric, dingy yellow above, becoming brown below, with a fragile, brownish ring.

■ The spores are rusty-brown in deposit, broadly ellipsoid 7.0-9.0 x 5.0-5.5 µm, verrucose, without a germ pore.

■ This species is distinguished by its tawny, fibrillose scales, and broad spores. Hesler (1969) studied a number of collections from Michigan, but a few collections have been found in Florida that fit his description, i.e., forming a fibrillose to membranous annulus, dextrinoid spores, with pleurocystidia and caulocystidia, and with a yellowish to ochraceous pileus bearing tawny scales.

Fig. 183. *Gymnopilus fulvosquamulosus* (x 0.4)

---

184   *Gymnopilus palmicola* Murr.

(?edibility)

■ The pileus is 2.0-5.0 cm in diameter, convex to plane, later depressed, pale rusty-brown to ochraceous, dry, floccose to scaly, with an even margin. The lamellae are adnate, similar but lighter in color to the pileus. The stipe is cylindric, 3.0-5.0 x 0.3-0.5 cm, yellowish, and slightly fibrillose.

■ The spores are rusty-brown in deposit, ellipsoid, 7.0-10.0 x 5.0-7.0 μm, and verrucose with coarse warts.

■ This species has been found on logs of palms in Florida and the subtropics. Its small size and habitat set it apart from other species.

---

185   *Gymnopilus penetrans* (Fr.: Fr.) Murr.

(?edibility)

■ The pileus is 3.0-5.0 cm in diameter, hemispherical to convex, becoming plane, chrome-yellow to golden, with even margins. The lamellae are adnate to sinuate, initially pale yellow but developing rusty spots with age. The stipe is cylindric, 4.0-6.0 x 0.4-0.7 cm, tapering upwards, light yellow with a whitish, fibrillar veil.

Fig. 184. *Gymnopilus palmicola* (x 2.0)   (Henry Aldrich)

■ The spores are rusty-brown in deposit, ellipsoid in face view, 7.0-9.0 x 4.0-5.5 μm, dextrinoid, verrucose and somewhat almond shaped.

■ This species is widespread throughout North America on conifers and hardwoods. Murrill (1972) noted that it was abundant on pine logs in northern Florida.

Fig. 185. _Gymnopilus penetrans_ (x 0.8)

Hebeloma

The pileus of species in this genus varies from cream to reddish-brown, and it is always viscid. The stipe is fleshy, dry, and annulate in some species. The spores are smooth to finely ornamented and clay-brown in color. They are all soil-inhabiting, some extremely toxic when eaten. There have been almost 20 species found in Florida. Only one will be treated here.

---

186   _Hebeloma mesophaeum_ (Pers.: Fr.) Quel.

(poisonous)

- The pileus is 1.0-4.0 cm in diameter, convex but expanding with age, viscid, creamy to gray-brown but darker brown on the disc. The lamellae are adnate to adnexed, close, light-brownish to grayish-brown, and with fine hairs on the margins. The stipe is cylindric, 3.0-8.0 x 0.3-0.5 cm, whitish at first but becoming brown towards the base, and the inner veil leaves a hairy annulus.

- The spores are yellowish to olive-brown in deposit, ellipsoid, 8.0-11.0 x 4.0-6.0 µm, and with a finely wrinkled surface.

■ This species is found on soil in various habitats, but has always been associated with pines which are probably its mycorrhizal partners.

Fig. 186. *Hebeloma mesophaeum* (x 0.8)

Inocybe

This genus of mushrooms contains soil-inhabiting species characterized by fibrillose to scaly caps and smooth, angular to nodular brown spores. The spore deposit is dull earth-brown, tobacco-brown, to dull yellow-brown. Many species resemble *Hebeloma*, but the pileus of species of the latter is viscid. There are close to 150 species described worldwide; more than 50 of them occur in Florida. Species of *Inocybe* are difficult to identify, often requiring a complex of microscopic characters.

A Key to Common Species of *Inocybe* in Florida
1. Pileus is yellow-brown with darker umbo; the stipe is 3.0-9.0 cm long .... *Inocybe fastigiata* (p. 218)
1. Pileus tawny-olive to cinnamon-buff
      .... *Inocybe subdecurrans* (p. 218)

187   *Inocybe fastigiata* (Schff.) Quel.

(poisonous)

- The pileus is 2.0-8.0 cm in diameter, broadly conical, becoming plane with a distinct yellow-brown or darker umbo, and becoming radially cracked with age. The lamellae are adnexed, pallid creamy-gray becoming drab. The stipe is 3.0-9.0 x 0.4-1.2 cm, slender, whitish to pale straw-colored.

- The spores are snuff-brown in deposit, somewhat reniform, 9.0-13.0 x 5.0-7.0 µm, and smooth.

- This species is found at the edge of woodlands and on shaded lawns throughout North America. It is found predominantly under hard-wood trees in Florida. It has been shown to contain high levels of muscarine, and for that reason is of concern for toddlers that love to nibble on things found on the lawn.

Fig. 187. *Inocybe fastigiata* (x 0.6)

Inocybe subdecurrans Ellis & Everh.   188

(?toxic)

- The pileus is 2.0-4.0 cm in diameter, initially ovoid, becoming convex then plane, surface dry, tawny-olive, becoming cinnamon-buff. The lamellae are decurrent, crowded, and similar in color to pileus. The stipe is cylindric, 2.5-4.0 x 0.3-0.5 cm, striate with fibrils, whitish to cinnamon buff, with a white mycelioid base.

- The spores are snuff-brown in deposit, ellipsoid, 8.0-10.0 x 5.0-5.5 µm, smooth and obtuse at both ends.

- This species is rather widespread across the United States. It is found occasionally in pine-oak forests of northern Florida.

Fig. 188. *Inocybe subdecurrans* (x 0.5)

The Agaricaceae

The concept of what genera belong in the Agaricaceae is currently in sharp dispute. Largent and Baroni (1988) include only three genera, *Melanophyllum, Cystoagaricus,* and *Agaricus.* However, Pegler (1983) and Breitenbach and Kranzlin (1995) include within the Agaricaceae genera previously placed in the Lepiotaceae. Under the latter concept, Hawksworth *et al.* (1995) recognize 37 genera in the Agaricaceae. I have chosen to follow those who restrict the Agaricaceae to those genera with free lamellae that are initially white but become pink and finally purple-brown to chocolate-brown, spores without a germ pore, and normally with a well developed annulus.

The one genus treated here, *Agaricus,* has numerous species throughout North America. Smith *et al.* (1979) estimate that there are probably more than 100 species in this country. There are approximately 35 species of *Agaricus* in the Mycological Herbarium at the University of Florida. A number of them will be treated here. I have followed Freeman (1979) in determining most of the species found in Florida. One of the field characters she uses to distinguish two groups of species in *Agaricus* is the morphology of basidiomata. In one group the basidiomata are thick-set, the length/width ratio of the pileus and stipe is less than one, and is referred to as "campestroid" type, and a second group that is thin-set and the pileus/stipe ratio is more than one, referred to as "placomycetoid" type.

A Key to Common Species of Agaricus in Florida

1. Pileus less than 4.0 cm in diameter 2
1. Pileus larger 5
    2. Pileus less than 1.5 cm in diameter
       .... *Agaricus diminutivus* (p. 226)
    2. Pileus larger 3
3. Pileus white with pale hazel scales, initially convex but becoming subumbonate............................. *Agaricus subalachuanus* (p. 231)
3. Pileus not as above 4
    4. Pileus pallid with yellowish scales; with a strong odor of peach or cherry pits ... *Agaricus cylindriceps* var. *aureus* (p. 225)
    4. Pileus pinkish-cinnamon with numberous purplish scales; no odors detected .... *Agaricus alachuanus* (p. 222)

5. Pileus up to 15.0 cm in diameter, campestroid, whitish with a yellowish tint and cracked surface ...... *Agaricus floridanus* (p. 227)

5. Pileus different, campestroid or placomycetoid 6

   6. Pileus less than 6.5 cm in diameter, pale vinaceous with a chestnut tinted disc .... *Agaricus rhoadsii* (p. 231)

   6. Pileus different 7

7. Mushroom placomycetoid 8

7. Mushroom campestroid 10

   8. Pileus white with yellowish tint; stipe bulbous and up to 13.0 cm long .... *Agaricus abruptibulbous* (p. 220)

   8. Pileus different 9

9. Pileus white with dark, floccose scales; stipe slender with a broad, cupulate base .... *Agaricus pocillator* (p. 229)

9. Pileus white with creamy disc; stipe narrow
   .... *Agaricus projectellus* (p. 230)

   10. Pileus reddish-brown with darker scales; flesh bruising blood-red .... *Agaricus hemorrhoidarius* (p. 228)

   10. Pileus not as above 11

11. Pileus convex, whitish to yellowish with rows of imbricated, plate-like scales .... *Agaricus alligator* (p. 223)

11. Pileus initially hemispherical, becoming convex, cream to yellowish-buff and smooth .... *Agaricus blazei* (p. 224)

---

189 *Agaricus abruptibulbous* **Peck**

(edible)

■ The pileus is smooth, ovoid, convex to plane, placomycetoid, reaching 10.0 cm in diameter, yellowish-white, becoming golden-tan with age. The lamellae are free, pink at first but become chocolate-brown. The stipe is 10.0-13.0 cm long, slender, with a superior ring, and pale golden when dry.

Fig. 189. *Agaricus abruptibulbous* (x 0.4)   (Sherri Angels)

■ The spores are chocolate-brown in deposit, ellipsoid, 6.0-7.5 x 4.5-5.5 µm, with a dark-brown wall.

■ This species in common in woodland habitats and is recognized from others growing under similar conditions by its lighter color. It has been confused with *A. silvicola.*, which has much smaller spores. Murrill (1972) says that it is common under oaks in Alachua County.

190 *Agaricus alachuanus* Murr.

(?edibility)

- The pileus is 3.0-4.0 cm in diameter, convex and slightly depressed, placomycetoid, buff with purplish scales, becoming tan with brown scales when dry. The free lamellae are deep chocolate-brown with age. The stipe is up to 4.0 cm long with a bulbous base.

- The spores are chocolate-brown in deposit, broadly ellipsoid, 4.5-6.8 x 3.0-4.5 µm, with a dark wall.

- This species is known only from Florida but is very common during rainy summer months beneath evergreen oaks on lawns and open woods around Gainesville.

Fig. 190. *Agaricus alachuanus* (x 2.5)   (Sherri Angels)

Fig. 191. *Agaricus alligator* (× 0.7)

Agaricus alligator Murr.   **191**

(?edibility)

■ The pileus is 6.0-10.0 cm in diameter, convex to plane, campestroid, with a white surface that darkens when handled, and becomes distinctly imbricate-scaly. The lamellae are free, close, and chocolate-brown with age. The stipe is equal, 7.0 x 1.7 cm, white, becoming yellowish, glabrous, with a median, membranous annulus.

■ The spores are broadly ellipsoid, 6.0-7.5 x 4.5-6.0 μm, smooth, with a dark wall.

■ This species is found on open grassy areas or on cultivated soil. It resembles *A. floridanus* Pk., but differs in having rows of scales on the pileus, thus "alligator," and the cap and stipe turn yellowish or brownish-yellow when handled. Although first discovered in the Gainesville area, it has subsequently been found along the Gulf Coastal plain.

(edible)

- The pileus is subcylindric to expanded, 7.0-9.0 cm in diameter, campestroid, creamy to ochraceous when fresh, drying a dull gold, with a finely scaly surface. The lamellae are free, at first pink but becoming chocolate-brown. The stipe is cylindric, 5.0-6.0 x 1.5-2.0 cm, bulbous, with a large, white medium annulus.

- The spores are chocolate brown in deposit, subglobose to ovoid, 5.3-7.0 x 4.5-5.3 µm, with a dark-brown wall.

- This is the most common summer *Agaricus* on the lawns, pastures, and golf courses around Gainesville. It is a choice edible species and is actively sought out by mycophagists in the area. It has also been found in other areas of the southeastern U.S. The late B.F. Isaacs (*pers. comm*) considered this species to be a synonym of *A. kauffmanii* Smith.

Fig. 192. *Agaricus blazei* (x 1.0)

Fig. 193. *Agaricus cylindriceps* var *aureus* (x 1.1)

Agaricus cylindriceps var. *aureus* Murr.   **193**

(?edibility)

- The pileus is cylindric, then expanding, up to 5.0 cm in diameter, campestroid, pallid with small yellow scales when young, becoming dull gold with golden-brown scales when dry. The lamellae are free and a deep chocolate-brown. The stipe reaches 3.0 cm in length, pallid to yellowish like the pileus, with a median annulus and a flattened base. The basidiomata turn gold when bruised and have a strong almond odor.

- The spores are chocolate-brown in deposit, ovoid to ellipsoid, 5.3-6.0 x 3.8-4.5 μm, with a dark thick wall.

- This species occurs on open lawns and open woods in the area, and is easily recognized by its amygdaline odor and golden coloration when bruised. It has also been found in a number of other southern states.

194   *Agaricus diminutivus* Pk.

(?edibility)

■ The pileus is very small, up to 1.5 cm, ovate, then plane to slightly umbonate, placomycetoid, pinkish-buff with a darkened disc, and pinkish then brownish fibrils, bruising yellowish. The lamellae are free, dull pink then brown. The stipe is cylindric, 3.0-6.0 x 0.3-0.6 cm, with a slightly bulbous base, whitish with brownish floccules, and a thin whitish ring.

■ The spores are deep brown in deposit, broadly ellipsoid, 4.5-5.5 x 3.5-5.0 µm, with a dark-brown wall.

■ It is found scattered on leaf litter in mixed forests throughout North America. It is distinguished from other Florida species by its smaller size, smaller spores, and its oak-pine forest habitat.

Fig. 194. *Agaricus diminutivus* (x 2.0)

Fig. 195. *Agaricus floridanus* (x 0.4)

Agaricus floridanus Pk.   **195**

(?edibility)

- ■ The pileus is campestroid, convex to plane, up to 15.0 cm in diameter, whitish with a yellowish center, and golden-yellow on drying. The lamellae are deep chocolate-brown, and free. The whitish buff stipe is cylindric, 8.0-10.0 x 1.0-1.5 cm, with a slightly bulbous, ochraceous base.

- ■ The spores are dark brown in deposit, broadly ellipsoid to ovoid, 6.0-7.5 x 4.5-5.3 µm, with a dark-brown wall.

- ■ This species is known only from Florida, where it has been found on numerous occasions growing on open grassy fields. Murrill (1972) recognized it in the field by its ochraceous stipe base.

Fig. 196. *Agaricus haemorrhoidarius* (x 0.5)

196	*Agaricus haemorrhoidarius* (Fr.) Kalch

(edible)

■ The pileus is 4.0-10.0 cm in diameter, convex, becoming plane, campestroid, with a deep reddish-brown to chocolate-brown color, and dense darker brown scales on the disc scattered towards the margin. The tissue quickly turns blood-red when bruised or cut. The lamellae are pinkish when young, becoming chocolate-brown with age. The stipe is 5.0-10.0 x 1.0-2.0 cm, only slightly bulbous at the base, whitish but turning blood-red when bruised.

■ The spores are deep purple-brown in deposit, ellipsoid, 4.5-7.0 x 3.0-3.5 µm, with a thick, dark-brown wall.

■ This species seems to be associated primarily with conifers and is found under pines during the summer, rainy season in Florida. It is easily distinguished from other forest-inhabiting species by its dark color and flesh that turns blood-red when bruised.

Agaricales

(poisonous)

■ The pileus is truncate-convex to plane, placomycetoid, 7.0-10.0 cm, white with dark floccose scales, and dull grayish-tan on the disc. The lamellae are free and deep chocolate with age. The stipe is slender, 6.0-8.0 x 0.6-0.8 cm with a shallow basal cup 1.5 cm wide and an apical, membranous annulus.

■ The spores are dark brown in deposit, ellipsoid, 4.5-6.0 x 3.0-3.8 μm, with a dark thick wall.

■ This species is easily recognized from other light brown, scaly species by its slender stipe with an abrupt, cupulate base. It is found in open woods throughout the Gulf Coastal plain, and it is most frequently associated with laurel oaks.

Fig. 197. *Agaricus pocillator* (x 1.0)

Fig. 198. *Agaricus projectellus* (x 0.7)

198   *Agaricus projectellus* Murr.

(edible)

■ The white to creamy pileus is placomycetoid, convex to plane, 6.0-
8.0 cm in diameter, with a smooth surface, or sometimes with fine
floccose scales, and with a projecting margin. The lamellae are free
and chocolate brown with age. The stipe is cylindric, 5.0-8.0 x 0.8-
1.5 cm, white with a median, membranous annulus.

■ The spores are dark brown in deposit, ellipsoid, 6.0-7.5 x 3.8-5.3
µm, with a dark thick wall.

■ This species is found in open lawns and pastures through northern
Florida during the summer months. The projecting margin of the
pileus and considerably shorter spores separate this from other
species of *Agaricus*.

Fig. 199. *Agaricus rhoadsii* (x 0.5)

Agaricus rhoadsii Murr.   199

(?edibility)

- The pileus is placomycetoid, truncate-conic to plane, up to 6.5 cm in diameter, pale purple becoming somewhat chestnut-brown on the disc with a whitish margin, and dry, fibrillose surface. The lamellae are whitish to dull pink, becoming chocolate-brown. The stipe tapers upwards, 7.0-8.0 x 0.6-1.0 cm, white, bulbous, with minute fibrils, and pale brownish scales below.

- The spores are purplish-brown in deposit, ellipsoid, 5.3-6.0 x 3.8-4.5 μm, with a dark-brown wall.

- Fresh specimens of *A. rhoadsii* have a distinct pale-purple color. They are found under oaks in high hammocks and heavily-wooded lawns.

Agaricus subalachuanus Murr.   200

(?edibility)

- The pileus is 3.0-3.5 cm in diameter, convex, becoming umbonate, placomycetoid, white with rosy-buff scales. The lamellae are free, close to crowded, whitish early, becoming deep chocolate-brown at maturity. The stipe is 3.0-3.5 x 0.2-0.3 cm, with a whitish, skirt-like annulus.

Fig. 200. *Agaricus subalachuanus* (x 1.0)   (Robert Williams)

- The spores are dark-brown in deposit, ellpisoid 6.0-7.0 x 4.0-4.5 µm, with a dark thick wall.

- This species is found on open fields and lawns during the early summer rainy season, and has been found throughout the Gulf coastal plain. Murrill (1942) noted that it was at times one of the most abundant species on open lawns and pastures.

The Strophariaceae

This family was traditionally recognized for fleshy mushrooms with attached lamellae, a purple-brown spore print and with smooth spores bearing an apical germ pore. Recent studies have shown that the spore color can vary from a pale tan to somewhat rusty-brown. There are 17 genera of Strophariaceae recognized worldwide. Largent and Baroni (1988) recognize 10 genera in their treatment of the family. Species of four genera will be treated below.

A Key to Common Genera of Strophariaceae in Florida

1. Spore deposit pale tan to rusty-brown .... *Pholiota* (p. 236)
1. Spore deposit violaceous-brown to chocolate-brown 2
    2. Sporulating on herbivore manure; with a distinct annulus; flesh turning blue when bruised .... *Psilocybe* (p. 238)
    2. Not as above 3
3. Pileus yellow-green to bronze, stipe long, growing on decaying wood or mulch .... *Naematoloma* (p. 232)
3. Pileus whitish to light brown, stipe stout, growing on soil, lawns and pastures, occasionally on mulch .... *Stropharia* (p. 239)

Naematoloma

These are small to medium-sized, yellow-green to fulvous-colored mushrooms with a grayish-violaceous, blackish to gray-brown spore print. The lamellae are pallid to green at first, becoming smoky-colored when mature. They are often found on decaying wood among deep mosses. The spores are smooth with an apical germ pore. Species of this genus have often gone under the name *Hypholoma,* but I am following Hawksworth *et al.* (1995) in placing them in *Naematoloma.*

The genus contains both poisonous and edible species, many of which are similar in appearance. Therefore, one must be precise in identifying species before attempting to eat them.

There are 37 species recognized worldwide, but Smith (1951) considered 21 in his treatment of North American species.

A Key to Common Florida Species of *Nematoloma*

1. Pileus small, 1.0-3.0 cm in diameter, convex, becoming plane, greenish-yellow .... *Naematoloma subviride* (p. 235)
1. Pileus larger 2
   2. Pileus 2.0-4.0 cm in diameter, cuticle a dull olive to maize yellow .... *Naematoloma capnoides* (p. 234)
   2. Pileus 3.0-8.0 cm in diameter, cuticle a dull orange-yellow to yellow-brown .... *Naematoloma fasciculare* (p. 234)

Fig. 201. *Naematoloma capnoides* (x 1.0)

201

Naematoloma capnoides (Fr.:Fr.) Karst.

(edible)

■ The pileus is 2.0-4.0 cm in diameter, convex becoming plane, moist when fresh, orange-yellow to reddish-orange, with enrolled margins. The lamellae are attached, cream-colored when young, then grayish to purple-brown with age. The stipe is 3.0-10.0 x 0.4-1.0 cm, cylindric, yellowish above, cinnamon-brown below with a median faint ring.

■ The spores are violet-brown in deposit, ellipsoid, 6.0-8.5 x 3.5-4.5 μm, and thick-walled with a germ pore.

■ This species grows in clusters, usually on moss-covered, decaying logs of conifers. Its size and bright yellow color distinguish it from other species in Florida.

202

Naematoloma fasciculare (Huds.:Fr.) Karst.

(poisonous)

■ The pileus is 2.0-8.0 cm in diameter, convex, becoming plane, surface smooth, dull, yellow-orange to orange-brown towards the disc, greenish-yellow towards the margins. The lamella are adnate, initially lemon-yellow but becoming greenish then purplish-brown

Fig. 202. *Naematoloma fascicularia* (x 0.3)   (Henry Aldrich)

as spores mature. The stipe is 5.0-10.0 x 0.3-0.1 cm, yellow to yellowish-green above, becoming reddish-brown below.

- The spores are purple-brown in deposit, ellipsoid, 6.5-8.0 x 3.5-4.0 μm, thick-walled with a germ pore.

- This species is very common in Florida, and is found growing on decaying stumps and logs of both hardwoods and conifers. It is most commonly found growing in clusters from partially buried wood.

Naematoloma subviride (Berk. & Curt.) Smith   **203**

(?edibility)

- The pileus is 1.0-3.0 cm in diameter, ovoid early becoming convex or umbonate, dry, glabrous, pale greenish-yellow, to somewhat olivaceous on the disc. The lamellae are adnate, crowded, greenish-yellow, becoming purplish-brown at maturity. The stipe is 3.0-4.0 x 0.2-0.3 cm cylindric, greenish-yellow, and pale olive-brown below.

- The spores are purple-brown in deposit, ellipsoid, 7.0-8.0 x 3.5-4.0 μm, thick-walled, with a germ pore.

- This species has been found throughout the tropics and subtropics where it is found growing in clusters on decaying logs. Murrill (1918) described the species as *Hypholoma flavovirens.*

Fig. 203. *Naematoloma subviride* (x 1.0)

Pholiota

Species of *Pholiota* are characterized by normally bright yellowish, rusty-yellow, to rusty-brown mushrooms that are typically 5.0-10.0 cm in diameter, but may become much larger. The pileus is often scaly or fibrillose, and some with a distinct, fibrous marginal veil. The stipe usually has a distinct annulus, but in some species it may become fragmented and inconspicuous. The spores are rusty-brown to earth-brown in deposit, smooth and typically with a germ pore.

Some species may resemble *Gymnopilus* or *Hypholoma*. Species of *Gymnopilus* differ in having a brighter, rusty to orange-brown spore deposit and ornamented spores. *Hypholoma* differs in having a dark grayish-olivaceous, olive-brown, or grayish spore print. *Pholiota* is a large genus, containing 105 species in North America (Smith & Hesler, 1968). Several are accessioned in the Mycological Herbarium at the University of Florida, mostly under the name *Flammula*. Two species of *Pholiota* will be described here.

A Key to Common Species of *Pholotia*

1. Pileus 4.0-15.0 cm in diameter, hemispherical to convex, ochre to orange with dark scales .... *Pholiota aurivella* (p. 236)

1. Pileus 1.5-10.0 cm in diameter, convex with an umbo, often viscid, pale green, turquoise to grayish .... *Pholiota polychroa* (p. 237)

---

204   *Pholiota aurivella* (Fr.) Kumm

(inedible)

■ The pileus is 4.0-15.0 cm in diameter, hemispheric to convex, with a broad umbo, ochra-orange to tawny, covered with darker scales which become appressed with a viscid to gelatinous cuticle. The lamellae are adnate to slightly sinuate, pale yellowish, but becoming rusty-brown. The stipe is 5.0-8.0 x 0.5-1.5 cm, yellowish to yellowish-brown, flocose above the annulus but becoming increasingly scaly below.

■ The spores are rusty-brown in deposit, ellipsoid, 7.0-9.5 x 4.5-6.0 µm, with a distinct apical pore.

■ This species grows in clusters on living or dead trunks of conifers and hardwoods. It is recognized by its viscid yellow pileus with darker brown appressed scales.

Fig. 204. *Pholiota aurivella* (× 0.3)   (Henry Aldrich)

Pholiota polychroa (Berk.) Smith   **205**

(inedible)

■ The pileus is 1.5-10.0 cm in diameter, initially obtuse to convex, expanding to become broadly convex with an umbo, with a viscid surface bearing superficial scales. It is pale green, turquoise, or becoming purplish-gray with yellowish hues. The lamellae are adnate to decurrent, initially purplish to pale cream-colored,

Fig. 205. *Pholiota polychroa* (× 0.7)   (Robert Williams)

becoming pale hazel-brown and purplish at spore maturation. The stipe is 2.0-6.0 x 0.3-0.5 cm, tapering downward, fibrillose, with scales covering the lower portion, light blue-green above and becoming darker, reddish-brown towards the base.

- The spores are brown to purplish-brown in deposit, oblong to ellipsoid, 6.0-7.5 x 3.5-4.5 μm, with a minute apical germ pore.

- This species is found on hardwood logs and stumps throughout southern and eastern North America. It is easily recognized in the field by its olive and green colors.

Psilocybe

The genus *Psilocybe* contains small to medium-sized mushrooms, seldom reaching beyond 10.0 cm in diameter. They are usually conical to convex, often umbonate, yellow-brown to brown in color, and viscid or subviscid. The spore deposit is purple-brown to dark brown, and the individual spores are smooth, yellow-brown to olive, thick-walled, with a prominent germ pore. In a world monograph of *Psilocybe,* Guzman (1983) recognized 144 species. A number of species have been confused with *Stropharia,* which is recognized largely on microscopic characteristics of the pileus cuticle and cystidial elements in the lamellae. The most common species in Florida, *Psilocybe cubensis,* is treated below.

---

206   *Psilocybe cubensis* (Earle) Sing.

(hallucinogenic/toxic)

- The pileus is 1.5-9.0 cm in diameter, broadly conical, becoming convex with a distinct umbo, with appressed fibrils, whitish to yellow-brown, darker on the umbo, viscid when moist, and bruising blue. The lamellae are adnate, pale tan initially, becoming dark purple-gray to almost black. The white to yellowish stipe is 4.0-15.0 x 0.4-1.5 cm, cylindric to tapering upwards, with a slightly bulbous base, and a persistent white, membranous ring that becomes purplish from the spore deposit.

- The spores are purple-brown in deposit, ellipsoid, 13.0-17.0 x 8.0-11.0 μm, thick-walled with a distinct germ pore.

■ This species was initially found growing around sugarcane mills in Cuba, thus the name "cubensis." It has subsequently been found on the dung of cows and horses throughout the Gulf Coastal states and Central America. It is one of a number of hallucinogenic mushrooms commonly referred to as "the magic mushrooms," but consumption may result in nausea, headache, prostration, and convulsion.

Fig. 206. *Psilocybe cubensis* (x 0.4)

Stropharia

Species of *Stropharia* are morphologically similar and grow in the same habitat with species of *Agaricus*, i.e., shaded lawns, open fields, and sparse woodlands. Some are also coprophilous. However, the distinctive purplish-brown to purplish-gray spore color, reflected in the gill color of mature specimens, set them apart from the initially pinkish, later chocolate-brown lamellae of *Agaricus*. The pileus color in species of *Stropharia* varies from pallid, yellowish-brown, violaceous-brown to bright orange in color. The stipes are fleshy-fibrous, with a membranous annulus. The distinct annulus sets *Stropharia* apart from *Hypholoma,* and the purplish-brown spores, from *Pholiota* with more rusty-brown spores. *Psilocybe* differs in having cystidia with yellowish inclusions, and normally a poorly formed annulus. Since a number of species of *Stropharia* are known to be toxic, many are untested and should be avoided. Two species will be considered below.

A Key to Common Species of Stropharia

1. Pileus 2.5-5.0 cm in diameter, whitish to yellowish, smooth; stipe 2.0-2.5 cm long .... *Stropharia bilamellata* (p. 240)

1. Pileus 1.0-4.0 cm in diameter, ochre to mustard-yellow, smooth, slimy to viscid; stipe 3.0-4.0 cm long... *Stropharia coronilla* (p. 241)

---

207   *Stropharia bilamellala* Pk.

(?edibility)

■ The pileus is 2.5-5.0 cm in diameter, convex becoming plane, with a dry surface that is whitish or yellowish and smooth. The lamellae are adnate and purplish-brown at maturity. The stipe is short, 2.0-2.5 x 0.6-0.8 cm, with a well-developed, white annulus showing gill impressions.

■ The spores are purplish-brown in deposit, ellipsoid, 10.0-10.5 x 5.0-6.0 μm, with a small apical pore.

Fig. 207. *Stropharia bilamellata* (x 0.8)   (Robert Williams)

■ This species is found throughout the eastern United States, and is especially common on grassy lawns and open fields around Florida.

Stropharia coronilla (Bull.:Fr.) Quel. **208**

(poisonous)

■ The pileus is small, 1.0-4.0 cm in diameter, convex, ochre-yellow to almost mustard-yellow, smooth and slimy to viscid when wet. The lamellae are adnate, brownish-violet, to purple-black with age. The stipe is 3.0-4.0 x 0.3-0.7 cm, cylindric, dry, white, bearing a median persistent membranous ring with gill impressions.

■ The spores are purple-brown in deposit, ovoid, 7.0-9.5 x 4.0-5.0 µm, with a small apical pore.

■ This species is also abundant on lawns, open pastures, and bordering woodlands. It is smaller and more viscid than other locally-occurring species.

Fig. 208. *Stropharia coronilla* (x 2.0) (Ulla Benny)

The Coprinaceae are usually small, conical to ovoid mushrooms with thin, fragile stipes. The lamellae are adnate to sinuate, and deliquesce in some genera. The spores are black to dark purple-brown, and have a distinct pore at their apices. They are saprobic on grassy lawns, leaf mulch, sawdust, and dung. Eleven genera are recognized worldwide; three have species very common in Florida. There are a number of choice edible species in *Coprinus* and *Psathyrella*. A number of species of *Panaeolus*, however, are toxic or hallucinogenic.

A Key to Common Genera of Coprinaceae

1. Gills black, deliquescing (inky); cap usually striate
   .... *Coprinus* (p. 242)
1. Gills not deliquescing, cap not striate 2
   2. Pileus conical to ovoid, lamellae blackish, mottled
      .... *Panaeolus* (p. 249)
   2. Pileus convex; lamellae not mottled .... *Psathyrella* (p. 253)

Coprinus

This group is known as the "inky-cap" mushrooms because of the autodigestion that takes place when the basidiomata mature. They normally have fragile, conical to bell-shape caps with radial striations and thin, fragile stipes. They are commonly found on decaying wood, leaf litter, humus, or on dung. Most of the species are edible and are found growing in large clusters. Some have been found to contain "coprine," a compound that will react when consumed with alcohol. Many of the symptoms experienced when consumed with alcohol are identical to to those experienced by individuals who are prescribed "antabuse" tablets to overcome alcoholism. Some species of *Coprinus* give an antabuse effect.

A Key to Common Florida Species of *Coprinus*

1. Pileus small, 1.5-3.0 cm in diameter, convex gray to pale hazel-brown; stipe hyaline to pallid .... *Coprinus floridanus* (p. 246)
1. Pileus and stipe different 2
   2. Pileus 2.0-5.0 cm in diameter, conical, pale grayish with white fibrils; stipe with white fibrils .... *Coprinus lagopus* (p. 247)

2. Not as above 3

3. Pileus 3.0-4.0 cm in diameter, white, flocccose, striate with an upturned margin ....*Coprinus alachuanus* (p. 243)

3. Not as above 4

    4. Pileus conic to convex, with gray squamules and radial folds; stipe 2.5-3.0 cm long .... *Coprinus capillaripes* (p. 244)

    4. Pileus and stipe not as above 5

5. Pileus ovoid to campanulate, white to whitish, splitting into brownish scales; stipe 10.0-20.0 cm long *Coprinus comatus* (p. 245)

5. Pileus honey-yellow; stipe 2.5-7.5 cm long
    .... *Coprinus micaceus* (p. 247)

Coprinus alachuanus Murr.   **209**

(?edibility)

■ The pileus is 3.0-4.0 cm in diameter, convex but slightly expanding, white becoming floccose and striate with an upturned margin. The lamellae are free, narrow, soon becoming black and deliquescing. The stipe is equal or tapering upwards, 7.0-8.0 x 0.3-0.5 cm, milk-white with a bulbous base.

Fig. 209. *Coprinus alachuanus* (x 1.0)

- The spores are black in deposit, subglobose, 10.0-11.0 x 9.0-9.5 µm, with a prominent germ pore.

- This species was found by Murrill (1942) growing on soil in a mesic hammock area near Gainesville. This species is somewhat similar to *C. niveus* Fr., which has larger spores and is basically dung inhabiting.

---

210   *Coprinus capillaripes* Murr.

(?edibility)

- The pileus is very small, approx 3.5-4.0 mm in diameter, conical, becoming covex, with a gray surface bearing squamules with folds and margins becoming upturned. The lamellae are free, somewhat distant, soon becoming black and deliquescing. The stipe is smooth, snow white, 2.5-3.0 cm x 0.1-0.2 cm, without an annulus.

- The spores are black in deposit, broadly ellipsoid, 10.0-11.0 x 7.0-8.0 µm, with a thick black wall and distinct germ pore.

- This is one of the smallest species of *Coprinus* found in this area. It is found on open grassy lawns and on pine bark mulch at the edge

Fig. 210. *Coprinus capillaripes* (x 2.0)

of lawns. *Coprinus disseminatus* (Pers.: Fr.) Gray is similar but has smaller spores, a larger pileus, and shorter stipe.

Coprinus comatus (Muell.: Fr.) Pers. **211**

(edible)

■ The pileus is 2.0-5.0 cm in diameter, initially cylindric to ovoid, expanding to become bell-shaped, white to whitish, with a silky surface splitting into silky radial fibrils or brownish scales, becoming blackish towards the margins. The lamellae are free, initially white, becoming grayish then black and deliquescing. The stipe is 10.0-20.0 x 1.0-3.0 cm, tapering apically and somewhat swollen at the base, white, with whitish, longitudinal fibrils, and a white, persistent annulus.

■ The spores are black in deposit, ellipsoid to broadly ellipsoid, 9.5-12.0 x 6.1-8.3 μm, with a smooth, dark, thick wall and distinct germ pore.

■ This species is commonly found growing in clusters on mulch, grass clippings, and other plant debris. In Florida it often occurs on mulched garden soils.

Fig. 211. *Coprinus comatus* (x 1.0)

Fig. 212. *Coprinus floridanus* (x 1.2)   (Ulla Benny)

---

212   *Coprinus floridanus* Murr.

(?edibility)

■ The pileus is 1.5-3.0 cm in diameter, very thin, broadly convex, with a gray or pale hazel-brown surface towards the disc, and prominently striate with upturned margins. The lamellae are adnexed, fairly close, initially white but becoming black and deliquescing with age. The stipe is 3.0-4.0 x 0.2 cm, almost hyaline, and slightly swollen at the base.

■ The spores are black in deposit, broadly ellipsoid, 9.5-10.0 x 5.5-7.0 μm, with brownish-black walls and a distinct germ pore.

■ This species has been found several times growing on rotting stumps and other decaying wood. It is also reminiscent of *C. disseminatus,* which is a slightly smaller mushroom with somewhat narrower spores.

Coprinus lagopus (Fr.) Fr. 213

(?edibility)

■ The pileus is 1.0-5.0 cm in diameter, conical but expanding with upturned margins, pale grayish and densely covered with white fibrils and radial furrows. The lamellae are free, close, initially grayish but becoming black and deliquescing. The stipe is 5.0-20.0 x 0.2-0.5 cm, cylindric, white and covered with whitish fibrils.

■ The spores are black in deposit, ellipsoid, 10.0-12.0 x 6.5-8.5 µm, with a thick black wall and an apical germ pore.

■ This species grows singlely or clustered on woody debris, and occasionally in grassy woodland areas. It has been found throughout North America. It is somewhat similar to *C. alachuanus*, but differs in having a more slender stipe and more globose spores.

Fig. 213. *Coprinus lagopus* (x 1.0)

Coprinus micaceus (Bull.: Fr.) Fr. 214

(edible)

■ The pileus is 2.5-5.0 cm in diameter, ovoid, becoming bell-shaped to convex, initially with a granular surface that becomes honey-yellow and a slightly darker disc. The lamellae are adnate, close, whitish to gray, becoming black and deliquescing. The stipe is 2.5-7.5 x 0.3-0.5 cm, fragile, white with whitish fibrils.

■ The spores are black in deposit, ellipsoid, 7.0-10.0 x 4.0-5.0 µm, with a thick dark wall bearing an apical germ pore.

■ This species is usually found in large clusters on decaying hardwood, stumps, and buried wood.

Fig. 214. *Coprinus micaceus* (x 0.5)

Fig. 215. *Panaeolus fimicola* (x 0.8)

Panaeolus

Species of *Panaeolus* differ from other Coprinaceae in that the pileus does not deliquisce and the spores do not mature simultaneously, leaving a purplish-black mosiac appearance on the lamellae. Most initially have conic grayish-brown to reddish-brown, striate caps and thin firm stipes. The spores may be smooth or ornamented, but all have a germ pore. Most species are dung-inhabiting, but may be found on manured soil, or on other rich humus habitats. Ten species are recognized worldwide, a number of them occur in Florida.

A Key to Common Florida Species of *Panaeolus*

1. Pileus 1.0-5.0 cm in diameter, yellowish-brown to dark brown, hygrophanous .... *Panaeolus fimicola* (p. 249)

1. Pileus not as above 2

   2. Pileus 1.0-4.0 cm in diameter, light grayish-brown with a darker disc, dull satiny .... *Panaeolus papilionaceus* (p. 250)

   2. Pileus not as above 3

3. Pileus 1.3-5.0 cm in diameter, whitish to yellow-buff, often with a frayed margin .... *Panaeolus phalaenarum* (p. 251)

3. Pileus 3.0-6.0 cm in diameter, pale buff-brown, with a striate margin .... *Panaeolus retirugis* (p. 252)

Panaeolus fimicola (Fr.) Gill   **215**

(toxic)

- The pileus is 1.0-2.5 cm in diameter, ovoid to conical, later convex to plane, with a hygrophanous, yellow-brown to dark-brown surface. The lamellae are narrowly adnate, grayish-beige, becoming brown-black. The stipe is 5.0-10.0 x 0.1-0.3.0 cm, cylindric, hollow, with a whitish apex that becomes brownish towards the base.

- The spores are black in deposit, broadly ellipsoid, 11.5-14.5 x 6.8-10.0 µm, with a thick red-brown wall bearing a germ pore.

- This species usually grows in clusters on manure piles or in manured pastures.

(toxic)

- The pileus is 1.0-4.0 cm in diameter, ovoid, becoming bell-shaped to almost convex, with a dull, satiny, light to dark grayish-brown surface that fades towards the margins with age. The lamellae are adnate, dark brown when young, becoming blackish and mottled with age. The stipe is 6.0-14.0 x 0.1-0.3 cm, hollow, gray-brown to dark brown, fragile and hollow.

- The spores are black in deposit, ellipsoid to almond shaped, 13.0-18.5 x 8.2-10.5 µm, thick-walled, brown, with a germ pore.

- This species is found mostly in clusters on manure of cattle and horses. It is the most abundant species throughout Florida. It is slightly darker in color and with a longer stipe than other species of *Panaeolus* in this area. This mushroom was previously known as *P. campanulatus* (Bull.:Fr.) Quel.

Fig. 216. *Panaeolus paplionaceus* (x 1.0)

Fig. 217. *Panaeolus phaleanarum* (× 1.0)

Panaeolus phalaenarum (Fr.) Quel.   **217**

(toxic)

- The pileus is 1.3-5.0 cm in diameter, ovoid to bell-shaped, whitish to yellow-buff, with a slightly frayed margin. The lamellae are adnate to slightly sinuate, initially grayish but becoming mottled black with age. The stipe is cylindric, 7.5-11.0 x 0.5-1.5 cm, smooth, without an annulus, and whitish to yellowish-white.

- The spores are black in deposit, broadly ellipsoid, 15.0-20.0 x 8.0-11.0 μm, with a brownish-black, thick wall and an apical germ pore.

- This is a common mushroom around northern Florida, and is found most often on horse and cow dung. It has traditionally gone under the name *P. solidipes* (Pk.) Sacc., and has also been confused with *P. semiovatus* (With.: Fr.) Wuns., a similar mushroom with a distinct white annulus.

(inedible)

- The pileus is 3.0-6.0 cm in diameter, ovoid at first, soon becoming bell-shaped, pale buff-brown on the disc, lighter, somewhat striate towards the margins, and becoming scurfy. The lamellae are adnate, crowded, purplish-gray at first, becoming blackish and mottled. The stipe is cylindric, 9.0-15.0 x 0.3-0.7 cm, hollow, whitish to pale gray, and becoming scurfy.

- The spores are grayish-black in deposit, broadly ellipsoid, 12.0-16.0 x 8.0-11.0 µm, with a darkened thick wall and an apical germ pore.

- This species is found on dung or heavily manured soil. Europeans have synonymized this species with *P. papilionaceus*, but the pileus of *P. retirugis* is slightly larger, buff-brown, and becomes scurfy, with spores that are smaller and more broadly ellipsoid.

Fig. 218. *Panaeolus retirugis* (x 0.3)

Psathyrella

These are small to medium-sized mushrooms, seldom more than 7 cm in diameter, with a fragile hygrophanous pileus. They are mostly convex to bell-shaped, dull pale-brown, yellow-brown, or darker. The spore deposit is dark chocolate-brown, purplish-gray to black, and may be smooth or ornamented. Some authors remove those with roughened spores and place them in *Lacrymaria*. This is a very large genus, with as many as 600 species described worldwide and more than 400 in North America (Smith 1972). The common species in Florida are included below.

A Key to Common Florida Species of *Psathyrella*

1. Pileus fawn-colored with darker disc .. *Psathyrella australis* (p. 253)
1. Pileus another color 2
  2. Pileus dull purple to reddish-brown
     ....*Psathyrella pennata* (p. 255)
  2. Pileus honey yellow to brownish but becoming dingy
     purple...................................*Psathyrella candolleana* (p. 254)

Psathyrella australis (Murr.) Smith   **219**

(?edibility)

■ The pileus is 1.0-3.0 cm in diameter, convex to subumbonate, smooth, hygrophanous, slightly striate, pale fawn color with a

Fig. 219. *Psathyrella australis* (× 1.0)

darker disc. The lamellae are adnexed, crowded, fawn to brownish. The stipe is cylindric, 4.0-6.0 x 0.2-0.3 cm, hollow, smooth, whitish, with a very slight veil early.

- The spores are purplish-brown in deposit, broadly ellipsoid, 7.0-9.0 x 4.0-5.0 µm, with a thicken wall and apical germ pore.

- This species grows in clusters on rotten wood and humus, and has been found on numerous occasions in northern Florida. Smith (1972) feels that it might be one of the variants of *P. candolleana* which is described below.

---

220   *Psathyrella candolleana* (Fr.: Fr.) Maire

(?edibility)

- The pileus is 3.0-7.0 cm in diameter, conical to convex, becoming broadly convex to plane, with a smooth surface that is moist, at first dark, honey-yellow but becoming a dingy purple-brown. The lamellae are narrowly adnate, initially light brown, but becoming darker. The stipe is cylindric, 6.0-10.0 x 0.4-0.8 cm, becoming hollow, whitish, and with an occasional, fibrillar annulus.

- The spores are purple-brown in deposit, ellipsoid to ovate, 7.0-9.0 x 4.0-5.0 µm, with a thickened wall and an apical germ pore.

- This species grows in clusters around old hardwood stumps or buried wood. It is one of the most common species of *Psathyrella* in North America. This species is probably what Murrill (1972) called *Drosophila appendiculata,* which he found common on leaf-mold and plant debris around Gainesville.

Fig. 220. *Psathyrella candolleana* (x 0.3)   (Ulla Benny)

(inedible)

■ The pileus is 1.2-3.5 cm in diameter, hemispherical, with a fibril-lose surface that is hygrophanous, dull, dark purple-brown, becoming radially wrinkled. The lamellae are adnate, light gray to beige, becoming darker and reddish-brown with age. The stipe is 2.0-4.0 x 0.2-0.3 cm, cylindric, with a whitish, squamose surface.

■ The spores are black in deposit, ellipsoid, 7.0-9.0 x 4.0-4.7 μm, coffee-brown without a germ pore.

■ This species is normally found in clusters on burned areas, and has gone under the name *Psathyrella carbonicola* Smith in North America.

Fig. 221. *Psathyrella pennata* (x 0.5)

Boletales

The "boletes" have traditionally been recognized as the poroid mushrooms, and until recent years contained only two families of Agaricales, the Boletaceae and Strobilomycetaceae. Singer (1986) divided the Agaricales into three suborders, placing the boletes in the Boletineae. Currently, Hawksworth *et al.* (1995) place them in the Boletales, which contains 11 families. Representatives of six of these families are common in Florida. The hymenial configuration of the Boletales is variable, ranging from mostly poroid to rarely gilled, or with folds. Spore deposits range from whitish, pink, ochraceous, cinnamon, olivaceous-brown, to smoky-black. Most species are believed to be ectomycorrhizal, although a few seem to be growing from decaying wood. I have relied largely on Singer (1977), Pegler (1986) and Both (1993) for keys and descriptions of the various groups of boletes encountered.

A Key to Families of Boletales in Florida

1. Spores short, smooth, subglobose, lacking a superhilar
    depression .... **Gyrodontaceae** (p. 256)
1. Spores usually cylindric, without superhilar depression 2
    2. Spore print black to brown and ornamented, or vinaceous to
        pink .... **Strobilomycetaceae** (p. 294)
    2. Spores not as above 3
3. Basidiomata usually robust, with a stout stipe, spores ovoid
    to fusoid-ellipsoid, usually smooth .... **Boletaceae** (p. 260)
3. Basidiomata usually small with a slender stipe, hymenium
    tubular to secondarily gilled, spores smooth or with
    longitudinal ridges .... **Xerocomaceae** (p. 285)

The Gyrodontaceae

These are medium to robust boletes with a tubular or labyrinthoid hymenium. The stipe is central or eccentric, stout and sometimes with a reticulate surface. The spore deposit is creamy to yellowish ochraceous to olive-brown, and the individual spores are subglobose to broadly ellipsoid. Nine genera are currently placed in this family; species of two of these genera will be treated here.

A Key to Some Florida Gyrodontaceae

1. Spore print cream to yellow; with central stipe 2
1. Spore print olivaceous brown; stipe eccentric
.... *Gyrodon merulioides* (p. 257)
2. Pileus and stipe yellow-chestnut brown
.... *Gyroporus castaneus* (p. 258)
2. Pileus and stipe white with pinkish tint
.... *Gyroporus subalbellus* (p. 259)

Gyrodon merulioides (Schw.) Sing.   **222**

(edible)

■ The pileus is 5.0-25.0 cm in diameter, broadly convex to plane, dull yellowish-brown to olive-brown, dry and subtomentose. The tubes

Fig. 222. *Gyrodon merulioides* (x 0.3)   (Walter Sundberg)

are 1.0-2.0 mm deep, decurrent, elongate and radially arranged, appearing almost gilled, bright to dull gold, and bruising slightly blue. The stipe is 1.0-6.0 x 0.1-0.3, laterally attached, and reticulate at the apex.

- The spores are brownish-yellow in deposit, broadly ellipsoid, 7.0-11.0 x 5.0-7.5 µm, smooth and thin-walled.

- This species is consistently found associated with ash, and is easily recognized by its lateral stipe and its shallow, elongate, wrinkled and radiating pores. It is found throughout Florida where ash trees are located.

---

223   *Gyroporus castaneus* (Bull.: Fr.) Quel.

(edible)

- The pileus is 3.0-8.0 cm in diameter, broadly convex to plane, yellowish to chestnut-brown, dry and finely tomentose. The tubes are initiallly white to whitish, becoming creamy to brown when bruised, small, up to 8 mm deep, and depressed near the stipe. The stipe is cylindric, 3.5-8.0 x 0.8-2.2 cm, yellowish to chestnut-brown, initially solid but becoming hollow.

- The spores are amber to citron-yellow in deposit, ellipsoid, 7.0-11.0 x 4.5-6.0 µm, thin-walled and smooth.

Fig. 223. *Gyroporus castaneus* (x 0.5)

- This species is found in open forests and in grassy areas near trees. Because of their constant association, it is likely ectomycorrhizal with oaks in this area. It is very abundant on shaded lawns and open parks around Gainesville.

Fig. 224. *Gyroporus subalbellus* (x 0.5)

Gyroporus subalbellus Murr.   **224**

(edible)

- The pileus is 3.5-10.0 cm in diameter, convex but becoming plane and often with a central depression, white but often with a pinkish to light buff color. The tubes are adnate, white to whitish, becoming cream to yellowish, 5.0-8.0 mm deep, not staining when bruised. The stipe is 3.3-8.0 x 1.1-3.0 cm, with an enlarged base, white with pinkish areas, solid, but sometimes developing cavities within.

- The spores are yellowish-buff in deposit, ellipsoid, 7.5-13.8 x 4.0-5.5 μm, thin-walled and smooth.

- This species was later described as *Gyroporus roseialbus* Murrill (1938). It is found in frequent association with both oaks and pines in northern Florida, and is easily recognized by the milk-white color of the pileus and tubes, along with the faint pinkish tints that develop on most collections.

The Boletaceae

The Boletaceae all have tubular hymenia that are adnate to free, and tubes that are circular to slightly angular. Their stipes are thick, often ventricose to bulbous. Spore deposits are ochraceous-cinnamon to olive-brown, and individual spores are mostly smooth, and commonly elongate to fusoid or rarely broadly ellipsoid. All appear to be ectomycorrhizal, and are most common in Florida around oaks and pines. The Boletaceae, which at one time encompassed most of the boletes, is now restricted to 13 genera. Three of these, *Boletus, Leccinum,* and *Suillus* are very common in Florida.

A Key to Genera of Florida Boletaceae
1. Pileus usually viscid to slimy; if dry, tubes are radially arranged .... ***Suillus*** (p. 282)
1. Pileus and tubes not as above 2
  2. Stipe scabrous, with dark tufts, tubes minute, spores usually 15.0 µm or more in length .... ***Leccinum*** (p. 277)
  2. Stipe not scabrous, often swollen at the base, spores variable in size .... ***Boletus*** (p. 260)

Boletus
The genus is characterized by large to robust basidiomata with white to yellowish flesh, which in some species may turn blue on bruising. Their stipes are powdery to velvety, often reticulate, sometimes smooth, but never scaly. They have an olive or olive-brown spore print and most spores are fusoid. There are 130 species worldwide, and all are probably ectomycorrhizal on various hardwood and conifer species. This is the largest and most complex group of boletes in Florida. Several of the most common species are described below.

A Key to Common Species of *Boletus*
1. Pore or pileus color red 9
1. Pore and pileus color similar, not red 2
  2. Contex white, not staining when bruised 3
  2. Contex yellow, bruising blue or not 4

Boletales

15. Pileus not as above 16

    16. Pileus deep red, fading ochraceous, minutely areolate; pores becoming greenish-yellow .... *Boletus fraternus* (p. 267)

    16. Pileus mixed reddish, brownish or pinkish; pores becoming olivaceous .... *Boletus rubricitrinus* (p. 275)

---

225   *Boletus aureissimus* (Murr.) Murr.

(edible)

■ The pileus is 8.0-15.0 cm in diameter, convex, becoming plane with a depressed center, bright lemon to mustard-yellow, with a pale yellow flesh. The tubes are pale lemon to cadmium-yellow, depressed around the stipe, 1.2-2.2 cm deep with small pores less than 1.0 mm The stipe is pale lemon to cadmium-yellow, the upper third with a distinct reticulum, and strongly bulbous at the base.

■ The spores are buff to yellow-olive in deposit, fusoid-ellipsoid, 12.0-13.7 x 3.0-5.0 µm, with a smooth, thin wall.

■ There is considerable controversy relative to the identification of this species. Singer (1945) considered it a variety of *B. auripes* Pk., but Murrill (1948) found that the types of *B. aureissimus* and

Fig. 225. *Boletus aureissimus* (x 0.7)   (Henry Aldrich)

B. auripes were quite different. Having seen both boletes in the field, we follow Murrill in considering it a distinct species. It is very common under evergreen oaks throughout northern Florida. It is considered one of the choice edible species of *Boletus.*

Fig. 226. *Boletus bicolor* (x 0.25)

Boletus bicolor Pk.   **226**

(edible)

■ The pileus is 5.0-28.0 cm in diameter, convex to plane, with a glabrous, dry surface, sometimes faintly areolate, initially apple red but becoming yellowish-red. The tubes are adnate to slightly depressed around the stipe, short, 0.6-1.3 cm deep, cadmium-yellow when young, becoming olivaceous with age, and staining intensely blue when bruised. The stipe is 4.0-15.0 x 1.0-3.5 cm, tapering towards the base, red to yellowish-red and slightly reticulate above, deep red and smooth below.

■ The spores are olivaceous in deposit, cylindric to fusoid, 9.5-12.0 x 3.6-4.4 µm, with smooth, thin greenish walls.

■ This species is found under oaks during rainy summer months. Both (1993) considers *Boletus rubellus* ssp. *bicolor* (Pk.) Singer to be a synonym. It is one of the most common boletes beneath evergreen oaks on the University of Florida campus.

227 *Boletus edulis* ssp. *clavipes* (Pk.) Pilat & Dermek

(edible)

■ The pileus is 6.5-12.0 cm in diameter, convex, somewhat viscid when wet, and reddish-brown to ochraceous-brown. The pores are intially white but become olivaceous. The stipe is clavate, 7.0-13.0 x 0.3 cm, pallid to dull reddish-brown, and with a very shallow reticulum.

Fig. 227. *Boletus edulis* ssp. *clavipes* (x 1.0)   (Robert Williams)

■ The spores are deep olivaceous in deposit, fusiform-ellipsoid, 12.0-18.0 x 4.0-6.0 µm, smooth, with thin walls.

■ This subspecies of B. edulis differs from the other varieties in that the stipe tapers upwards, is bulbous at the base, and lighter in color. It has been found largely beneath pines in northern Florida, but has also been located in mixed forests.

Boletus fairchildianus Sing.   **228**

(?edibility)

■ The pileus is 4.0-15.0 cm in diameter, broadly convex to plane, purplish-red to deeper red, with faded margins. The tubes are yellow with "Pompeian red" mouths, and turn strongly blue when bruised. The stipe is 5.0-12.0 x 1.5-3.5 cm, tapering downward, lemon to mustard-yellow, and longitudinally striate.

■ The spores are olive-brown in deposit, fusoid, 12.5-17.3 x 4.5-7.5 µm, with smooth, thin walls.

■ This species is found under live oaks both in north and south Florida. It was first described as B. rubricitrinus var. fairchildianus Singer (1947), but was later elevated to species rank (Singer, 1977). They differ in that B. rubricitrinus has yellowish tubes,

Fig. 228. Boletus fairchildianus (x 0.3)

while those of *B. fairchildianus* are red. Until recently, *B. fairchildianus* has been found only in south Florida. With its large size and brilliant colors, this is truly one of the most beautiful of the boletes.

---

229   *Boletus floridanus* (Sing.) Sing.

(toxic)

■ The pileus is 5.0-15.0 cm in diameter, initially convex, becoming plane and often with a central depression, with a "Corinthian" red surface, at first smooth, later becoming dull red with small cracks. The tubes are yellow within, bright "Corinthian" red on the pores, fading with age, 6.0-9.0 mm deep, depressed around the stipe, turning blue when bruised. The stipe is 4.0-8.0 x 1.7-2.7 cm, deep red but fading with age, highly inflated below center, and prominently reticulate with an elongate mesh extending over the length of the stipe.

Fig. 229. *Boletus floridanus* (x 0.5)   (Robert Williams)

- The spores are olive-brown, ellipsoid-fusoid 13.2-16.7 x 4.5-5.3 µm, smooth with a thin wall.

- This species is found associated with evergreen oaks on shaded lawns and at the edge of open woodlands. It is a remarkable bolete because of the brilliant red color of the pileus, tubes, and deeply reticulate stipe. This combination of characters separate it from other red boletes in the area. Singer (1945) first considered it a subspecies of *B. frostii* Russell, but later concluded that it was a distinct species.

Fig. 230. *Boletus fraternus* (x 1.0)   (Ulla Benny)

Boletus fraternus Pk.   **230**

(?edibility)

- The pileus is 2.8-6.4 cm in diameter, broadly convex to plane, often areolate, deep red, discoloring to ochraceous-brown, and bruising blue when cut. The tubes are yellow, becoming greenish, 4.0-14 mm deep, and slightly depressed around the stipe. The stipe is 2.8-6.4 x 0.5-1.2 cm, yellow above, ochraceous-brown below, and with scant longitudinal fibrils.

- The spores are olive-brown in deposit, narrowly elliptic, 11.0-14.0 x 4.0-6.0 µm, thin-walled and smooth.

- This species is frequent on lawns and open woods beneath oak trees. It appears scattered, or in clusters during the summer rainy season. *Boletus rubricitrinus* is similar but has a larger pileus which bears brownish blotches.

---

231   *Boletus fumosiceps* (Murr.) Murr.

(?edibility)

- The pileus is 8.0-13.0 cm in diameter, convex but becoming plane, smooth or finely tomentose in places, and buffy-brown to smoky-brown. The tubes are whitish, becoming gray-brown to yellowish-brown, with pores of a similar color, and depressed around the stipe. The stipe is 3.0-6.0 x 2.5-4.0 cm, tapering downward, and with straw-colored reticulations all over.

- The spores are olive-brown in deposit, ellipsoid-fusoid, 11.0-12.5 x 3.2-4.0 µm, with a smooth, thin wall.

- This species is often found in sandy soils beneath evergreen oaks; mostly laurel oaks around north Florida. It is similar to *Boletus griseus* Frost, but differs in having fine reticulations on the stipe, a tapering stipe, and more narrow spores.

---

232   *Boletus granulosiceps* Sing.

(edible)

- The pileus is 3.0-7.5 cm in diameter, convex to plane and finally depressed in the center, dull brown to grayish-brown, and with finely appressed fibrils. The tubes are lemon to golden yellow, and turn blue on bruising. The stipe is 3.0-5.0 x 0.6-0.8 cm, pallid to yellow with brownish ribs or fibrils.

- The spores are olive-brown in deposit, ellipsoid-fusoid, 8.8-13.0 x 4.5-5.5 µm, with a thin, smooth wall.

- Prior to this study, this species had been found only in hammock areas of south Florida. It has since been found in Alachua County

Fig.231. *Boletus fumosiceps* (× 0.4)

Fig. 232. *Boletus granulosiceps* (× 0.7)

in low mesic hammock areas. It is somewhat similar to *B. subsolitarius,* but is slightly larger, darker in color, and with darker granules or fibrils on the stipe.

Boletus hypocaricinus Sing.　　　　　**233**

(?edibility)

■ The pileus is 8.0-8.5 cm in diameter, broadly convex to pulvinate, dark umber with cinnamon-brown margins, and distinctly tomentose. The tubes are yellow, with minute, reddish-brown mouths, and readily turn blue on bruising. The stipe is bulbous, 8.0-8.5 x

Fig. 233. *Boletus hypocaricinus* (x 0.5)   (Sherri Angels)

4.5-5.2 cm, apex yellowish but entirely red towards the base, with slightly raised areas but not reticulate.

- The spores are olive-brown in deposit, narrowly ellipsoid, 8.5-11.5 x 3.5-3.8 µm, with a thin, smooth wall.

- This species has been found only under live oaks, *Quercus virginiana*, in the Gainesville area.

---

234   *Boletus luridellus* (Murr.) Murr.

(?edibility)

- The pileus is 4.0-12.0 cm in diameter, convex to plane, amber to darker brown, becoming ochraceous with age, with tissues quickly turning blue on bruising. The tubes are adnate or depressed around the stipe, 1.0 cm deep, lemon-yellow, becoming greenish with age, mouth of tubes yellow to very pale yellowish-green. The stipe is 4.5-9.5 x 1.0-3.0 cm, apically lemon-yellow and faintly reticulate but becoming dull brown below.

- The spores are olive-brown in deposit, fusoid, 12.5-17.3 x 4.5-5.5 µm, with smooth, thin walls.

- This species is found on open, shaded lawns or in sparcely wooded areas of mesic hammocks. It is usually associated with various oaks and pines in both north and south Florida. Most of the collections were first described as *B. subsensibilis,* which was placed in synonymy by Singer (1947). Singer also considered this species closely related to *B. rubricitrinus* and was tempted to place it there.

Fig. 234. *Boletus luridellus* (x 0.3)   (Robert Williams)

Boletus luridiceps (Murr.) Murr.   **235**

(?edibility)

- The pileus is 7.0-11.0 cm in diameter, broadly convex to plane, subtomentose, dull brown to cinnamon-brown, with even margins. The tubes are adnate, slightly depressed near the stipe, 1.0 cm deep, bay to dull-brown, becoming blue on bruising. The stipe is swollen, tapering downwards, 7.0-8.0 x 2.5-3.5 cm, lemon-yellow, becoming dull brown with reddish blotches.

Fig. 235. *Boletus luridiceps* (x 0.3)

- The spores are olive-brown in deposit, narrowly ellipsoid, 10.0-11.0 x 3.0-3.2 µm, with a smooth thin wall.

- This species has been found only under laurel oaks in the Gainesville area. Murrill (1945) compared it with *B. subvelutipes*, which is pale yellow to orange-brown having deep red tubes and larger spores.

236   *Boletus oliveisporus* (Murr.) Murr.

(?edibility)

- The pileus is 6.0-15.0 cm in diameter, convex becoming plane, dark fulvous with a bay tint, with an initially smooth surface that often becomes blotched and somewhat areolate. The tubes are yellowish with a faint olive-green tint, and turn blue when bruised. The stipe is 4.0-8.5 x 0.1-0.5 cm, apex more or less yellow and smooth, reddish in the midsection with floccules, and reddish brown at the base.

- The spores are olive-brown in deposit, fusoid and narrowly cylindric, 11.0-15.0 x 4.0-4.8 µm, with a smooth, thin wall.

- This species was initially found on pine stumps surrounded by pines and scrub oaks (*Quercus minima*). It is similar to *B. luridellus* but does not have the coloration and zone of reticulations on the stipe.

Fig. 236. *Boletus oliveisporus* (x 0.5)

Boletus pulverulentus Opat. 237

(?edibility)

- The pileus is 4.0-8.5 cm in diameter, tomentose, cushion-shaped to plane, becoming dark brown to copper-brown. The tubes are initially yellowish-brown, bluing slowly when bruised, and turning darker. The stipe is 4.0-5.0 x 0.6-1.5 cm, bright yellow at the apex, creamy below, floccose and becoming reddish when handled.

- The spores are olive in deposit, fusoid, 11.0-14.7 x 4.0-6.0 μm, with a smooth, thin wall.

- This species is found in high and mesic hammocks in northern Florida. It is common in open areas around laurel oaks and other evergreen oaks. It is easily recognized by its copper-brown pileus and tubes that turn dull blue and darken with age.

Fig. 237. *Boletus pulverulentus* (x 0.5)

Boletus purpurellus Murr. 238

(?edibility)

- The pileus is 6.0-7.0 cm in diameter, convex to cushion-shaped, purple-red, smooth, quickly turning blue when cut. The tubes are lemon to mustard-yellow, 0.7 cm deep, and slightly depressed around the stipe. The stipe is yellow above with longitudinal streaks, becoming purple-red and scurfy below.

Boletales

Fig. 238. *Boletus purpurellus* (x 0.6)

- The spores are olive-brown in deposit, fusoid, 12.0-15.0 x 5.0-6.0 µm, with smooth, thin walls.

- This species has been found consistently associated with laurel oaks on the campus of the University of Florida and on a number of lawns throughout the area. It is somewhat like *Boletus rubricitrinus*, but is much smaller and has a definite deep purple-red as opposed to a reddish-brown color. The spores of *B. rubricitrinus* are also somewhat smaller.

---

239   *Boletus rubellus* var. *fraternus* (Pk.) Sing.

(?edibility)

- The pileus is 1.3-4.7 cm in diameter, convex to pulvinate, smooth, deep red to brick-red, sometimes fading to pinkish-red or yellowish at the margins. The tubes are initially "pinard yellow," becoming yellowish-green with age, adnate and depressed around the stipe, bluing readily when bruised. The stipe is 3.0-7.0 x 0.2-1.1 cm, initially yellowish towards the apex; becoming deep red around the base.

- The spores are olive-brown in deposit, fusoid, 10.0-14.5 x 4.0-5.5 µm, with smooth, thin walls.

- This species is found on lawns, around flower beds, and on moist embankments in wooded areas. On lawns it appears to be associ-

ated with evergreen oaks. It is a beautiful little bolete, representing one of the smallest of the red-capped species found in this area. It is near *B. purpurellus* but has a smaller stipe and pileus, less of a scurfy stipe, and a lack of purple in the pileus cuticle.

Fig. 239. *Boletus rubellus* var. *fraternus* (x 0.5)

Boletus rubricitrinus (Murr.) Murr.   **240**

(?edibility)

■ The pileus is 4.0-15.0 cm in diameter, convex to pulvinate or plane, deep brownish-red, often with deep colors fading to brownish-olive and often becoming mottled with age, turning blue when bruised, dry with a very fine tomentum. The tubes and tube mouths are lemon to greenish-yellow, depressed around the stipe, and reaching 1.0 mm in diameter. The stipe is 4.0-15.0 x 1.5-3.7 cm, pale ochraceous with fine reddish longitudinal striations towards the base and deep burgundy scales below, and yellow, often with minor reticulations near the tubes.

■ The spores are olive-brown in deposit, ellipsoid to fusoid, 12.5-18.8 x 4.8-7.7 µm, with smooth, thin walls.

Fig. 240. *Boletus rubricitrinus* (x 0.3)

- This is another very common, large, red-capped bolete found beneath oaks and pines throughout Florida. *Boletus fairchildianus* was initially considered a variety of *B. rubricitrinus,* but the tube mouths of *B. fairchildianus* become red and the pileus color differs.

---

241   *Boletus underwoodii* Pk.

(?edibility)

- The pileus is 5.0-11.0 cm in diameter, convex, then expanding, jasper red to deep orange-red, dry but somewhat viscid when moist, with an areolate to folded surface. The tubes are initially sulphur-yellow, bluing when bruised, tube mouths red tinged early, becoming bright red with age. The stipe is 5.0-8.0 x 1.8-2.2 cm, yellowish at the apex but becoming bright red below with longitudinal rows of deeper red fibrils.

- The spores are olive-brown in deposit, ellipsoid to subfusoid, 11.5-13.5 x 3.5-4.2 µm, with thin, smooth walls.

- This species was first described as *Suillellus subluridus* Murr., later considered *Boletus miniatoolivaceous* var. *subluridus* Sing., and finally determined to be *B. underwoodii* Pk. It is found beneath evergreen oaks throughout north Florida. It closely resembles *Boletus floridanus* in which the pileus, tubes and stipe are also red.

Fig. 241. *Boletus underwoodii* (x 0.6)

Boletus floridanus, however, has very distinct reticulations on the stipe, a smooth, non areolate pileus, and larger spores.

Leccinum

The very roughened or scurfy stipes with tufts of hyphae, or small scales that darken with age set this genus apart from other boletes. The tube mouths are circular and range from yellow to yellow-brown. There are 30 species described worldwide, a number of these occur in Florida. Murrill described many of these species in the genus *Ceriomyces*.

A Key to Common Species of *Leccinum*

1. Pileus and flesh white 2
1. Pileus and flesh yellow 4
    2. Pileus changing reddish-violet to gray
       .... *Leccinum chalybaeum* (p. 279)
    2. Pileus unchanged when cut 3
3. Pileus white to pallid, not areolate .... *Leccinum albellum* (p. 277)
3. Pileus rosy-buff, areolate .... *L.albellum f. reticulatum* (p. 278)
    4. Flesh yellow becoming pinkish-olivaceous; pileus
       yellowish-brown .... *Leccinum rugosiceps* (p. 280)
    4. Flesh yellow, unchanging when bruised 5
5. Pileus brown to ochre-brown; pores vivid yellow; stipe pallid with yellowish to brownish scales ... *Leccinum subglabripes* (p. 281)
5. Pileus chestnut brown with paler spots; pores whitish or whitish-yellow .... *Leccinum roseoscrabrum* (p. 280)

Leccinum albellum (Pk.) Singer   **242**

(edible)

■ The pileus is 2.0-5.2 cm in diameter, convex to plane, white to pale grayish-white, and smooth. The tubes are white to pale gray, depressed around the stipe, 5.0-8.0 mm deep, with round pores. The stipe is 4.0-9.0 x 0.5-1.2 cm, slightly tapering upwards, white to pale gray with darker squamules.

- The spores are olive-brown in deposit, narrowly ellipsoid, 12.5-23.0 x 4.2-5.8 µm, thin-walled and smooth.

- This species has been found from New York to Florida and west to Missouri. In Florida, it grows under various oaks. It is distinguished from other local species of *Leccinum* by its white color and slender, scabrose stipe.

Fig. 242. *Leccinum albellum* (x 1.0) (Terry Henkel)

---

243 *Leccinum albellum* f. *reticulatum* Murr.

(edible)

- The pileus is 2.0-5.0 cm in diameter, white to creamy-buff on the disc, with an areolate surface. The tubes are white to pale creamy-

Fig. 243. *Leccinum albellum* f. *reticulatum* (x 0.8)

white, 0.5-0.9 cm deep, depressed near the stipe. The stipe is more or less cylindric, 4.0-8.0 x 0.9-1.4 cm, with creamy-gray scales.

- The spores are olive-brown in deposit, narrowly ellipsoid, 12.5-23.0 x 4.2-5.8 µm, thin-walled and smooth.

- This form of *L. albellum* is also found beneath oaks in mesic hammock areas in northern Florida.

Fig. 244. *Leccinium chalybaeum* (x 0.4)   (Robert Williams)

Leccinum chalybaeum Sing.   **244**

(edible)

- The pileus is 4.5-8.5 cm in diameter, broadly convex to plane, pinkish buff to sordid-cinnamon, viscid when wet, and bruising reddish-violet to grayish-purple to black. The pores are intially whitish, later becoming beige. The stipe is 4.0-6.5 x 1.3-2.1 cm, initially a dingy white, later with brownish scales that turn black.

- The spores are mellous-brownish in deposit, fusoid, 16.3-17.7 x 5.5-6.2 µm, thin-walled and smooth.

- This species is distributed throughout north Florida and is found growing beneath evergreen oaks. It is distinguished from other species by its white tissues that turn reddish-violet to gray when bruised or cut.

Leccinum roseoscabrum Singer & Williams

(?edibility)

■ The pileus is 6.0-6.3 cm in diameter, convex, brown to chestnut brown, and often with paler spots. The pores are whitish to yellowish-white, and slightly depressed around the stipe. The stipe is 6.2-9.0 x 1.2-3.2 cm, tapering upwards and curved at the base, and scabrous on whitish to yellowish ground tissue.

■ The spores are brown in deposit, fusoid, 13.5-17.0 x 3.5-5.7 μm, smooth and thin-walled.

■ This species appears to be ectomycorrhizal with live oaks, and has been found thus far only in south Florida.

Fig. 245. *Leccinum roseoscabrum* (x 0.5)   (Robert Williams)

246   *Leccinum rugosiceps* (Pk.) Singer

(edible)

■ The pileus is 6.2-15.0 cm in diameter, convex to broadly convex, mustard-yellow but ochraceous-brown towards the disc, smooth and becoming wrinkled to areolate. The tubes are pale greenish-

Fig. 246. *Leccinium rugosiceps* (x 0.4)

yellow, depressed around the stipe, with tube mouths similar in color. The stipe is 6.0-9.0 x 1.4-3.0 cm, inflated in the middle, and light mustard-yellow.

■ The spores are olive-brown in deposit, ellipsoid-fusoid, 14.0-17.0 x 4.8-5.2 μm, with a thin smooth wall.

■ This species is easily recognized by its mustard-yellow color and wrinkled to areolate pileus. It is frequently found in mixed forests and beneath oaks in shaded lawns in northern Florida.

Leccinum subglabripes (Pk.) Sing.   **247**

(edible)

■ The pileus is 4.0-10.0 cm in diameter, convex, reddish, becoming ochraceous to chestnut-brown, with a dry, and smooth surface. The tubes are bright golden-yellow, depressed around the stipe, up to 1.0 cm deep, small and circular. The stipe is 8.0-9.5 x 0.8-1.4 cm, pale mustard-yellow with strong pompeian-red to brick-red spots or squamules.

- The spores are buffy-olive in deposit, fusoid to ellipsoid, 13.0-18.5 x 5.0-6.0 µm, with thin, smooth walls.

- This species is found associated with oaks in mesic hammocks around northern Florida. Both (1993) describes at least two other varieties that occur in Florida.

Fig. 247. *Leccinum subglabripes* (x 0.5)

Suillus

The pileus of most species of this genus is viscid to slimy, and many have a pellicular (slimy) veil that will form an evanescent annulus. In others, the pileus is dry but the pores are elongate and radially arranged. All have a yellow-brown to olive-brown spore deposit. A number of species are common in Florida, most appear to be mycorrhizal on pines.

A Key to Common Species of *Suillus*

1. Pellicular veil forming a mucilaginous annulus, pileus ochre to cinnamon-buff .... *Suillus cothurnatus* var. *cothurnatus* (p. 283)

1. Pellicular veil lacking, no annulus present 2

    2. Pileus cinnamon to pinkish gray, without darker squamules .... *Suillus granulatus* (p. 285)

    2. Pileus yellow, covered with darker appressed squamules .... *Suillus hirtellus* ssp. *thermophilus* (p. 285)

(edible)

The pileus is 1.5-6.5 cm in diameter, initially subconic to convex, becoming slightly umbonate and plane, dingy brown, becoming orange to dark yellow-brown, viscid and smooth with a mucilaginous marginal pellicular veil. The tubes are similar in color to the pileus, becoming honey yellow, adnate, 7.0-8.0 mm deep and somewhat oblong. The stipe is 2.5-7.0 x 0.4-0.7 cm, cylindric, initially whitish, becoming yellowish with orange tints, and darker glandular dots, and a mucilaginous annulus.

The spores are yellowish in deposit, ellipsoid 7.5-9.8 x 2.7-3.5 µm, with thin smooth walls.

The accompanying illustration is of the winter variety and differs from the summer variety, *S. cothurnatus* var. *cothurnatus*, in being darker and more olivaceous-brown.

Boletales

Fig. 248. *Suillus corthunatus* var. *corthunatus* (x 1.0)   (Robert Williams)

Fig. 249. *Suillus granulatus* (x 0.4)

Fig. 250. *Suillus hirtellus* var. *thermophilus* (x 0.9)   (Robert Williams)

Suillus granulatus (Fr.) Kuntze **249**

(edible)

■ The pileus is 5.0-15.0 cm in diameter, broadly convex, slimy when wet, smooth, buff to pale cinnamon-brown. The circular tubes are adnate, pale yellow with cream to pale yellow mouths, and approximately 1.0 cm deep. The stipe is 4.0-8.0 x 1.0-2.5 cm, whitish, becoming yellow above and dingy cinnamon-brown below, covered with brownish dots.

■ The spores are dingy-cinnamon in deposit, ellipsoid, 7.0-10.0 x 2.5-3.5 µm, somewhat inequilateral in profile.

■ This species grows scattered or in clusters beneath pines, and is common during the summer rainy season in Florida.

Suillus hirtellus ssp. thermophilus Singer **250**

(edible)

■ The pileus is 5.0-6.0 cm in diameter, convex to plane with a slight umbo, cinnamon becoming maize to sulphur-yellow, subviscid, and minutely hirsute. The tubes are 5.0-8.0 mm deep, depressed around the stipe, deep colonial-buff to olive-ochre, becoming dark olive-buff or maize yellow at their mouths. The stipe is 5.0-6.0 x 0.6-0.9 cm, cylindric with a root-like base, maize to mustard-yellow with numerous cinnamon-brown glandular dots.

■ The spores are deep olivaceous in deposit, ellipsoid to fusoid, 7.5-10.2 x 3.0-3.2 µm, thin-walled and smooth.

■ This subspecies is found in mixed oak-pine forest in hammocks under *Pinus palustris*. It appears to be endemic to the lower southeastern United States. It is recognized in the field by its bright maize-colored pileus with deep red tints.

The Xerocomaceae

The Xerocomaceae are small to medium-sized boletes with a slender, smooth stipe, a hymenial area of either yellowish tubes or lamellae, spores that are smooth or ribbed and are olive-brown in deposit. Seven genera have been placed in this family at one time or another. Species of three, *Boletellus, Phylloporus,* and *Xerocomus*, are common in Florida.

A Key to Common Florida Xerocomaceae
1. Hymenial area gilled ....***Phylloporus*** (p. 289)
1. Hymenial area tubular...2
   2. Basidiomata medium to large, shaggy to squamulose; spores with longitudinal striations ....***Boletellus*** (p. 286)
   2. Basidiomata small to medium, tomentose; spores fusoid, without striations ....***Xerocomus*** (p. 292)

Boletellus
Species of *Boletellus* are medium to large boletes in which the pileus is covered either with low matted fibril or fibrils that form large wooly scales. They have tubes that are initially yellow, but soon become honey-yellow to olivaceous. The spores are sometimes smooth or mostly with longitudinal ribs. The spore print is deep olivaceous-brown to blackish. Because of their ornamented spores and deep olive-brown to blackish spore print, Singer (1945) placed these species in the Strobilomycetaceae. Pegler and Young (1981), however, placed the genus in the Xerocomaceae based largely upon spore color and morphology. The current Dictrionary of the Fungi (Hawksworth *et al.,*1995) includes them among the genera of Xerocomaceae. There are 38 species, mostly tropical and subtropical, six of which are reported from Florida. Two are included here.

A Key to Common Florida Species of *Boletellus*.
1. Stipe not strongly reticulate to lacerate ... *Boletellus ananas* (p. 286)
1. Stipe strongly reticulate to lacerate .... *Boletellus russellii* (p. 288)

---

251   *Boletellus ananas* (Curtis) Murr.

(edible)

■ The pileus is 4.5-9.5 cm in diameter, convex, strongly reddish or yellowish-red, fibrillose with fibrils forming large wooly scales,

Fig. 251. *Boletellus ananas* (x 0.7)   (Robert Williams)

becoming purplish-brown, and strongly bluing when bruised. The tubes are large, irregular, yellowish, becoming reddish-brown, depressed around the stipe, and with a yellow-brown pore surface. The stipe is 6.0-14.0 x 0.5-1.5 cm, tapering upwards, smooth, whitish above, becoming faintly buff below and reddish-buff around the slightly swollen base.

■ The spores are black in deposit, broadly ellipsoid, 13.8-25.5 x 7.0-11.0 μm, with strongly projecting longitudinal wing-like ridges that sometimes interconnect, and with an indistinct germ pore.

■ This species has been found in all types of forests throughout the southeastern U.S., but in north Florida it appears most common among pines. The tufts of pinkish, pyramidal scales on the pileus are reminiscent of the brownish tufts found in *Strobilomyces*, making this bolete an easy one to spot in the field.

Fig. 252. *Boletellus russellii* (x 0.4)   (Sherri Angels)

---

252   *Boletellus russellii* (Frost) **Gilbert**

(?edibility)

■ The pileus is 3.5-10.0 cm in diameter, convex to broadly convex, brown to reddish-brown, strongly tomentose, becoming cracked and fibrillar. The tubes are small, pale mustard-yellow, with tube mouths taking on a pinkish tint, becoming depressed around the stipe. The stipe is slender 6.0-8.0 x 1.4-2.0 cm, dull reddish-brown with deep lacerations or interconnected ribs that are buff-pink above and more reddish below.

■ The spores are dark olive in deposit, broadly ellipsoid, 16.0-19.5 x 8.0-11.0 μm, with longitudinal wing-like ribs that do not interconnect.

■ This is the same bolete that Murrill (1909) called *Ceriomyces russellii,* and later accessioned in the Mycological Herbarium at the University of Florida as *Frostiella russellii.* Murrill never published *Frostiella,* but recognized that it differed from *Boletellus* in having olive rather than black spores and lacking a veil. In Florida it is found consistently associated with laurel oaks in various habitats mixed with sabal palms and other tree species.

Phylloporus

This is the only genus of Boletaceae that has lamellae instead of tubes. They differ from other gilled mushrooms by the physical and chemical nature of the pileus cuticle and the configuration of the gill trama. There are ten species known worldwide, three of which occur in Florida.

A Key to Common Species of *Phylloporus* in Florida

1. Lamellae not bruising blue .... *Phylloporus boletinoides* (p. 289)

1 Lamellae turn blue when bruised 2

   2. Pileus maroon to hazel-brown .... *Phylloporus foliiporus* (p. 290)

   2. Pileus deep reddish-brown

            .... *Phylloporus rhodoxanthus* ssp. *americanus* (p. 291)

Phylloporus boletinoides Smith & Thiers   **253**

(edible)

■ The pileus is 2.0-7.5 cm in diameter, convex, becoming plane with incurved margins and somewhat depressed at the disc, buff, hazel-brown to vinaceous-brown, not turning blue when bruised. The lamellae are decurrent, broadly spaced, with transverse veins, and are pallid to olive-buff. The stipe is 3.0-5.5 x 0.5-1.0 cm, tapering downward, yellowish at the apex but darker cinnamon-brown towards the base.

■ The spores are yellow-to olive-brown in deposit, ellipsoid to subfusoid, 11.0-14.5 x 3.5-6.0 μm, smooth with thin walls.

■ This species is often found growing beneath pines in low hammock areas. It differs from other species of *Phylloporus* in not

Fig. 253. *Phylloporus boletinoides* (x 1.0)   (Robert Williams)

turning blue when bruised, by its olive-buff lamellae, and lamellae that are more contorted with connecting veins. While the pileus shape and color are somewhat similar to *Phylloporus foliiporus*, the lamellae of the latter are bright yellow and bruise intensely blue.

---

254   *Phylloporus foliiporus* (Murr.) Sing.

(edible)

■   The pileus is 2.0-14.5 cm in diameter, convex but becoming plane with incurved margins, reddish to dull brown, and darker olive-

Fig. 254. *Phylloporus foliiporus* (x 0.5)

brown with age. The lamellae are decurrent, broadly spaced with forks or connecting veins, whitish to yellowish and bruising intensely blue. The stipe is 1.7-5.0 x 0.5-2.0 cm, tapering downward, dull cinnamon-brown above but darker below.

■ The spores are reddish-brown in deposit, subfusoid to ellipsoid, 11.0-15.0 x 4.5-6.0 μm, with thin, smooth walls.

■ This species has been associated with both pine and oak species around north Florida. It is a bolete found during both summer and winter rainy seasons. As noted in comments above, it closely resembles *P. boletinioides* in the field but, in addition to having lamellae that blue intensely, it is usually a slightly larger bolete that is darker in color, has a more yellowish hymenium, and a darker colored stipe.

Phylloporus rhodoxanthus ssp. *americanus* Sing. **255**

(edible)

■ The pileus is 2.5-7.5 cm in diameter, convex, becoming plane with an incurved margin, reddish-brown, and sometimes becoming areolate. The lamellae are decurrent, widely separated, with receded crossveins, bright yellow, and bruising blue. The stipe is 4.0-8.0 x 0.5-1.0 cm, tapering downward, reddish to rusty-yellow, and somewhat darker towards the base.

Fig. 255. *Phylloporus rhodoxanthus* ssp. *americanus* (× 1.0)　　　　(Henry Aldrich)

- The spores are yellowish to olive green in deposit, narrowly ellipsoid, 11.0-13.5 x 4.0-4.8 µm, with thin, smooth walls.

- This species is widely scattered throughout North America. It is highly variable with at least four subspecies recognized at one time or another (Singer, 1945). Of the other common species of *Phylloporus* in Florida, this species is recognized by a distinct reddish pileus and more yellowish stipe.

Xerocomus

Species of *Xerocomus* are rather small boletes with a hymenial configuration of wide, angular pores, somewhat intermediate to *Phylloporus* and *Boletinus*, a more or less tomentose pileus, and a thin stipe that is usually smooth or rarely scabrous. The spores are variable in size, subcylindrical to fusoid, and always with an olivaceous-brown deposit. There are 40 species described worldwide, seven occurring in Florida, but only one of them, *Xerocomus hypoxanthus*, is very common in the area.

Xerocomus hypoxanthus Sing.   **256**

(?edibility)

■ The pileus is 11.0-14.0 cm in diameter, convex, becoming plane, pale reddish-brown, tomentose, and tissues turn blue slightly when bruised. The tubes are bright yellow, slightly depressed around the stipe, and with somewhat elongate tube pores. The stipe is 2.0-3.0 x 0.2-0.4 cm, yellow with minor brownish scurfiness.

Fig. 256. *Xerocomus hypoxanthus* (x 0.8)   (Robert Williams)

- The spores are brownish-olive in deposit, subfusoid, 11.0-14.0 x 4.0-5.2 µm, with a smooth, thin wall.

- This species is found predominantly in mesic hammocks, growing on old palm trunks and on humus and plant debris. It is similar to *Xerocomus illudens* but does not have the course network of ridges on the stipe.

The Strobilomycetaceae

The Strobilomycetaceae has been in a state of taxonomic flux in recent years, with as few as one and as many as eleven genera placed within it. Genera such as *Boletellus* and *Phylloboletellus* have recently been transferred to the Xerocomaceae and members of the Boletaceae, such as *Tylopilus*, are now included in the Strobilomycetaceae. It is a highly variable family with considerable variation in the pileus, tubes, stipes, and spores. The most characteristic feature of the family include vinaceous, purple-brown to black spore deposits, with smooth to ornamented spores that have exosporal folds, ridges, or reticulations. Species of *Austroboletus*, *Strobilomyces* and *Tylopilus* will be considered here.

A Key to Common Florida Strobilomyceteacae

1. Spore deposit a dark reddish brown; spores wrinkled with small indentations .... *Austroboletus* (p. 294)
1. Not as above 2
   2. Spore deposit brownish-black to black; spores subglobose to ellipsoid, and ornamented; pileus shaggy
      .... *Strobilomyces* (p. 296)
   2. Spore deposit pinkish, violaceous to hazel-brown or cinnamon; spores thin-walled and smooth .... *Tylopilus* (p. 298)

Austroboletus

Species of *Austroboletus* look similar to certain species of *Tylopilus* in the field. They differ, however, in having a much darker spore print, and the spores are pitted when examined under the microscope. There are 13 species known worldwide; only a couple occur in Florida. One of these will be treated below.

(?edibility)

- The pileus is 4.5-10.0 cm in diameter, convex, whitish to yellow-buff, and areolate with age. The tubes are pinkish at maturity and the tissue is bitter to the taste. The stipe is 4.5-14.5 x 0.7-3.0 cm, light yellow and with deep lacerations.

- The spores are cinnamon to olive-brown in deposit, fusoid, 14.5-18.0 x 6.5-8.3 µm, with a wrinkled wall that appears pitted.

- This species has at one time or another been placed in *Boletus*, *Boletellus*, *Tylopilus*, or *Porphyrellus*. It is distinguished from other whitish to pinkish boletes by the deeply-lacerated stipe and pitted spores. It has been associated with both pine and oak species in various parts of Florida.

Boletales

Fig. 257. *Astroboletus subflavidus* (x 0.8)   (Robert Williams)

Strobilomyces

Species of *Strobilomyces* are distinguished in the field by their brown-ish to black basidiomata, in which the pileus is covered with dark, pyramid-like clusters of tufted fibrils. The tube area is initially flesh-colored, becoming grayish-brown and the stipe is normally fibrillous to scaly. The spore deposit is brownish-black to black, and the spores are globoid to broadly ellipsoid and ornamented or reticulated. There are nine species known worldwide, three of them reported from Florida. Two of these will be considered below.

A Key to Common Species of *Strobilomyces* in Florida

1. Pileus covered with rigid spines or pyramids; spores with
    short ridges or isolated warts .... *Strobilomyces confusus* (p. 297)

1. Pileus with wooly scales that have a broad base, spores with
    a reticulate surface .... *Strobilomyces floccopus* (p. 297)

Fig. 258. *Strobilomyces confusus* (× 0.7)

Strobilomyces confusus Sing.   **258**

(edible)

- The pileus is 3.0-8.5 cm in diameter, initially convex, becoming plane, brownish-black with thin, rigid blackish spines. The tubes are whitish-gray, becoming blackish with aging spores, slightly depressed around the stipe, becoming cinnamon-brown where touched. The stipe is 4.2-7.8 x 1.0-2.0 cm, brownish gray, reticulate above, and shaggy to wooly below.

- The spores are black in deposit, globose to subglobose, 10.5-12.5 x 9.7-10.2 µm, with short, brown ridges or warts.

- This species has been found only in eastern North America, extending from Massachusetts to Florida. It occurs on shaded lawns and in various forests of north Florida, and is common under both pines and oaks. It is less common than *S. floccopus*, a species that occurs in similar habitats.

Strobilomyces floccopus (Vahl: Fr.) Karsten   **259**

(edible)

- The pileus is 4.0-12.0 cm in diameter, convex, becoming plane, dark brown to black, with large, appressed, pyramid-like scales, and tissues becoming brick-red when bruised. The tubes are whitish-gray, becoming black with age, often slightly depressed but becoming decurrent. The stipe is 6.5-13.5 x 0.8-2.5 cm, brownish-black, reticulate above but with floccose scales.

- The spores are black in deposit, ellipsoid, 11.0-15.3 x 8.5-12.0 µm, with a raised, snuff-brown reticulum.

- This species is worldwide in distribution. It has traditionally gone under the name *Strobilomyces strobilaceus* in North America. It is more frequently found under hardwood species in Florida, and is common in mesic hammocks throughout the area.

Boletales

Fig. 259. *Strobilomyces floccopus* (x 0.7)

Tylopilus

Species of *Tylopilus* are medium to large boletes with a flesh to buff or salmon-buff spore deposit and spores with a thin, smooth wall. They usually have a smooth to slightly tomentose pileus and stipe. The tissues do not turn blue when bruised, but will occasionally turn reddish-brown. In Florida, they appear to be ectomycorrhizal with both oak and pine species. Until recently, the genus was considered in the Boletaceae. There are 18 species recognized worldwide, 16 of which have been found in Florida. Nine are treated below.

A Key to Common species of *Tylopilus* in Florida
1. Pileus shaggy, fibrillose-squamulose, yellow to orange yellow
.... *Tylopilus conicus* (p. 300)

1. Pileus not shaggy, fibrillose 2

    2. Stipe distinctly reticulate 3

Tylopilus alboater (Schw.) Murr.   **260**

(edible)

■ The pileus is 6.0-12.0 cm in diameter, blackish-brown to black with a grayish bloom, and faintly tomentose. The tubes become pinkish-gray then blackish with age, and are deeply depressed around the stipe. The stipe is 4.0-10 x 1.5-2.5 cm, gray to black, often with a whitish bloom, sometimes reticulate at the apex and velvety below.

Fig. 260. *Tylopilus alboater* (x 0.5)

- The spores are a deep rosy-salmon in deposit, ellipsoid, 9.0-13.0 x 4.0-4.8 μm, with thin, smooth walls.

- This species is usually found beneath oak trees in open forests or on shaded lawns. It is easily distinguished from other *Tylopilus* in Florida by its black pileus and stipe.

---

261   *Tylopilus conicus* (Rav.: B. & C.) Beards.

(?edibility)

- The pileus is 2.5-9.5 cm in diameter, conical to convex, bright yellow to pallid pink, with shaggy, fibrillar scales on the cuticle. The tubes are grayish to vinaceous fawn, de-pressed around the stipe, and with tube mouths of similar color. The stipe is more or less cylindric, 4.0-7.0 x 0.6-1.8 cm, whitish at the base and pinkish-cinnamon above.

- The spores are pale reddish-brown in deposit, fusoid, 14.2-17.7 x 4.0-6.0 μm with thin, smooth walls.

- This species is common in pine flatwoods and cut-over forests of northern Florida. It is distinguished from other species of *Tylopilus* by its shaggy, yellow pileus.

Fig. 261. *Tylopilus conicus* (x 0.7)

(Robert Williams)

Fig. 262. *Tylopilus felleus* (x 0.5)

Tylopilus felleus (Bull.: Fr.) Karst.   **262**

(?edibility)

■ The pileus is 4.5-12.0 cm in diameter, convex to plane, cinnamon brown, slightly darker on the disc, and becoming areolate with age. The pores are initially white and become white to pinkish. The stipe is 4.5-8.0 x 1.5-3.0 cm, dull to olivaceous-brown, with a darker reticulation.

■ The spores are fawn to reddish-brown in deposit, fusoid, 10.0-15.0 x 4.2-4.5 μm, smooth, and with a thin wall

■ While many agaricologists do not report this species from Florida, Murrill (1948) stated that it occurs in northern and central parts of the state. It occurs in conifer and mixed forests.

Fig. 263. *Tylopilus ferrugineus* (x 0.6)

---

263   *Tylopilus ferrugineus* (Frost) Sing.

(?edibility)

■ The pileus is 4.0-10.0 cm in diameter, convex to plane, reddish brown to chocolate-brown, minutely velvety, contex white, becoming pinkish when bruised. The tubes are white, becoming pinkish, depressed around the stipe, with small, angular pores. The stipe is 3.5-7.5 x 1.5-2.0 cm, cylindric to slightly swollen, reddish to chocolate-brown, sometimes violaceous, smooth except towards the apex where it may become slightly fibrillose.

■ The spores are hazel to reddish-brown in deposit, broadly ellipsoid, 8.3-13.0 x 3.5-5.0 µm, with a smooth, thin wall.

■ This is a common bolete in northern Florida, and is usually found in abundance beneath laurel and water oaks during the summer rainy season. It is easily recognized by its chocolate-brown pileus and milk white tubes that bruise pink when handled.

(inedible)

- The pileus is 4.5-13.0 cm in diameter, broadly convex to plain, initially white, becoming yellowish to pale brownish-yellow, or staining pinkish when bruised, and bitter to the taste. The tubes are white to pinkish white, becoming salmon-pink when bruised, and somewhat depressed around the stipe. The stipe is 4.5-11.0 x 1.3-4.0 cm, white but becoming brownish-yellow with age, and sometimes tapering upwards.

- The spores are creamy-buff in deposit, ellipsoid to fusoid, 7.5-9.5 x 2.3-3.5 µm, with thin, smooth walls.

- This is one of the few whitish to pinkish species of *Tylopilus* in Florida. It is somewhat similar to *T. rhoadsiae* which has a brownish pileus, reticulated stipe, and larger spores. It is found frequently associated with laurel and water oaks on shaded lawns, or at the edge of mixed forests.

Boletales

Fig. 264. *Tylopilus peralbidus* (x 0.5)

Fig. 265. *Tylopilus plumbeoviolaceus* (x 0.5)

---

265   *Tylopilus plumbeoviolaceus* (Snell & Dick) Sing.

(inedible)

■ The pileus is 6.5-15.0 cm in diameter, broadly convex to plane, initially purple-lilac, becoming gray to gray-brown, smooth, and with a bitter taste. The tubes are creamy to purplish-brown, with pinkish-tan pores, and depressed around the stipe. The stipe 4.0-9.0 x 3.2-5.6 cm, smooth, but marbled or striped with lilac-purple areas.

■ The spores are lilac-buff in deposit, fusoid to cylindric, 9.5-14.0 x 3.0-3.8 μm, with thin, smooth walls.

■ There are two species of *Tylopilus* in Florida that are dark purple-brown to purplish-black, *T. alboater* and *T. plumbeoviolaceous*. The pileus in *T. alboater* is tomentose, distinctly darker in color, without a violaceous tint, and the stipe is not marbled as in *T. plumbeoviolaceous*. It is common under evergreen oaks on shaded lawns and open forests of north Florida.

---

266   *Tylopilus rhoadsiae* (Murr.) Murr.

(inedible)

■ The pileus is 6.0-9.0 cm in diameter, broadly convex to plane, white with pale brown to ochraceous-brown areas towards the

Fig. 266. *Tylopilus rhoadsiae* (x 1.2)   (Robert Williams)

margin, and with a bitter taste. The tubes are whitish, becoming pinkish, deeply depressed near the stipe, with pore mouths of similar color. The stipe is 5.5-9.5 x 1.7-2.7 cm, cylindric, white with brownish reticulations.

■ The spores are honey-yellow in deposit, fusoid, 11.0-13.7 x 3.7-4.5 µm, with thin, smooth walls.

■ This species is found around pines or along the edge of open mixed forests and lake shores in northern Florida. It is recognized from other species of *Tylopilus* in the area by its white, slender, and deeply lacerate/reticulate stipe.

Tylopilus tabacinus (Snell) var. *tabacinus* Sing.   **267**

(edible)

■ The pileus is 4.5-17.5 cm in diameter, broadly convex to plane, tobacco brown, finely tomentose, becoming slate-violet to brownish with age. It has an unpleasant, fishy odor. The tubes are initially whitish, becoming pale tobacco brown, with mouths of

Fig. 267. *Tylopilus tabacinus* var. *tabacinus* (x 0.5)   (Robert Williams)

similar color. The stipe is bulbous below, 4.0-16.0 x 2.5-6.0 cm, with a strong wide mesh, hazel-brown reticulum above that becomes less distinct below.

■ The spores are fawn to wood-brown in deposit, fusoid to narowly ellipsoid, 11.8-14.5 x 4.2-4.5 µm, with smooth, thin walls.

■ This species is common under evergreen oaks on shaded lawns or in open woods. While some have confused it with *T. ferrugineus*, the pileus color is a lighter tobacco brown, the tubes become a pale tobacco brown, and it has a fishy odor.

---

268   *Tylopilus tabacinus* var. *amarus* Sing.

(edible)

■ The pileus is 4.0-7.0 cm in diameter, broadly convex to plane, pinkish to pale brown, with a distinct bitter taste. The tubes are whitish to pale grayish-buff, turning brownish when bruised, and depressed around the stipe. The stipe is 4.0-7.0 x 2.2-3.5 cm, basically cylindric, with a pinkish-buff ground color, and the surface bearing a brownish to pinkish-buff reticulum.

- The spores are hazel to fawn brown in deposit, subfusoid, 11.8-14.5 x 4.0-5.0 µm, with thin, smooth walls.

- While Singer (1947) and Both (1993) report it growing in the same habitat as the typical variety of *T. tabacinus*, i.e., high hammocks and shady lawns, I find it is common beneath live oaks near rivers and lakes in north and central Florida.

Fig. 268. *Tylopilus tabacinus* var. *amarus* (x 1.0)

Cooking with Mushrooms

As noted in the preface, most native "Southerners" have had a great aversion to mushrooms over the years. They look upon mushrooms as being those fleshy fungi bought fresh or in cans in the supermarket. All other mushrooms found in the lawns, fields, and forests are toadstools; and we know from legends, of course, all toadstools are poisonous. There is a growing number of individuals, however, who have learned that most of the wild toadstools are in fact edible, and many of them are preferable to the common button mushrooms found in the markets. Aside from their taste, aroma, and texture, wild mushrooms have nutritional qualities that are appealing to the health conscious. The protein content of mushrooms fall between that of animal and vegetable sources. All essential amino acids are present in mushrooms, as well as many non-essential amino acids. Mushrooms are low in fat, but all classes of lipids are represented. One pound of fresh mushrooms provides approximately 140 calories. Water-soluble vitamins are generally well represented in mushrooms, and all essential minerals, except iron, are present in mushrooms. More and more exotic mushrooms are being cultivated and are now available in farmer's markets and grocery stores. There is a growing interest in using exotic species and in collecting edible mushrooms in the field. Chefs have found that many of the wild mushrooms impart distinct flavors to their meals and often "spice up" the appearance of various dishes.

There are many mushroom cookbooks available in most bookstores, and our newspapers and magazines often have attractive recipes on cooking with mushrooms. One of the better cookbooks is *Hope's Mushroom Cookbook,* which can be obtained from the author (Hope Miller, 209 Pine Drive, Blacksburg, VA 24060). She discusses the use of mushrooms as appetizers, in soups, salads, sauces, and in main dishes incorporating beef, pork, lamb, poultry, fish, cheeses and vegetables. She has granted permission for me to use many of these recipes below.

Since a large majority of mushroom recipes have focused on the use of the common button mushroom, *Agaricus* spp., I wish here to concentrate on favorite recipes for some of the wild mushrooms found in Florida. A word of caution, **amateurs should not attempt to consume wild mushrooms unless they have had their identity confirmed by a professional or someone with long experience.** To get confirmation of mushrooms collected from the field, dig mushrooms from the substrate and record features of the fresh specimens. Keep separate from others you intend to use for food. With those for cooking, one should remove the soiled bases of stipes before placing them in the collecting basket; or else all of your collection will become soiled. Examine the cut base of the stipe to determine if there are any insect pores. In Florida, there is a race to see who can consume mushrooms first; you, the insects, or the rodents. Determine if insects have invaded the upper stipe and pileus; if so, discard them.

Armillarias: Species of the honey agarics, *Armillaria* spp., are prized edibles used in a number of dishes. They are often somewhat more fibrous than other mushrooms and require longer cooking times. They are especially good in the following recipe:

Mushroom Loaf

2 lbs of *Armillaria mellea* or *A. tabescens*
1 large onion, thinly sliced
2 Tbl of butter
$1/_2$ cup of dry bread crumbs
2 eggs, lightly beaten
$1/_4$ lb butter or margarine, melted
$1/_2$ tsb of salt
dash of pepper

Sauté half of the onion in 2 tablespoons of butter until golden brown. Save several large mushroom caps for garnish. Chop remaining mushrooms, including stipes and remaining onion; mix with bread crumbs, salt, pepper, and remaining butter. Stir in eggs and sautéed onions. Press entire mixture in a well-greased loaf pan. Arrange mushroom caps on top and press slightly. Bake for 1 hour at 350° F. Let stand several minutes; slice and serve with mushroom gravy.

Boletes: There are nearly 20 genera and hundreds of poroid mushrooms referred to as "boletes ." Most boletes are highly prized edibles, and those that are toxic largely cause gasterointestinal irritation. Boletes with red tube mouths or stain blue when bruised should be avoided, since some species with these features are toxic. Many find boletes to be their favorite wild mushroom and many recipes call specifically for them.

Recipes

Boletes and Lemon Chicken Breasts

1 lb of chopped boletes
3 Tbl of butter or margarine
$1/2$ cup of chopped onions
2 whole chicken breasts, skinned, split and boned
2 Tbl flour
$2/3$ cups of dry white wine
$1/2$ cup of water
$1/4$ tsp of tarragon
$1/8$ tsp of pepper
$1/4$ cup of lemon juice

Sauté mushrooms in butter; add onion and cook until golden. Remove from pan and reserve. Flour chicken breasts and brown on both sides. Add rest of ingredients plus the mushrooms; simmer, covered, about 10 minutes or until chicken is done. Serve with rice and salad.

Bolete and Chicken Soup

6 cups of chicken stock
$1/2$ cup of celery, finely chopped
2 Tbl of minced onion
1 cup of sliced *Boletus edulis*
2 oz of egg noodles

Heat chicken stock; add celery and onion and simmer for 2 minutes. Add rest of the ingredients and cook until noodles are tender. (Yields 6 servings).

Cantharelles: Species of *Cantharellus* and *Craterellus* are highly prized for food worldwide. They have an excellent flavor and can be used in side dishes, sauces, and sautéed with meats and vegetables.

Mushroom Sauce

$3/4$ lb of cantharelles, chopped
3 Tbl of butter or margarine
3 Tbl of flour
1 tsp of salt
$1/4$ tsp of pepper
$1 1/2$ cups of half and half
$1/2$ Tbl each of lemon juice and sherry

Sauté mushrooms in butter or margarine for 5-6 min; stir in flour, salt and pepper. Slowly add half and half while cooking, stirring continually until thick and smooth. Add lemon juice and sherry. This sauce is especially good over rice, young irish potatoes, pasta or chow-mein noodles.

Chanterelle Biscuits

2 cups of flour
5 tsp of baking powder
4 Tbl shortening
$1/2$ tsp salt
$1/4$ cup each of milk and chopped onions
$1/2$ cup of Parmesan cheese and cooked chantarelles
$1/4$ cup of butter, melted

Mix flour, baking powder, and salt. Cut in shortening. Add onion, cheese, and mushrooms; knead lightly. Add milk and blend. Form a ball and knead lightly. Press out to a thickness of $1/4$ to $1/2$ inch and cut out with a biscuit cutter. Brush both sides with melted butter and bake in a hot oven (400° F) for 12-15 minutes or until golden brown.

Chicken and Chanterelles

2 chicken breasts, skinned, boned and cut into strips (save chicken bones)
2 each stipes of celery and carrots, sliced
3 cups of water
3 Tbl each of minced shallots and unsalted butter
1 lb of fresh chanterelles cut into bite-sized pieces
$1/4$ cup of dry vermouth
$1/3$ cup of heavy cream
parsley

Combine chicken bones, celery, carrots, and water; bring to a boil. Simmer mixture, skimming froth occasionally for one hour. Reduce chicken stock over high heat to about 1 cup; strain and reserve. Cook shallots in butter over moderate heat for 2 minutes or until softened. Add mushrooms and toss to coat with butter. Add reserved stock and cook until liquid is reduced by half. Add vermouth and reduce liquid to about 2 Tbl. Add cream, salt, and pepper; cook stirring until sauce is thickened. Stir in chicken and cook mixture until chicken is just cooked through. Transfer mixture to a heated serving dish and sprinkle with parsley.

Coprinus: The "inky cap" or "shaggy mane" mushrooms should not be eaten in combination with alcohol. If so, uncomfortable symptoms usually result (see Coprine toxin in the next section). Species of *Coprinus* have a delicate texture and are not desirable for a number of mushroom dishes. The following recipes call specifically for species of *Coprinus*.

Recipes

Cream of Shaggy Mane Soup

1 qt of fresh sliced *Coprinus comatus*
2 Tbl of butter or margarine
$1/_2$ cup each of flour and butter or margarine
2 qt of milk
$1/_2$ tsp each or salt and pepper
a pinch of cayenne pepper

Sauté mushrooms in butter in a non-stick frying pan until completely cooked. Reserve the liquid. Melt butter in a large sauce pan; stir in flour. When bubbly, add milk and stir continuously until thick. Add mushrooms, liquid, salt, pepper, and cayenne. Heat thoroughly. Serve hot with a dot of butter in the center. (Yields 4 servings).

Herbed Mushroom Paté

3 cups of chopped onion
4 Tbl of butter
1 lb of chopped *Coprinus comatus*
$1/_2$ tsp of salt
1 tsp of dry mustard
$1/_2$ tsp of dill weed
freshly ground pepper to taste
3 Tbl dry white wine
2 cups of cottage cheese
8 oz of softened cream cheese
paprika and parsley

Sauté onion in butter until soft; add mushrooms and spices. Stir and cook uncovered for 5 minutes. Add wine and cook for 5 minutes more; set aside. In a blender, purée cottage cheese until smooth. Pour into a large bowl. Cream the cream cheese until it is soft enough to blend well with the cottage cheese. Combine the two in a large bowl. Purée the mushroom mixture until very nearly smooth. Add to cheese mixture, stirring well. Place the mixture in buttered casseroles or in 2 loaf pans buttered and lined with buttered wax paper. It will be softer if cooked in a casserole. You can slice it if it is cooked in loaf pans. Cool in the pan and then remove and peel off paper. Chill, covered, before serving. Sprinkle with paprika and chopped fresh parsley. Serve with toast slices or crackers.

Lactarius: Several species of *Lactarius* are choice edible mushrooms. They have a distinct tastes, a nutty texture, and go especially well with vegetable dishes that call for almonds or other nuts.

Mushrooms with Cheese Sauce

5 large mushrooms
2 oz of olive oil
1 minced garlic clove
3 stipes of diced celery
1 each of carrot, onion, green pepper and red pepper, diced
6 diced ripe olives
$1/4$ cups each of Parmesan cheese and seasoned bread crumbs

Remove mushroom stipes and par-boil caps; set aside. Sauté diced vegetables in olive oil until onions are tender. Toss with cheese and bread crumbs. Stuff mushroom caps and place in a baking dish. Cover with cheese sauce and bake at 350° F for 10 minutes.

Cheese sauce:

1 cup of milk
2 oz of grated sharp cheese
1 oz each of butter and flour, browned together to form a roux
salt and pepper to taste

Heat milk and add cheese. Stir constantly until cheese melts. Mix roux into mixture and stir until sauce thickens.

Oyster mushrooms: A number of species of *Pleurotus* are edible and are preferred by many. They are a common item in the produce area of most supermarkets and at farmer's markets since they are actively cultivated by those growing exotics. Their shelf-life, however, is shorter than most cultivated mushrooms.

Pleurotus Chowder

$1/_2$ lb of *Pleurotus*, chopped
$1/_2$ cup of finely chopped onion
4 Tbl butter or margarine
1 cup raw potato cubes
salt and pepper to taste
dash each of mace, chives, Tabasco© sauce
$1/_4$ tsp of thyme
2 cups of milk
2 well beaten egg yolks
$1/_4$ cup of sherry
2 cups of sour cream
croutons and parsley

Sauté mushrooms and onions in butter until onions are translucent and mushrooms are tender. Add potato cubes and cook over low heat until potatoes are tender, approx. 12 to 15 minutes. Add seasoning; gradually stir in milk and bring to a boil. Remove from heat; gradually add rest of the ingredients, one at a time. Return to heat and bring to a boil. Serve at once with croutons and garnish with parsley. (Yeilds 4-5 servings).

Baked Clams with Mushroom Sauce

$1/_2$ cup each of chopped onion and oyster mushrooms
$3/_4$ cup of butter or margarine
3 cups of clams
$1/_4$ tsp of paprika
$1/_2$ tsp of salt
$1/_3$ cup of chopped parsley
1 $1/_2$ cup of medium white sauce
buttered bread crumbs

Sauté mushrooms and onion until onion is translucent. Add clams and cook for 5 minutes. Combine rest of ingredients and add to clam mixture. Pour into a greased casserole and cover with buttered bread crumbs. Bake at 450° F for 20 to 25 minutes. (Yields 6 servings).

Shiitake: While other species of *Lentinula* are edible, *L. edodes*, the popular shiitake mushroom, is well known worldwide. Its texture is firmer than most other edible mushrooms, and combined with its taste, shiitake is preferred for a number of mushroom dishes.

Shiitake Cream Sauce

4 to 6 oz of fresh shiitake
2 finely chopped shallots
1/4 lb of butter or margarine
1 minced garlic clove
8 to 12 oz of heavy cream

Remove and discard stipes from mushrooms. Chop mushrooms into medium-sized pieces. Sauté shallots and garlic in butter until translucent. Add mushrooms and cook until dry. Add cream and reduce this mixture to the desired degree of thickness. Serve over fresh broiled fish, chicken breasts, or veal chops. (Yields 4 servings).

Green Beans and Shiitake

2 oz of dried shiitake
3 Tbl each of soy sauce and dry sherry
1 Tbl sugar
4 slices of fresh ginger root
5 tsp sesame oil
2 lbs of green beans; thin ends

Soak mushrooms in hot water until soft and pliable, about 20 to 30 minutes. Discard stipes. In a large pan, combine mushrooms, 2 Tbs of soy sauce and sherry, sugar, ginger, and 1 cup of water. Bring to boil; reduce heat and simmer, covered, over low heat until mushrooms have absorbed all of the liquid, about 15 minutes. Drain. Mix beans with remaining sesame oil and arrange in a serving dish. Spoon mushrooms and juice across beans. Serve warm. (Yields 8 servings).

Grilled Shiitake

4 slivered garlic cloves
2 cups of fresh shiitake, with stipes removed
1 Tbl + 1 tsp reduced-calorie tub of melted margarine
2 tsp of thyme
1 tsp rosemary
salt and pepper to taste

Insert 4 slivers of garlic into the lamellae of each shiitake cap. Place mushrooms, stipe sides up, in a small baking pan. Pour melted margarine evenly over mushrooms. Sprinkle with the remaining ingredients. Let stand for 10 minutes. Spray broiler pan with non-stick cooking spray. Place mushrooms, stipe sides up, on grill and grill at medium heat for 4 minutes. Turn and grill 4 minutes longer until tender. (Yields 4 servings).

Recipes

Tomato Stuffed Mushrooms

12 large shiitake mushrooms (2 to 3 inches)
$1/4$ cup of butter or margarine
2 chopped green onions or shallots
$1/2$ small, minced garlic clove
2 medium tomatoes, peeled
salt and pepper to taste
$1/2$ cup each of soft fresh bread crumbs and boiling water

Remove mushroom stipes and chop finely. Place mushroom caps in greased shallow baking pan. In frying pan, heat butter and add onions, garlic, and mushroom stipes. Sauté about 5 minutes. Meanwhile cut the tomatoes in half and squeeze gently to remove the seeds. Finely dice the tomato pulp and add to onion mixture with salt and pepper. Remove from heat and stir in the bread crumbs. The mixture should be soft but will hold together. Mound tomato mixture in cups. Pour the boiling water into the pan around the mushrooms. Bake, uncovered, for about 15 minutes at 350° F or until heated through. Serve by placing on platter surrounded a meat entrée. (Yields 6 servings).

Lemon Pepper Mushrooms

8 large shiitake mushrooms
1 Tbl each chopped chives, light mayonnaise, and vegetable oil
2 Tbl lemon juice
1 $1/2$ tsp lemon pepper

Select large, firm mushrooms and wipe with a damp cloth. Remove stipes and chop very fine. Combine with the remaining ingredients in a bowl. Stuff mushrooms with the mixture. Bake at 450° F in a shallow pan 8 to 10 minutes. Serve immediately. (Yields 4 servings).

Dishes With Various Mushrooms: In addition to the button mushrooms (*Agaricus* spp), several wild mushrooms are used in a variety of dishes. For many of these dishes, species of *Armillaria*, *Boletus* and allies, *Cantharellus*, *Craterellus*, *Lactarius*, *Lentinula*, *Macrolepiota*, *Pleurotus*, and others are preferable.

Cheesy Mushroom and Broccoli Dip

1 (10 oz) pkg of frozen, chopped broccoli
3 Tbl of butter or margarine
$1/_4$ cup each of fresh mushrooms, chopped celery, and chopped onion
1 (10 $3/_4$ oz) can of cream of mushroom soup
1 (6 oz) piece of processed cheese food with garlic,
cut into cubes with a dash of hot sauce

Cook broccoli according to package directions and drain well. Melt butter in a large fry pan and sauté vegetables and mushrooms until tender. Add the cooked broccoli and remaining ingredients and cook over low heat, stirring until cheese melts. Serve warm over corn chips.

Mushroom Turnovers

3 Tbl minced onions
1 $1/_2$ cups of finely chopped mushrooms
2 Tbl melted butter or margarine
1 Tbl flour
$1/_4$ tsp thyme or dill
3 Tbl sour cream cream cheese pastry (recipe below)

Sauté onion and mushrooms in butter. Add flour and spices; cook one minute longer. Make sure the flour is blended well. Add sour cream and set aside.

Cream cheese pastry:

$1/_2$ cup of soft butter or margarine
3 (3 oz) packages of softened cream cheese
1 $1/_2$ cups of all purpose flour

Combine butter and chream cheese; beat well. Add flour and mix until smooth. Chill several hours. Roll pastry to 1/8 inch thickness on a lightly floured board; cut into 3-inch rounds. Place one tsp of mushroom mixture into center of each circle. Moisten edges of circles with water and fold in half. Press edges with fork dipped in flour. Prick top with fork. Place on ungreased baking sheets and bake at 425° F for 10 to 12 minutes or until lightly browned. (Yields 2 $1/_2$ dozen).

Sautéed Mushrooms

3 chopped green onions with tops
$1/_4$ cup of melted butter or margarine
1 lb of fresh, sliced mushrooms
$1/_4$ cup of dry white wine

1/4 tsp each of salt and pepper
1/8 tsp of garlic powder
2 tsp of Worcestershire™ sauce

Sauté green onions in butter until tender. Stir in remaining ingredients. Cook over low heat until mushrooms are tender, 30 to 35 minutes. (Yields 4 servings).

Cheesy Mushroom Appetizers

1/2 cup of butter or corn oil
1 1/4 lbs sharp cheese shredded
2-oz jar of jalapeño cheese spread
5-oz jar of American processed cheese spread
1/4 tsp each of onion powder and dry mustard
1/2 tsp each of salt and Worcestershire™ sauce
1 tsp chopped pimiento
1 cup of mushrooms, chopped and sautéed
1 1/4 cup of flour

Beat butter and cheese until blended. Stir in spices, pimiento, sauce, and mushrooms. Add flour and mix. Roll into small balls, approximately 1 tsp per ball. Place on greased cookie sheet and bake at 350° F for 20 minutes. Serve warm.

Mushroom Jewel Salad

1/2 lb of fresh mushrooms (boletes, cantharelles, or lactarius)
2 1/2 cups of boiling water
2 (3 oz) pkg of lemon gelatin
1/2 cup of bottled Italian salad dressing
3 Tbl lemon juice
1/2 cup each of diced apple and diced celery
lettuce

Place mushrooms in boiling water; bring to boiling point; cover, and simmer for 5 minutes. Drain off cooking liquid and pour it over gelatin. Stir to dissolve. Set mushrooms aside. Stir in salad dressing and lemon juice into gelatin mixture. Refrigerate until mixture is consistency of unbeaten egg white. Spoon a thin layer of gelatin into 6-cup mold. Press a few mushroom slices into side of mold. Chill until firm. Stir apple and celery into remaining gelatin. Pour a layer of gelatin over mushrooms; chill. Stand a row of mushrooms around side of mold and carefully spoon gelatin mixture into mold to reach top of mushrooms. Chill until firm. Repeat with a second layer. Chill until ready to serve. You may also just stir poached mushroom slices, apples, and celery into slightly thickened gelatin. Pour into 6-cup mold and refrigerate until firm. Unmold onto letttuce-lined serving plate. (Yields 8 portions).

Cashew Mushrooms

$1/_4$ cup of butter or margarine
$1/_2$ lb of thinly sliced mushrooms
$1/_3$ cup of salted cashews, coursely chopped
2 garlic cloves, minced
1 $1/_2$ tsp of cornstarch
1 tsp of water
$1/_3$ cup of sour cream

Melt butter in large frying pan over medium heat. Add mushrooms and cook approximately 4 minutes until tan in color. Add cashews and garlic; stir and cook an additional 2 minutes. Blend water and cornstarch; add sour cream and mix well. Add to mushroom mixture, stirring constantly until cream is heated thoroughly. Remove from heat and serve immediately. (Yields 4 servings).

Beef Teriyaki

1 flank steak (approx. 1 $1/_2$ lbs)
$1/_3$ cup each of dry sherry and chicken broth
$1/_2$ cup of soy sauce
1 garlic clove, minced
1 tsp sugar
1 medium sized sweet potato, peeled and thinly sliced
12 small mushrooms cut in half
1 sweet green pepper, cut into squares
4 green onions, cut into 1 inch pieces
1 Tbl vegetable oil
1 cup of fresh bean sprouts

Marinate steak for 15 minutes in a sauce made from sherry, chicken broth, soy sauce, garlic, and sugar. Use 2/3 of the sauce for marinade. Reserve the rest for later. Drain steak; pat dry and broil 4 inches from heat, 2 to 3 minutes on each side. Keep warm. Heat oil in a wok or skillet; add sweet potato slices and fry for 1 minute. Add rest of the vegetables except sprouts and fry for 2 to 3 minutes until crisp/tender. Stir into bean sprouts on heated platter. Serve with reserved teriyaki sauce and rice. (Yields 6 servings).

Mushroom Toxins

The major problems we have with mushroom posionings in Florida are children, immigrants, the elderly, those seeking mushrooms for recreational purposes, and the psychologically disturbed. Benjamin (1995) estimates that there are at least 400 species of poisonous mushrooms known. Many of these occur in Florida. Most hospitals and poison control centers are not equipped, and their staffs are not trained to identify mushrooms and determine if they are toxic or edible. Ideally, it would be best to get a rapid, accurate identification of a suspected mushroom, and to have someone who is familiar with the history of a particular species to determine if it is harmless, and if not, what kind of mushroom toxin(s) it possesses. Once toxic elements have been identified, most medical laboratories can administer proper treatments for many.

There are eight basic groups of mushroom toxins based upon their mode of activity. Three groups cause cellular destruction: (1) **cyclopeptides**, (2) **monomethylhydrazine**, and (3) **orellanine**; two groups affect the autonomic nervous system: (4) **coprine** and (5) **muscarine;** two groups affect the central nervous system: (6) **pantherine** and (7) **psilocybin/psilocin**; and one group (8) that causes **gasterointestinal irritation**. (Lincoff and Mitchell, 1977; Benjamin, 1995).

(1) **Cyclopeptide poisoning (amanitoxins and phyllotoxins).** Six amanitoxins and five phyllotoxins have been identified as the toxic principles in the most poisonous of mushrooms. These toxins are thermostable and are not removed on cooking; neither are they removed on drying. These cyclopeptides inhibit **RNA polymerase** and bring about cell destruction. The liver, kidney and central nervous system are affected. Individuals who have ingested mushrooms with cyclopeptides may not be aware for some time that they eaten "a bad one," because symtpoms may not appear until 6 to 12 hours, or even as late as 48 hours. The first symptoms include sharp abdominal pain, nausea, vomiting and watery diarrhea or bloody stools. Excessive thirst is also a symptom. By the third or fourth day, jaundice, renal shutdown, convulsions, and coma occur. Symptoms of meningitis appear with dilated pupils, stiffness of neck, and twitching of facial muscles precede convulsions. From 5-10 mg. constitute a lethal dose. Therefore, one mushroom cap could kill a healthy adult. Liver and kidney stabilization and liver transplants have been used to treat some cases. Efforts should also be made to prevent further toxin absorption, enhance toxin elimination, and management of electrolytes and fluid levels.

- Several species of *Amanita, Galerina, Lepiota,* and a few of *Conocybe* have been shown to contain high levels of cyclopeptides. The most common Florida species include *A. bisporiga, A. hygroscopica, A. suballiacea, A. tenuifolis, A. verna,* and *A. virosa.* There are a number of species of *Conocybe* found in Florida, but the toxicity for most is unclear. Parents of toddlers that "munch on things' found in the grass should be cautious during the rainy season when a number of these species are present.

(2) **Monomethylhydrazine (MMH) poisoning (gyromitrin).** MMH is a hemolytic toxin and is very toxic to the central nervous system. It is also a gasterointestinal irritant and damages the liver. MMH has a long and puzzling history. A party of five pick what they thought were prized, edible mushrooms, for example, and all consume similar servings. Two become violently ill, three enjoyed them with no problem. The chef, however, became the most violently ill, although he did not consume any mushrooms. It was not until the space age arrived that the answer to the erratic nature of mushroom poisoning by species of *Gyromitra* and *Helvella* was forthcoming. Previously, the poisoning had been attributed to helvellic acid, gyromitrin, or other compounds isolated from these fleshy ascomycetes. It was found that during the fueling of space rockets with hydrazine gases that the rocket technologists experienced all sorts of weird but critical symptoms. Those in the medical profession were able to determine the type of poisoning to be identical to that experienced by those who had eaten specimens of *Gyromitra* and *Helvella.* Mycologists reexamined the toxic principle in these fungi and found that in fact they did contain monomethylhydrazine.

- It is now known that the threshold level of toxicity to MMH differs from one individual to another; which explains why only certain individuals from the same party became ill and the others did not. We now know why the chef became violently ill; some of the hydrazine gases were driven off during cooking. Symptoms do not occur for 6 to 12 hours after exposure to MMH, often too late to receive proper treatment. Nausea, vomiting, and diarrhea with abdominal pain is experienced. In severe cases, jaundice, rapid pulse, high fever, dizziness, faintness, loss of coordination, and rarely coma or death occur. Patients who are severely poisoned experience signs of liver toxicity after three to four days. Renal failure occurs in some individuals. Treatment for MMH is much like that described above for cyclopeptide poisoning.

Toxins

(3) **Orellanine or cortinarin poisoning.** This type of mushroom poisoning is caused by a number of species of *Cortinarius.* One of the characteristic features of orellanine poisoning is the long delay of symptoms from the time mushrooms are ingested. Symptoms usually do not appear before the third day after consumption, and may not occur for three weeks (Benjamin, 1995). The prime symptoms include nausea, vomiting and anorexia which is followed within a few days by frequent urination and a burning thirst. These symptoms are often accompanied with exhaustion, lethargy, and lack of appetite. Some experience "flu-like" symptoms of chills and musculoskeletal pain. Severe cases have resulted in renal and kidney failure.

■ Other than the routine treatments for liver and kidney failure, no specific treatment for orellanine poisoning has been developed. In severe cases, damage is irreversible; in milder cases renal function may be reestablished within two to four weeks. Steriods and other treatments have not proven successful.

■ Currently, orellanine toxins are known only in certain species of *Cortinarius,* largely *C. orellanus, C. orellanoides,* and *C. speciosissimus.* Several other species, however, are suspected of containing this toxin. The exact chemical nature of the toxin is unclear, some claiming a bipyridyl structure and others a cyclopeptide structure (Lamke, 1991).

(4) **Coprine.** Coprine is a unique, naturally-occuring amino acid that blocks various metabolic pathways in the human body. It affects the metabolism of alcohol in the body, stopping at the acetaldehyde stage. Acetaldehyde causes vascomotor effects that impact the autonomic nervous system. Symptoms typically occur within a half-hour to one hour after the consumption of alcohol if certain species of *Coprinus* have been eaten within the past 4 to 5 days. Symptoms can also occur if mushrooms are consumed with alcohol, or a short time afterwards. Fortunately, with a rapid onset of symptoms, one can get quick medical attention. When acetaldehydes form, there is a flushing of the face, a throbbing of the neck, swelling of the hands and feet, followed by a strong metallic taste in the mouth, and sometimes chest pains. In severe cases, the loss of muscle tone, respiratory difficulty, and coma may occur. Because of the strong metallic taste and related symptoms, coprine poisoning is referred to as the **antabuse** effect, because it is similar to the symptoms experience by alcohol patients who are on the "antabuse" tablets.

- Coprine poisoning has been restricted to certain species of *Coprinus, C. atramentarius, C. insignis, C. quadrifidus,* and *C. variagatus,* members of a group of mushrooms known as "inky caps" because of the autodigestion of the cap during maturation. Coprine has not been found in *C. comatus,* the shaggy mane mushroom found in Florida and in other areas of the country. While our awareness of the "coprine/alcohol" reaction is a 20th century discovery, the Yuroba people of Nigeria have been aware of this for ages (Oso, 1975), because their name for *Coprinus africanus* is **Ajeimutin** (aje = eat + imu = without drinking + otin = alcohol)!

(5) **Muscarine poisoning.** Muscarine was the first mushroom toxin to be identified when it was first isolated from *Amanita muscaria* (Eugster, 1960), although we now know that this mushroom has only a trace amount of this toxin. Muscarine poisoning causes prolonged sweating, watery eyes, and salivation. Symptoms begin usually within 1 hour, very often within 30 minutes, enabling one to receive medical attention. In severe cases, a slow pulse, a fall in blood pressure, and blurred vision occurs. Muscarine effects the **cholinestrase** level in the body, much like the effects of phosphate insecticides. Atropine, an alkaloid isolated from the nightshade, *Atropa,* completely counteracts muscarine and is used as a antidote.

- The largest number of species that contain muscarine belong to *Clitocybe* and *Inocybe.* More than 15 species of *Clitocybe* contain muscarine, including *C. gibba* and *C. hydrogramma* which are common in Florida and close to 10 species of *Inocybe.* Since many of the species of *Inocybe,* like *I. fastigiata,* are small mushrooms found in shaded lawns, they should be of concern to parents of toddlers who love to munch on things from the lawn. Very small amounts of muscarine have also been found in numerous other genera of mushrooms.

(6) **Pantherine (ibotenic acid and muscimol).** "They neither sow nor plow; they live only on fish and fowl for which there is a great wealth there...they eat certain fungi in the shape of fly agarics, and thus they get drunk worse than vodka, and for them that's the very best banquet" (Wasson 1968). The psychotropic principles in mushrooms causing pantherine poisoning have been identified as isoxazole derivities, ibotenic acid and a closely-related decarboxylation product muscimol (Tyler, 1971). Muscimol is 5-10 times as potent as ibotenic acid in the central nervous system. Symptoms

occur within 30 minutes to 2 hours in the form of dizziness and lack of coordination. Individuals stagger as with alcohol intoxication. With large consumption, hypertension, muscle cramps, and spasms may occur that last up to 24 hours, ending with a deep, coma-like sleep. One mushroom cap is capable of giving incoordination. And yes, a hangover headache may occur.

■ Seven species of *Amanita* have been shown to contain pantherine, the most common of which are *A. muscaria* and *A. pantherina*. A common Japanese mushroom, *Tricholoma muscarium* also contains this toxin. Three pantherine-containing species occur in Florida, *A. muscaria, A. gemmata,* and *A. strobiliformis.*

(7) **Psilocybin/psilocin (tryptoamine) poisoning.** When Roger Heim, a French mycologist, joined Gordon Wasson on his 1955 trip to Mexico, he was able to identify a number of psychoactive mushrooms, mainly species of *Psilocybe*. Heim was instrumental in getting cultures and specimens of *Psilocybe* to Albert Hofmann at the Sandoz Laboratory in Basal, Switzerland. Hofmann *et al.,* (1959) discovered that the hallucinogenic compounds in these mushrooms were two closely-related indolic compounds, psilocybin and psilocin that were similar to LSD in their structure and mode action. Psilocybin contains a phosphorus group, psilocin does not.

■ The onset of symptoms occurs within 10 to 30 minutes and are usually expressed as exhilaration and uncontrollable laughter, followed by visual hallucinations. Some experience a meditative state accompanied with confusion, loss of muscle tone, vertigo, and severe muscle cramps. The principal physiological effects of these compounds seem to be to occupy the serotonin receptor site at synaptic junctions, in this manner interferring with the transmitter-receptor system to the brain. Case studies in Florida have shown that continuous use of psilocybin/psilocin containing mushroom results in personality changes, whereas overuse has resulted in severe "flashbacks" that required rigorous medical attention to overcome.

■ Nearly 25 species of *Psilocybe,* a dozen species of *Panaeolus,* and a few species of *Conocybe, Inocybe, Gymnopilus,* and *Pluteus* have been shown to have psilocybin and psilocin.

(8) **Gastrointestinal irritants.** Quite a large number of mushrooms have species that will cause gastrointestinal irritation. Unfortunately, in very few of them has the active toxin been identified. Another thing that comes into play with this type of mushroom

poisoning is that personal sensitivity and the threshold level of a particular compound one can accept without adverse consequences varies from one individual to the next. Mushrooms produce an enormous number of secondary metabolites. Some act as an emetic, i.e., causes vomiting, others produce diarrhea and abdominal pain, while others produce both. Bresinsky (1977) outlined nine broad catagories of toxic compounds that may cause these problems: terpenoids, anthroquinones, oxolans, nitrogen heterocyclics, amides and peptides, hydrazine and others with N-N bonds, polysaccharides, lipids, and sterols.

■ Species of *Agaricus* contain some of our most highly prized edibles; yet there are almost a dozen species that cause GI problems. A number of the latter occur in Florida, and can sometimes be recognized by an odor of peach seed kernals, anise, phenol, or similar pungent odors. Although considered edible by most, some people cannot eat *Armillaria mellea*. My family has had no problem with a sister species, *A. tabescens*, which is found in abundant clusters during autumn months in Florida. Some of the most highly prized wild mushrooms are members of the Boletales, or boletes. There has been considerable documentation that some of the red-tubed species of *Boletus* such as *B. luridus, B. eastwoodiae,* and *B. frostii* are toxic. Some others in which the tubes turn blue when bruised should also be eaten with caution. W. A. Murrill, who lived in Gainesville, FL for almost 30 years, ate all of the tasty boletes he found. He always parboiled mushrooms for 5-10 minutes and poured off the water before cooking them.

■ *Chlorophyllum molybdites,* the green-spored Morgan's *Lepiota,* is responsible for the greatest number of cases of mushroom poisoning in North America, and in Florida. This is probably due to the fact that it is easily confused with choice edible species such as *Lepiota procera* and *L. rhacodes,* and it is one of the most common mushrooms found on lawns and pastures throughout the country, with the exception of the Pacific Northwest. When eaten raw, *C. molybdites* produces severe symptoms, including bloody stools, within a couple of hours. When cooked well, or parboiled and decanting the liquid before cooking, others eat and enjoy it. Eilers and Nelson (1974) found a heat-labile, high molecular weight protein which showed an adverse effect when given by intraperitoneal injection into laboratory animals.

■ Several species of *Entoloma* have been implicated in mushroom poisoning, but the species most widely documented is *E. sinuatum.* Symptoms usually develop from a half hour to two hours after consumption, causing vomiting, diarrhea, and headache. There have also been reports of liver and psychological disturbance (Benjamin, 1995). Currently, it is not known precisely what toxic principles may be involved, but Maki *et al.* (1985) suggested that muscarine, muscaridine, and choline may be implicated in *E. rhodopolium*. Species of *Entoloma* produce a rosy to salmon spore print, strikingly similar to *Pluteus*, which has a number of choice edible species. *Entoloma* can be distinguished, however, by having sinuate lamellae, knobby spores, and being soil inhabiting, and mycorrhizal, whereas species of *Pluteus* have free lamellae, smooth spores, and are wood inhabiting saprobes.

- Several species of *Lactarius* are choice, edible mushrooms, easily recognized by the exudation of milk when the flesh is broken. However, at least a dozen species have toxins that may cause severe gastrointestinal irritation. Noteworthy of these in Florida are *L. chryorheus* and *L. glaucescens*. A number of the peppery species have sesquiterpenes that incite great irritation of the lips, tongue, and throat when consumed raw. Boiling and decanting the water before cooking, however, rids the mushrooms of these compounds.

- The jack-o-lantern fungus, *Omphalotus olearius*, has a long history of mushroom toxicity. Because of its bright yellow color and decurrent lamellae, it shows a striking resemblance to species of *Cantharellus*. Symptoms of *Omphalotus* poisoning occur within 1 to 3 hours, resulting in nausea, abdominal pain, dizziness, lethargy, and headache. There is usually a rapid recovery. One toxic compound, a sesquiterpene referred to as illudin, has been isolated from *O. olearius* (Benjamin, 1995).

- Because of their texture and relatively poor taste, species of *Russula* are not often collected for food. Most of the bitter or peppery *Russula* can cause GI problems, *R. emetica* foremost among them. While the toxic compound has not been documented, sesquiterpenes, like those in *Lactarius* are suspected.

- Numerous other groups of mushrooms have species that cause gastrointestinal irritation. For a more extensive list of these, refer to Lincoff and Mitchel (1977) and Benjamin (1995).

Bibliography

Akers, B. 1997. *A Systematic study of Lepiotaceae of Florida.* PhD Dissertation, Southern Illinois University, Carbondale, IL, 252 pp.

_____ and W. Sundberg. 1997. *Leucoagaricus hortensis:* some synonyms from Florida. Mycotaxon 62: 401-419.

Baker, T. 1990. *The word "toadstool" in Britain.* The Mycologist 4: 25-29.

Baroni, T. J. 1981. A revision of the genus *Rhodocybe* Maire *(Agaricales).* Beih. Nova Hedwigia. Heft 67: 5-194.

Bas, C. 1969. Morphology and subdivision of *Amanita* and a monograph of its section *Lepidella.* Persoonia 5: 285-579.

Benjamin, D. R. 1995. *Mushrooms: poisons and panaceas.* W. H. Freeman and Co., New York, 422 pp.

Bigelow, H. E. 1982. North American species of *Clitocybe.* Part I. Beih. Nova Hedwigia. Hefte 72: 5-280 pp.

_____. 1985. North American species of *Clitocybe.* Part II. Beih. Nova Hedwigia. Hefte 81: 281-471.

Both, E. E. 1993. *The Boletes of North America,* a compendium. Buffalo Museum of Science, Buffalo, N.Y., 431 pp.

Breitenbach, J. and F. Kränzlin. 1995. Fungi of Switzerland. Vol 4. Edition Mykologia Lucerne, Lucerne, Switzerland, pp. 368.

Bresinksy, A. 1977. Chemotaxonomie de Pilze. Pp. 25-42. In: *Beitrage zur biologie der niederen Pflanzen.* eds. W. Frey, H. Hurka, and F. Oberwinkler. Gustav Fischer, New York.

Cooke, W. B. 1961. The genus *Schizophyllum.* Mycologia 53: 575-599.

Eilers, F. I. and L. R. Nelson. 1974. Characterization and partial purification of the toxin of *Lepiota morgani.* Toxicon 12: 557-563.

Eilers, F. I., D. Te Strake Wagner-Merner, and J. W. Kimbrough. 1980. Rare occurrences of large mushrooms (*Tricholoma* sp.) in Florida. Florida Scientist 43: 50-54.

Eugster, C. H. 1960. The chemistry of Muscarine. Adv. in Organic Chem. 2: 427-455.

Freeman, A. E. H. 1979. *Agaricus* in the southeastern United States. Mycotaxon 8: 50-118.

Guzman, G. 1983. The genus *Psilocybe,* a systematic revision of the known species including the history, distribution and chemistry of hallucinogenic species. Heih. Nova Hedwigia. Heft 74: 6-439.

Halling, R. E. 1986. An annotated index of species and infraspecific taxa of Agaricales and Boletales described by William A. Murrill. Mem. N. Y. Bot. Gard. 40: 1-120.

Hawksworth, D. L., P. M. Kirk, B. C. Sutton, and D. N. Pegler. 1995. Ainsworth and Bisby's Dictionary of the Fungi. 8th Ed., CAB International, Oxon, UK, 616 pp.

Hesler, L. R. 1967. *Entoloma* in southeastern North America. Beih. Nova Hedwigia. Hefte 23: 1-196.

_____. 1969. North American species of *Gymnopilus*. Mycol. Mem. 3:1-117.

_____ and A. H. Smith. 1963. North American species of *Hygrophorus*. The University of Tennessee Press, Knoxville, TN, 416 pp.

_____ and _____. 1983. *North American species of Lactarius*. The University of Michigan Press, Ann Arbor, 841 pp.

Hofmann, A., R. Heim, A. Brack, H. Kobel, A. Frey, H. Ott, T. H. Petrizilka, and F. Troxler. 1959. Psilocybin and psilocin, zwei psychotrope Wirkstoffe aus mexikanischen Rauschpilzen. Helv. Chim. Acta 42: 1557-1572.

Jenkins, D. T. 1986. *Amanita of North America*. Mad River Press, Eureka, CA, 197 pp.

Kibby, G. and R. Fatto.1990. *Keys to the species of Russula in Northeastern North America*. Kibby-Fatto Enterprises, Somerfield N.J., 61 pp.

Lamke, K. F. 1991. Human Poisoning by Mushrooms of the genus *Cortinarius*. Pp.497-521. In: *Handbook of natural toxins: Toxicology of Plant and fungal compounds*. Vol. 6, eds. R. S. Keeler and A. T. Tu. Marcel Dekker, New York.

Largent, D. L. and T. J. Baroni. 1988. *How to Identify Mushrooms to Genus VI: Modern Genera*. Mad River Press, Eureka, CA, 277 pp.

Lincoff, G. and D. H. Mitchel. 1977. *Toxic and Hallucinogenic Mushroom Poisoning*. Van Norstrand-Rienhold, Co., N.Y., 267 pp.

Maas Geesteranus, R. A. 1988. Conspectus of the Mycenas of the Northern Hemisphere 9, Section *Fragilipedes*. Proc. Konink. Ned. Akad. Van Wetenschappen 91: 43-314.

Maki, T., K. Takahashi, and S. Shibata. 1985. Isolation of the vomiting principles from the mushroom *Rhodophyllus rhodopolius*. J. Agric. .. Food Chem. 33: 1204-1205.

Miller, O. K. Jr. 1968. A revision of the genus *Xeromphalina*. Mycologia 60: 156-188.

Murrill, W. A. 1909. The Boletaceae of North America 1. Mycologia 1: 1-14.

_____. 1918. The Agaricaceae of Tropical North America, VIII. Mycologia 10: 62-85.

_____. 1938. New Florida Agarics. Mycologia 30: 362-364.

_____. 1939a. Oligocene Island Fungi. Bull. Torrey Bot. Club. 66: 151- 160.

_____. 1939b. Some Florida gill fungi. J. Elisha Mitchell Soc. 55: 361-372.

_____. 1942. New Fungi from Florida. Lloydia 5: 136-157.

_____. 1943. More New Fungi from Florida. Lloydia 6: 207-228.

_____. 1945. New Florida Fungi. J. Florida Acad. Sci. 8: 181-183.

_____. 1946. New and Interesting Florida Fungi. Lloydia 9: 315-330.

_____. 1948. Florida Boletes. Lloydia 11: 21-35.

_____. 1951. *Species of Florida Basidiomycetes*. Florida Agric. Exp. Sta. Bull. 478, Gainesville, FL., 36 pp.

_____. 1972. *Keys to the fleshy basidiomycetes of Florida*. Ed. J. W. Kimbrough. University of Florida, Gainesville, 199 pp.

Oso, B. A. 1975. Mushrooms and the Yuroba people of Nigeria. Mycologia 67: 311-319.

Pegler, D. N. 1983. *Agaric flora of the Lesser Antilles*. Supp. Kew Bulletin 9: 1-688.

_____1986. *Agaric Flora of Sri Lanka*. Kew Bulletin Additional Series XII: 1-519.

_____, D. J. Lodge, and K. I. Nakasone. 1998. The pantropical genus *Macrocybe* gen. nov. Mycologia 90: 494-504.

_____ and T. W. K. Young. 1981. A natural arrangement of the Boletales with reference to spore morphology. Trans. Brit. Mycol. Soc. 76: 103-146.

Phillips, R. 1991. *Mushrooms of North America*. Little, Brown, and Co., Boston, 319 pp.

Pomerleau, R. 1980. *Flore de Champignons au Quebec et Regions limitropes*. Les Editions La Presse. Ltée. Montreal, 652 pp.

Shafer, R. 1972. North American Russulas of the Subsection Foenentianae. Mycologia 64: 1008-1053.

Singer, R. 1945. The Boletineae of Florida with notes on extralimital species. II. The Boletaceae (Gyroporoideae). Farlowia 2: 223-303.

_____. 1947. The Boletineae of Florida with notes on extralimital species. III. The American Midland Naturalist 37: 1-135.

_____. 1956. Contributions towards a monograph of the genus *Pluteus*. Trans. Brit. Mycol. Soc. 39: 145-232.

_____. 1977. *The Boletineae of Florida*. J. Cramer Publ., Hirschberg, Germany, 567 pp.

_____. 1986. *The Agaricales in modern taxonomy*. 4th Ed., Koeltz Scientific Books, Koenigstein, 981 pp.

Smith, A. H. 1951. The North American species of *Naematoloma*. Mycologia 43: 467-521.

_____. 1972. The North American species of *Psathyrella*. Mem. New York Bot. Gard. 24: 1-633.

_____. and L. R. Hesler. 1968. *The North American species of Pholiota*. Hafner Publ. Co., N. Y., 402 pp.

_____, H. V. Smith, and N. A. Weber. 1979. *How to know the gilled mushrooms*. Wm. C. Brown Co., Dubuque, Iowa, 334 pp.

Tulloss, R. E. 1998. *Seminar on Amanita*. NAMA98, Pub. by the author, Roosevelt, N. J., 184 pp.

Tyler, V. E. Jr. 1971. Chemotaxonomy in the Basidiomycetes. Pp. 29-62. In: *Evolution in the Higher Basidiomycetes*. Univ. Tennessee Press, Knoxville, TN.

Wasson, E. G. 1968. *Soma: Divine Mushroom of Immortality*. Harcourt Brace Javonovich, Inc., New York, pp. 381.

Weber, G. F. 1961. William Alphonso Murrill. Mycologia 53: 543-557.

Weber, N. S. and A. H. Smith. 1988. *A field guide to Southern Mushrooms*. Univ. of Michigan Press, Ann Arbor, 280 pp.

Glossary

Acrid: a very sharp bitter or peppery taste.

Adnate: gills attached to the stipe their full width.

Adnexed: gill attachment in which the gill edge curves upward on the stipe and only a portion of the gill is attached.

Agaric: a general term applied to gill-forming mushrooms.

Allantoid: sausage-shaped.

Amanitin: a high molecular weight cyclopeptide in certain deadly toxic species of *Amanita* that inhabits RNA polymerase and causes cell destruction.

Amygdaliform: almond-shaped, as spores of some Lepiotaceae.

Amyloid: turning blue to blue-black when mounted in an iodine solution.

Annulus: a fibrous or membranous ring left on the stipe by the inner veil.

Apical pore: a germ pore in the apex of a spore.

Appendiculate: structures with appendages.

Appressed: pressed closely to the surface, i.e. as in fibrils or scales.

Arachnoid: cobwebby like a spider web.

Areolate: a surface with cracks and platelets.

Ascending: curved upwards.

Basidiomata: sporulating structures in Basidiomycetes, preferred over basidiocarp.

Basidia: club-shaped structures on gills and pores of agarics and boletes on which basidiospores are attached.

Basidiospores: spores formed on basidia.

Bolete: a general term given to pore-forming mushrooms, the Boletales.

Bulbous: swollen or enlarged; applied to the base of stipes.

Caespitose: growing in clusters or large groups.

Campanulate: bell-shaped.

Campestroid: have a broad, stout stature as in certain species of *Agaricus.*

Cap: the expanded portion of the mushroom at the apex of the stipe; also referred to as the pileus.

Capitate: having an enlarged tip or head.

Cartilaginous: having a tough, leathery consistency of cartilage.

Chantrelles: a common name applied to members of the Cantharellaceae.

Cheilocystidia: cystidia located at the edge of gills.

Clamp connections: a hyphal branch that loops across a septum from one cell to another that will allow the passage of nuclei.

Clavate: club-shaped.

Concolorous: of the same color.

Conic or conical: cone-shaped.

Context: the internal tissue of the pileus, gill, or stipe.

Convex: rounded like an inverted bowl.

Coprine: a naturally occurring amino acid in species of *Coprinus* that renders them toxic when consumed with alcohol.

Coprophilous: grows on the dung of animals.

Corrugate: with rounded ridges or folds.

Cortina: a cobwebby veil in certain mushrooms.

Cotton blue: a common fungal stain usually in a lactic acid/phenol solution.

Crenate: margins with rounded teeth.

Crowded: applied to gills that are almost touching.

Cuspidate: applied to a pileus with a sharp, tooth-like projection at the center.

Cuticle: a thin, waxy surface layer.

Cyanophilic: a bluing reaction of cells or tissues mounted in cotton blue.

Cystidium: a sterile element among basidia in the hymenium.

Decurrent: referring to gills that extend down the stipe.

D

Deliquesce: a process of autodigestion where the tissues liquefy.

Denticulate: a structure on which there are small teeth.

Depressed: the middle of the pileus sunkened below level of the margin.

Dextrinoid: a chemical reaction in which structures turn reddish to reddish-brown when mounted in Melzer's iodine.

Dimitic: with two kinds of hyphae, thin-walled generative hyphae and thick-walled skeletal hyphae.

Disc: the central portion of the pileus.

Distant: a term applied to widely spaced gills.

Eccentric: off-centered or to one side.

Echinulate: applied to surfaces with small, pointed spines.

Ectomycorrhizae: symbiotic (mutually beneficial) relationship between the fungus and tree species.

Ellipsoid: longer than broad, or narrowly ovoid.

Epigeous: growing above ground.

Evanescent: fragmenting and usually disappearing with age.

Fascicle: arrangement in a small group.

Ferruginous: a rusty-red color.

Fibrillose: covered with long, delicate hairs.

Fibrous: composed of dense interwoven fibrils.

Filamentous: long, thread-like in shape.

Floccose: surface with a cottony appearance.

Free: gills that are not attached to the stipe.

Fulvous: a reddish, cinnamon-brown color.

Funnel-shaped: shaped like a funnel, infundibuliform.

Furfuraceous: covered with bran-like particles.

Fuscous: a dark, smoky-brown color.

Fusiform: tapering at both ends, i. e. spindle-shaped.

Gelatinous: jelly-like in consistency.

Gills: blades beneath the pileus on which spores are borne, see lamellae.

Glabrous: smooth, without any type of hairs or pubescence.

Glandular dots: closely matted hairs, often with secretions, that form conspicuous dots on a surface; for example the stipe of *Leccinium*.

Globose: somewhat spherical or round.

Granulose: when the surface is covered with granules.

Gregarious: growing close together but not touching.

Gymnohymenial: the hymenial area of a mushroom that is exposed at all stages of development.

Hazel: the color of the hulls of mature hazel nuts.

Hemiangiohymenial: mushroom development in which the stipe elongates, enlarges at the apex, and the hymenium develops within the swollen apex.

Heteromerous: tramal tissues composed of sphaerocysts and filamenous hyphae.

Hilum: basidiospore scar marking the point of attachment to the sterigmata.

Hirsute: surface covered with long, course hairs.

Homoiomerous: tramal tissues composed of filamentous cells only.

Hyaline: unpigment and clear under transmitted light.

Hygrophanous: appears water-soaked.

Hymenium: the spore-bearing layer of gills or pores of agarics and boletes.

Hyphae: microscopic, filatmentous threads which branch and develop into mycelium.

Hypogeous: grows below ground.

Imbricate: overlapping plates or shingle-like.

Incurved: a pileus margin that curves downward and inwards.

Inferior annulus: an annulus that is attached rather low on the stipe.

Inrolled: the pileus rolls inwards; more than incurved.

Labyrinthoid: having a maze-like arrangement of the hymenium.

Lacerate: surface appearing torn or cut.

Lamella: the blade or gill on which basidia and spores are borne.

Lateral attachment: attachment of the stipe to the side of the pileus.

Latex: milk or juice that exudes from a broken or cut basidioma.

Luminescent: emits light, or glows in the dark.

Marginal veil: the membrane-like structure on the margin of the pileus that remains as the pileus edge detaches from the stipe.

Marginate: with a well-formed margin.

Melzer's reagent: an iodine/potassium iodide/chloral hydrate solution used to determine dextrinoid and bluing reaction (see amyloid).

Mesic: a moderately moist habitat.

Monomethylhydrazine: a highly toxic hydrazine gas that is found in many species of *Helvella* and *Gyromitra*.

Monomitic: only one type of cell in a tissue, i. e. generative hyphae only.

Muscarine: toxic quarternary ammonium compound in certain species of *Amanita, Conocybe,* and *Inocybe.*

Mycelium: filamentous threads that make up the spawn or vegetative phase of a mushroom.

Nodulose: with bumps or knobs.

Notched: where the gills at the point of attachment to the stipe have a small notch; also referred to as sinuate.

Ochraceous: a dingy, dull, yellowish-brown color.

Olivaceous: the color of a green olive.

Orellanine: a bipyridal or cyclopeptide-like compound found in toxic species of *Cortanarius.*

Pallid: a very pale shade of a color, or otherwise whitish.

Pantherine: the toxic compounds in certain species of *Amanita* containing ibotenic acid and muscimol.

Partial veil: the veil that extends from the stipe to the pileus margin.

Pellicular veil: a slimy partial veil common in species of *Suillus.*

Phyllodin: a high molecular weight cyclopeptide in certain *Amanita* species that inhibits RNA polymerase and causes cell destruction.

Pileate: having a cap or pileus.

Pileus: the technical term for the cap of a mushroom.

Placomycetoid: have a slim stature with a somewhat thin pileus; characteristic of certain species of *Agaricus.*

Plane: having a more or less flat surface.

Pleurocystidia: cystidia found among the basidia within the hymenium.

Pleurotoid: to describe mushrooms with a lateral stipe.

Polypores: a general term applied to many of the Aphyllophorales.

Primordium: the small, button stage of a mushroom.

Pruinose: covered with a fine powder.

Pseudoangiohymenial: mushroom development in which the hymenium is initially exposed but by rapid growth and inrolling of the pileus but is soon enclosed as the pileus margin adheres to the stipe.

Pseudosclerotium: a large, firm structure composed of a woody substrate impregnated with a fungus and its metabolites; found in species of *Lentinus*.

Pubescent: surface with fine, soft hairs, i. e. downy.

Punctate: surface with small recessed dots or depressions.

Reniform: kidney-shaped.

Reticulate: with a net-like pattern on the surface.

Rhizoid: a root-like structure.

Rhizomorph: thread or cord-like structure composed of numerous hyphae.

Rimose: a cracked surface pattern; like a dry lakebed.

Rugose: coarsely wrinkled.

Saccate: bag-shaped; used in describing a mushroom volva.

Scabrous: surface roughened with erect scales.

Scurfy: with bran-like scales; also called furfuraceous.

Serrate: with a saw-toothed edge.

Serrulate: with a fine saw-toothed edge.

Sessile: without a stipe; attached directly to the substrate.

Sinuate: lamella attachment in which there is a notch in the lamella where it meets the stipe.

Solitary: basidiomata growing separated or apart from others.

Spawn: the mycelium from which a mushroom develops.

Sphaerocysts: clusters of globose cells within tissues of Russulaceae.

Spinose: with sharp, spiny processes.

Squamose: a surface with rather large scales.

Squamulose: a surface with small scales.

Statismosporic: a spore that lacks a mechanism of forceful discharge.

Sterigmata: pointed protrusions at the apex of basidia on which spores are borne.

Stipitate: bearing a stalk or stipe.

Striate: with radial lines, ridges, or grooves.

Substrate: the substance on which basidiomata develop.

Superior annulus: an annulus attached at the apex of the stipe and hangs around it as an apron.

T

Tapered: becoming narrower, either upwards or downward.

Tawny: a very pale tan to yellowish-brown.

Tomentose: with soft, densely matted to wooly hair.

Trama: internal tissues of structures of the basidiomata.

Translucent: somewhat clear, allowing the passage of light.

Trimitic: a tissue with generative, skeletal, and binding hyphae; typical of many of the tough, corky Aphyllophorales.

Truncate: with a blunt, flat end.

Tuberculate: a surface with small bumps or outgrowths.

U

Umber: a very dark, dull, reddish-brown.

Umbo: the center of the pileus with a hump or protrusion.

Umbonate: the state of having an umbo.

Undulate: with broad wavy edges.

Universal veil: the peridium or outer membrane that completely encircles a developing basidioma with angiohymenial development.

Upturned: used to describe the upward growth of the pileus margin.

V

Veil: a thin membrane-like tissue that covers the lamella or pileus.

Verrucose: having a wart-like or nodular surface.

Velutinous: with a fine, velvety surface.

Ventricose: a structure that is broad in the middle and tapers at each end; i. e. fusoid.

Vinaceous: the color of the stain of red wine.

Violaceous: the color of purplish violets.

Viscid: a sticky but not slimy surface.

Volva: the remains of the universal veil around the base of the stipe; often cupulate or sometimes fragile and mealy.

Volval patches: remains of the universal veil on the surface of the pileus.

Z

Zonate: a surface with zones of different colors or textures.

Index

Index

Index